NO LIGHTS, NO SIRENS

ROBERT
CEA

NO LIGHTS, NO SIRENS

The Corruption and Redemption of an Inner City Cop

WM

WILLIAM MORROW

An Imprint of HarperCollinsPublishers

HarperCollins books may be purchased for educational, business, or sales promotional use. For information please write: Special Markets Department, HarperCollins Publishers Inc., 10 East 53rd Street, New York, NY 10022.

FIRST EDITION

Designed by Renato Stanisic

Printed on acid-free paper

Library of Congress Cataloging-in-Publication Data

Cea, Robert, 1961–
    No lights, no sirens : the corruption and redemption of an inner city cop / by Robert Cea.— 1st ed.
        p. cm.
    ISBN 0-06-058712-1 (acid-free paper)
    1. Cea, Robert, 1961– 2. Police—New York (State)—New York— Biography.   3. Police corruption—New York (State)—New York.
4. Police misconduct—New York (State)—New York. I. Title.

HV7911.C43A3   2005
363.2'092—dc22
[B]   2004063153

05   06   07   08   09   DIX/RRD   10   9   8   7   6   5   4   3   2   1

For
Lisa, Nicholas, and Olivia

CONTENTS

AUTHOR'S NOTE

Dates and certain locations have been changed. Street names and aliases remain the same. Let no cop ever be questioned or tried beyond my own admissions, and let no perp walk free behind any misinterpretation of his absolute guilt.

NO LIGHTS, NO SIRENS

Prologue

Was this the end, finally?

We were on a rooftop littered with empty crack vials and forties, his knee jammed into my solar plexus, making breathing impossible. The air I could inhale was filled with a coppery-tasting fluid—blood, my blood—and the harder I tried to breathe, the more I coughed out red lather. He lifted me, to throw me from the roof, but realized he'd have to follow me down. I'd cuffed our wrists together. I couldn't see for the veil of red from when he'd bitten cleanly through both of my nasal chambers. The skin that was once the outer part of my nose had torn from my face and flattened. As I drew in breath, the skin tissue was pulled in and out. The pain was excruciating.

Anywhere this scumbag mutt could exact pain he did. His huge right hand freely hit the upper part of my body. I was trying not to focus on the pain, taking comfort in knowing that I was receiving exactly what I'd set out for that late afternoon—to have all of the sins ripped from my body by an animal as dirty and as sinful as I'd become. It was a ghetto exorcism in the very place where it had all begun so many years before, the place where I had been baptized by fire as a young New York City cop, the streets of the Badlands in Red Hook, Brooklyn.

My body suddenly became cold, numb. I was sure that I was going to die on that quiet rooftop and I was so fucking happy about it. I wanted to die—I deserved to die. With each vicious punch, I began to see black-and-white snapshots of what once was my life. Standing proudly in front of One Police Plaza in my dress blues . . . my first gun collar . . . my first drug arrest . . . the medals that had accumulated so easily . . . the first bag of smack I'd given away . . . the poor junkie snitch I was accused of murdering . . . my wife, Mia, holding our baby.

The sudden realization of defeat and sorrow washed over me and I wondered how I'd gotten here. When was the exact moment I no longer was the cop, but had become the criminal?

The Beginning

It was the early eighties. New York City was just starting to recover from the bankrupt years of the seventies, though the crime rate was at an all-time high and continuing to rocket out of proportion. Mayor Ed "How am I doing?" Koch was too busy self-promoting or writing books to realize just how bad the city really was. Of course, New York has always been a dangerous and volatile place, but things were out of control: 1,826 murders, 3,747 rapes, and 100,667 robberies in 1981. The murder rate would climb to 2,445 by 1989. To top it off, an average of five police officers a year were murdered. Yes, New York City was a war zone, and crack had not even reared its ugly head, at least not yet. When it did, things would get much, much worse before they got better. I was heading right for it. My number had been called by the department; I was entering the New York City Police Academy and I couldn't wait.

My older brother, Jeff, had already been on the job for over a year. He was exactly where he wanted to be: The juice, the action, it was what made it all so real for him. It's what he had wanted to do his whole life, be a cop, and it's what I had wanted to do since I could remember. Jeff has a great physical presence—he's a natural leader—and with his uniform on and the medals that were starting to accumulate over his shield, he seemed larger than life. I would follow him anywhere. I wanted to feel that juice. I wanted to know that what I was about to do had some powerful meaning behind it. The long and short of it: I just wanted to help people.

Jeff worked on the Lower East Side of Manhattan, and at that time it was a virtual drugstore. The operation pressure points and TNT drug initiatives that solely targeted narcotics trafficking and street-level sales hadn't yet been established, so the dealers and the junkies ran the show. Jeff would call me up on a Friday when he was doing a four-to-twelve tour and I would hang out with him on his foot post. I was a second-year student in college, and having been raised in a working-class section of Brooklyn, this gray, dark world was very unfamiliar to me. I was mesmerized by the tight, narrow streets where tenement buildings were piled one on top of the other, so close together that, looking up from the ground, they all seemed to meld into scarred brick monoliths. The burned-out storefronts, the garbage trailing from the doorways to the streets. The rat-infested alleys, the dark and dangerous courtyards where murder was a simple afterthought, the abandoned buildings where the walking dead fucked, sucked, and skin-popped to live. These images triggered something deep inside me. I was hooked, and there was no turning back.

Each borough has its main thoroughfare: Fordham Road, the Bronx; Broadway, Manhattan; Queens Boulevard, Queens; Hyland Boulevard, Staten Island. And Flatbush Avenue, Brooklyn. Flatbush is the main artery carrying lifeblood through the center of the borough, running the entire length, south to north, for approximately eleven miles. It is said to be the longest avenue in the world. The south end connects Brooklyn to Rockaway, Queens, via the Marine Park Bridge; the north end connects Brooklyn with Manhattan via the Manhattan Bridge. Every couple of miles, the neighborhoods flow from good to bad, a microcosm of the borough. The neighborhoods at the south end of Flatbush, where I was raised, run from Flatlands to Marine Park. Clean mom-and-pop stores, wide streets with spotless one-family houses dot the area. As you travel north, Flatbush Avenue narrows and snakes through the middle of Brooklyn, from East Flatbush through Crown Heights. Overcrowded and unkempt four-story apartment buildings, liquor stores, and "pot spots" are on every corner. Farther north, the dangerous urban landscape gives way to 526 acres of rolling meadows and luxuriant greenery: Prospect Park. Flatbush Avenue cuts through the eastern end of the park, and it is here that the affluent neighborhood of Park Slope begins. The tree-lined streets consist of four-story brownstones, turn-of-the-century mansions, and art deco apartment buildings.

Some people have been born and died on this avenue. If there really are eight million stories in New York, this avenue owns half of them.

The drive down Flatbush Avenue this morning seemed different to me. Yes, it was the same place I'd walked and driven down for the past twenty years. Same people, same pristine storefronts—Ebinger's Bakery, Joe's candy store, Gus's delicatessen, Louie's meat market, the family-run businesses that made the borough famous, stores I'd shopped at since I was a child. Yet now, even though I hadn't had one day of training, I started to look at it all from a different perspective. I created scenarios in my head. If a man was robbing Joe's, how would I stop him before anyone got hurt? A woman is screaming in an alley, two ways in, which is the safest and quickest route? The thought that I would be out there in those streets in six short months, making it a better place to live, filled me with incredible purpose. I was now looking at men and women twice my age as if I were their keeper. I wanted to chase away the monsters that had stalked these streets for so many years. I thought of the three thousand other recruits who were coming on to the job with me this day. Were they thinking and feeling the same thoughts I was?

My destination, the police academy, on Twentieth Street, off Third Avenue, in Manhattan, was a place I'd been to many times to watch the cadets going home after a long day of what I thought was as priceless an education as any an Ivy League school had to offer. I recognized the incredible bond that these young recruits had with one another, the mutual respect and camaraderie forged at the institution where every cop who's a member or has ever been a member of the NYPD has studied and trained. I was about to join this unique union of men who would run into out-of-control situations while everyone else was running out. My brother, Jeff, and the rest of these men and women were my heroes. I could not wait.

I arrived at the academy at 0630 hours on July 12, 1982. I proudly wore my cadet uniform: navy blue pants, light blue shirt, navy tie, and black clunky shoes. If you were from out of town and saw a group of us walking down the street, you'd probably think we were headed to a bus-drivers' convention. There was nothing to identify us with the greatest police force in the world other than a cheap NYPD tie clip.

The academy is a boxy structure, six stories of gray cement walls dressed with black slate tile framing the double glass doors. If it weren't for all the uniformed cops moving in and out of those front doors, the building could be mistaken for some social services department. I entered the muster deck in the covered atrium and noticed a hundred or so class numbers taped to the wall. We'd been assigned our classes back at Brooklyn College when we were officially sworn in. Mine was Company B, Class 82-79. Home.

I soaked everything in, ate it up with knife and fork. Hanging on the wall next to the double doors was the NYPD flag with its five green-and-white alternating stripes representing the five boroughs, and its twenty-four stars in a field of blue representing the original towns and counties of the city. In bold letters the flag read *"Fidelis Ad Mortem,"* Latin for "Faithful unto Death." It bounced around in my head like a stray .22, making what we were about to do seem all that more important. The Devotion of yourself so completely to the cause of keeping the peace, to the point that you'd be willing to die for it. I certainly would.

The recruits started to line up in front of the class numbers. I clocked my classmates. An overweight black guy named Lester Knowles who didn't look like he'd been in-country very long. A tall, good-looking cat I'd seen smoking a Di Nobili on Second

Avenue less than a half hour before, even though it was forbidden to smoke in public in uniform. I checked his nameplate: "Pirelli." He looked as though he was clocking his classmates for who might be a degenerate gambler or have some imperfection he might be able to capitalize on, someone he could quite possibly run a game on. I enjoyed watching him watch everyone else.

Billy Devlin fell in line. He was dark Irish, about twenty-one, my age. He looked even more attuned to his surroundings than me and I sensed immediately that we shared the same vision. I could also tell that he'd been working out with weights, which told me he was smart enough to know he'd need an edge in the street. Now, was that edge needed because of a flaw he felt he had, or did he just want to cover every base? He caught me checking him out and smiled, then lowered his head respectfully. I did the same, and then I looked back at Mister Cool, Pirelli. This time he caught me watching him. I saw his mood darken slightly, but I did not look away. I didn't want him to think I was some punk from Long Island, or "Cupcake Land" as it was referred to. I, probably like him, was from Brooklyn, and once you give a guy from Brooklyn even the slightest hint of weakness, you're pretty much his bitch for the duration, and six months in Academy Land was way too long to be anybody's bitch. He smirked at me, then dramatically dropped his leather bag to the ground, holding out the palms of his hands as if he were about to be cuffed. I smiled at the hard-core Brooklyn act. He slowly smiled, and then we both laughed. That's when we heard a piercing whistle cut through the air. At that moment, we were the property of the city of New York.

Our company instructor, Sergeant Tom O'Lary, did roll call every morning and every afternoon. If you were to see him on the A train, you'd think accountant, software programmer, quite possibly sous-chef at Alain Ducasse, he was so nondescript. Unless you looked in his eyes. There you'd find a completely different story. He had what we called the thousand-mile gaze—Sergeant Tom had seen it all, looked into the abyss and come out on the other side. Leopardlike, his eyes were clocking everyone. Not just the recruits in his class but also every recruit in the atrium and every civilian walking past the muster deck. He seemed to be thinking continuously, working out some problem, neutralizing situations before they might actually occur. Very few of the instructors had that look.

After Sergeant Tom completed roll call of the thirty recruits in 82-79, we filed into the building one class at a time. Perfect formation; not one recruit looked anywhere other than at the shoulders in front of him. That is, of course, everyone except me and Patty Pirelli. I was looking at him, and he was looking at the perfect ass of a female probationary police officer (PPO). *I give him a week before he gets bounced,* I thought. Of course, I couldn't have been more wrong.

I shared my locker with none other than Mister Cool himself, Pirelli, and Billy Devlin. I was a minimalist, with a small towel, travel soap, my shorts, top, and sneakers. Devlin, the same. Pirelli, however, was packed as if he was ready to go on the lam at a minute's notice. Shampoo, hair conditioner, hair gel, three types of brushes, skin toner, two beach towels, cologne, toothbrush, toothpaste, skin moisturizer, and exfoliating lotion. *Exfoliating lotion?* When we questioned him about it, his answer was quite succinct, as if he'd put a lot of thought into it.

"Just because my paycheck says white-man's welfare, that doesn't mean I have to look or smell the fuckin' part. You see some a the third-world gorillas they hired in this class? Last thing I want is some honey going down on me and her getting a taste a Lester Knowles. His fuckin' balls look like they ain't seen soap since before electricity, and where that Cro-Magnon's from, I don't even think they got that luxury yet." We laughed. It was all about the *puta* for Patty and looking and smelling good. We knew Patty had wood for Lester Knowles, not because Patty was a racist, but because it was a given that he pretty much hated anyone who wasn't Italian. No, Lester irked Patty because appearance wasn't at the top of Lester's list. Lester had enough trouble understanding the English language; personal hygiene, that would have to wait. Patty didn't let little things like the possibility of getting thrown out of the academy stop him from letting everyone know his distaste for the poor recruit. The drugstore on Twenty-third Street was making a small fortune on all the soap that Pirelli was buying and leaving on Lester's locker before every gym class started. Lester, naturally, never received the soap, as the nearest recruit would swipe it off the locker before Lester got the message. Every moment, Patty was obsessing about Lester's bathing habits. "Betcha' this fuckin' baboon is sellin' the soap. I find out the cocksucker is making money off of my good graces, I'm gonna drown the prick in the pool."

Billy could not help himself, he only made it worse. "You know, Patty, chlorine is a natural enhancer."

"Fuck is a natural enhancer?" Patty wasn't sure he wanted to know what Billy's answer was going to be.

"That means that whatever Knowles has on his body, like skin rashes, some kind of dysentery, athlete's foot, crotch rot, whatever, the chlorine will enhance what he's got, and anyone near him in the water will get it too." Pirelli's upper lip curled slowly, as if he'd just smelled his first ripe DOA. Slowly he smiled.

"Then I'll fuckin' cap Magilla Gorilla." Crazy thing was, though he was smiling, something told us he meant it.

Of course, O'Lary keyed on this special relationship from day one, and he had the two of them sitting next to each other for the duration. "Learn to love your brother PPOs," he'd say. Not so coincidentally, they were also made gym partners. That meant that for every training exercise we did in the gym, they were paired up. We all had to bite the insides of our lips to keep from laughing as Patty and Lester would be used time and time again to demonstrate the proper way of getting out of headlocks or leg locks around the neck. Patty was always made to be the victim to Lester's aggressor. Lester's armpits dripped with perspiration as he wrapped his meaty, hairy arm or leg around Patty's head. Patty was rendered helpless not because of Lester's strength, but because the hair under Lester's armpits was actually braiding together into tiny dreadlocks. The odor was brutal.

O'Lary somehow heard of Devlin's lesson to Patty about, "natural enhancers" in the pool. Now, the pool wasn't the cleanest to begin with, and one day we just happened to be the last class in gym, which meant that there were 2,970 different types of germs all being "enhanced" in the pool by the time we got there. We were there to practice water rescue, and Patty looked as though he was going to faint. He didn't want anything to do with that pool. Our first lesson was to show the buoyancy of different body types. A Chinese recruit, Deacon Chin, was told to stand at the edge of the pool, and then our pal Lester Knowles was picked. O'Lary scanned the recruits. "All right, who wants to volunteer for the exercise?" Now Pirelli was no midget, he was six foot three on a bad day, but for the life of me today I could not find him in the crowd of two hundred shorter recruits. O'Lary, without looking or waiting for a volunteer, pointed through about twenty PPOs, a building stanchion, a lifeguard's chair, and an even taller instructor. And there was Patty, trying desperately not to be seen. Wasn't gonna happen.

"Yes, that works for me, Asian, black, and a big white guy. Go next to your brother PPOs, Pirelli." Patty was in quite the jumble fuck. He made his way slowly to the pool.

"C'mon, puppy, you look like you done your share of partying poolside, only difference is here you're gonna learn something." Patty neared the edge of the pool. No one said a word.

O'Lary explained that we were going to witness a natural phenomenon. "What you guys should do is jump into the water like you're doing a cannonball; once you hit the water, keep your arms wrapped around your legs, try to let your body float back up to the top of the water." O'Lary looked at Pirelli, who was at this point a really interesting shade of green. "You okay, puppy?" Patty looked away and didn't answer. "What is it, you can't swim?" At this point, Patty's embarrassment was changing his complexion from green to purple. Lester, who didn't have a clue, spoke in his very thick Haitian accent.

"That okay, Patty, me born in da water, man. Ya grab whole a me, man, you feel like you go under, Lester man pull you right up top, man."

Patty squeezed his eyes closed, then charged toward the edge of the pool as if he'd just stepped on a land mine. He jumped to the farthest point away from where he thought Lester was going to be, then sank quickly toward the bottom. Lester and Chin followed; sure enough, the most buoyant was Chin, who rose to the top of the water almost as soon as he hit it, then Patty came up halfway, and Lester, he kept sinking. Lester must've had his eye on his gym buddy above him, because before he reached the bottom, he started to quickly swim back up toward Patty, who was just suspended in the water and not moving. Lester must've thought Patty was overcome. Patty, sensing Lester moving toward him like an oily torpedo, rocketed out of the water like a surface-to-air missile. It looked as though he was actually running on top of the water to get out. He bolted past the instructors and the recruits, grabbing his, my, and Devlin's towels. He was in a zone, trying to scrub off the diseases he was sure he'd just contracted. O'Lary was trying to keep a straight face as he explained what had occurred. "So if you are assigned to a water-bordering precinct, you know who to go to first, and who not to grab on to for help. However, if you happen to be in the precinct with PPO Pirelli, pray he is in the water, because that boy, like Jesus himself, can walk on friggin' water." The class exploded in laughter while Patty furiously scrubbed, oblivious.

Two things occurred that day—everyone had a newfound respect for Lester because of his desire to help a fellow cop in need, and Patty Pirelli received a nickname that has stayed with him for twenty years: JC, short for Jesus Christ.

The academy was structured into three classes, social science, law, and police science. Social science focused on the different cultures, religions, and beliefs of the many people who lived in the most diverse city in the world. I always prided myself on being street savvy, having been raised in Brooklyn, "the second largest city in the world," but it was laughable what I did not know. I learned about the Hasidim in Crown Heights, the rituals of the Santeria, snippets of different languages, key phrases and buzz words to look out for, and street slang. It was all fascinating to me.

Law class broke down into two categories, CPL (criminal procedure law) and penal law. CPL was the course that taught us what we legally could and could not do. For instance, the time limit a police officer needed to acquire a search warrant, what due process of law meant, when we were able to stop and frisk, when we were able to effect an arrest. Patty Pirelli had an acute knowledge of what the police could and could not do. When asked by our law teacher, John Iannello, about his keen understanding of this, Patty clammed up. But as Patty and I got closer, I came to understand exactly who he was and where he was from.

Patty was an anomaly of sorts. His uncle "Joe Sap" was a respected and feared capo in the Genovese crime family, the strongest of all mob families since Giuliani took dead aim at "Dapper Don" John Gotti, and the Gambinos. Joe Sap was what is known in the streets as a gangster's gangster. It's been said that he personally hog-tied a very mean street guy, took him to his corrugated-box factory, placed the poor sap's head in a compressor, and squashed it into a flattened stream of pulp. That's how he earned his name, Joe Sap—he saps the saps. Patty had his uncle's traits—hair-trigger temper, and he could knock you the fuck out with either hand. Sap loved his nephew, so Patty would always have work when he retired or the job "retired" him. I understood their relationship, though it was an area I really did not want to know that much about. But guaran-fucking-teed, had I asked him, in a millisecond Patty would've given me the goods on himself and his uncle. We would come to develop an unconditional trust in each other.

Penal law was the definition of charges and their classifications, literally hundreds of penal codes and what they meant. My favorite was 265.02–03: "In possession of a loaded firearm." I read every statute on firearms. I imagined that was the purest form of police work, finding a man with a gun. Why would anyone carry a gun unless he was going to use it? What interested me and a handful of other recruits even more, however, was how you would go about finding that man with a gun and what to do once you acquired your target. This we learned in police science class. O'Lary was our teacher, and we'd heard nobody did it better than he and his partners when he was on patrol.

Police science is basically the nuts and bolts of your daily routine on the street. All the paperwork and then some, and of course what to look for while on foot post or in an RMP (radio motor patrol), a patrol car. Has that derelict really been shopping for a wedding band for the last two hours or is he casing the store for a robbery? What do you do if you see a wanted car that was used in connection with a homicide? How would you stop, approach, question, and arrest five individuals all carrying heavy armament? This is the class that taught you how to survive on the street. My favorite.

During the lessons, we would get visits from some of Sergeant Tom's old partners. They would come in, talk to us, and share war stories. One afternoon a police officer named John Conroy came in. Everyone stood at attention awhile longer than usual in the presence of the uniformed cop who stood larger than life before us. He was solidly built, around six feet tall, and maybe thirty-five years old. His hair was light brown and a little messy. His shoes were scuffed, as if they'd seen a lot of tussling in the mud. He didn't seem as though he paid much attention to his uniform or his appearance. His gun belt was minimal: his six-shot .38, two sets of handcuffs, a flashlight, and plenty of rounds on his bandolier-type holster. Tucked inside his belt buckle was a shorter .38-caliber revolver, his backup.* He was "a working cop," though he did not seem like the in-your-face types we all had recognized from television and movies. Then again, neither did Sergeant Tom. These guys were a different breed: low key, covert, never notice them until the cuffs are on. This is what I aspired to, to be on that same mission, that same quest for good and righteousness, and to do it the right way, like these two demigods in front of us. And here they were giving us their particular

* This was before all of the NYPD's rank and file were issued the Glock 17, the mother of all small-arms firepower.

knowledge about life and death on the inside. *We* were finally on the inside.

Conroy's leather medal device above his shield ran all the way up to just below his chin. He had placed a thin metal bar behind the device, sliding it through the backs of the medals and in between the leather so that it would not flap over. The highest medal, at the top of the rack, was a light green bar bordered with gold piping; in the center of the medal was a gold star. We knew the bar to be the combat cross. From our teachings with Sergeant Tom, we understood that medal to be revered. It meant that the recipient was in a fight to the death with an armed assailant who was firing on him, or his partner, and that they had overcome the situation. The gold star in the center of the medal meant Conroy had been awarded two of them. Below the combat crosses was a row of different-colored medals that looked like enameled train tracks: blues, greens, whites with gold trim. Some had different-colored multiple stars on them, bronze, silver, and light green. The last was the exceptional-merit medal, given in conjunction with the combat cross or the medal of valor, the solid blue bars that Conroy also wore. John had four exceptional merits. We were, to say the very least, in awe. You could tell that even though Sergeant Tom was Conroy's superior officer, Conroy ran the show, and to all of us and most of the other instructors in the academy, Sergeant Tom was pretty much "the shit" on patrol— the medals above *his* shield were a testament to that. If that were the case, then who in the hell was Officer John Conroy?

After a nervous salute from Conroy, we were all told to be seated. He seemed a little uncomfortable around all of us. He was clocking everybody. I assumed that upon entering the classroom he knew how many windows there were, how many men there were as opposed to women, how many of them were minorities.

Sergeant Tom placed his hand on Conroy's shoulder and smiled. "This is Police Officer John Conroy. Mega Man, King Kong, what the Rastafarian brothers kindly and simply refer to as the beast, or beas, if you're cruising in the Badlands. They like to drop their *t*s." Conroy smiled, at that. "Now, sooner rather than later you're all gonna get your wings, and as far as I'm concerned, there is no one left on this job who can give the real four-one-one on what it's like to be out there. So if you have any questions, now is the time to ask my partner in crime, John Conroy."

Conroy did not like the attention, and he did not look anyone in the eye long enough for them to gauge what he was thinking. The standard questions were asked. What central booking was like, how to act in court, what it was like to make an arrest. No one had the balls to ask the really good questions, the ones we all wanted to know, and then Patty raised his hand.

"What did you get the cross for?"

Sergeant Tom smiled at Conroy. "That's Pirelli, one of our glory fighters."

Conroy paused and thought about his answer.

"Pulled a livery cab over on Eastern Parkway. Perp in the backseat transporting quantity coke," he said casually. "He drew on us, we were quicker, which is what you always want to be."

The class laughed. I figured the door was opened, so why not ask? I raised my hand. "Why'd you pull the cab over?" He gave Sergeant Tom the slightest of looks, then he smiled and looked directly into my eyes. *Did I key into something here, was I getting even further on the inside?* I wondered.

"The gentleman matched a photo of a perp wanted for a homicide." There was something here that wasn't being said, some unspoken language, something I felt I needed to know.

"But the man wasn't the one wanted for the homicide?"

"That's right, it wasn't him. It also wasn't his day, it was our day."

"You could do that? Pull the car over because you think it's a different guy?"

O'Lary jumped in. "That's called a good-faith stop, as long as you have one of these . . ." He moved to his desk and pulled a short form from the mountain of papers scattered all over it. He snapped it high in the air. "This little baby is your lifesaver on the street, the UF250. As long as you fill this piece of paper out after every stop you make, no one can say that you were being duplicitous in your police work. It is the stop, question, and frisk report. After every stop, after every arrest, this paper must be filled out. If not, something or someone can come back and take a piece out of your ass."

I was there, on the edge of something dark. I tried to raise my hand again and ask more about that paper, about being "duplicitous in your police work." That was something I'd never heard of before. I mean, how could you be duplicitous on the job? Billy Devlin raised his hand; Sergeant Jack was glad someone else was asking the question.

"Sir, do you have any advice for us once we get out there?"

Without batting an eye, Conroy said these six simple words, which I never forgot: "End of tour, you sign out."

thought about those words as I ran with a hundred other cadets the next morning. It was scorching hot even though it was only 7:20 in the A.M. The sun was slowly moving past the Brooklyn Bridge and toward New Jersey. The traffic above was light, though it wouldn't be long before the morning rush hour had cars and tempers overheating on the span above me. As I ran, I looked up at the massive stone expanse. That bridge always gave me a sense of pride. After all, it was the city's first bridge, built more than a hundred years before, and it wasn't called the Manhattan Bridge, or the New York Bridge, no, it was called the Brooklyn Bridge. It immediately gave the place where I grew up its own identity. I always felt like I was a part of something special; I think that everyone who was ever brought up in the borough feels that same sense of distinct belonging. But as I was running with the recruits that morning, I felt a strange distance from my home, even though it was less than two thousand feet to the south. The time I had spent in the academy had given me the feeling that it was a part of my past that was slowly being swallowed beneath this new shell that was covering my skin, my thoughts, and my soul. My home was with the 37,000 cops in New York City, wherever that was on any given day; that was now my home.

• • •

The clock was winding down toward the end of the greatest six months of my life. Before going into battle, we all had to be prepared for the mean New York streets. Sergeant Tom was in a rare mood this day. He was jazzed at what we were going to experience that hot summer evening.

"We can sit in this classroom and talk about what happened when I entered the apartment and Nat E. Dread took a shot at me, or what it's like to encounter your first microwaved infant, or how we collect body parts from a multiple catastrophic car crash—or plane crash, for that matter. We'd all like to think, 'Ah, simple patrol-guide stuff, bang it right out.' We know the paper we need to fill out, the notifications that have to be made, we got it all together. After all, we're graduates of the finest police academy in the world." He slowed down, looked around the room, into every recruit's eyes. He tapped his left temple slowly and almost whispered this: "Garbage in, garbage out, guys. Garbage in, garbage out."

He then took us on a trip to the medical examiner's office, not ten blocks from the police academy. The purpose: to man all of us up before we actually saw atrocities in the street. We gathered around the corpse on the examiner's table. Then, unbelievably, the pathologist cut open the dead man's skull and removed the brain. On down the body he went, removing other vital organs. It was the most horrific thing I had ever seen. I instantly found a flaw within myself: I could not stomach the carnage that violent death generally leads to. As I heard the buzz saw rip into the man's head, heard the bones cracking, watched the brain scraped free, then dropped into a metal scale, I vomited all over the ME's shiny linoleum floors and then some. To make matters worse, one of the workers at the morgue was an old high school friend, Mickey Farrell, who I hadn't seen in years. I was sure that everyone in Brooklyn would soon know about the little mishap.

Ultimately, though, I worried that maybe this job wasn't really for me, and that is what scared the shit out of me more than anything else. At the end of the day, I waited in the darkened doorway of the Chinese laundry situated across from the academy. The clouds overhead were threatening to clean the dirty streets of Gramercy Park in a very big way. Twentieth Street that time of night looked like Coney Island in February, boarded up and deserted. One by one, the instructors exited in their street clothes, making it hard to differentiate who was who. But I had an uncanny knack for knowing the gaits and walks of most of the instructors in the B company.

Sergeant Tom stepped outside holding on to an umbrella. *The only instructor smart enough to check the weather report in the morning.* I thought. He walked east across Twentieth Street toward Second Avenue; his left hand held the umbrella, right hand tucked into his light London Fog raincoat, probably holding on to his five-shot DT special. I followed him from across the street, trying to determine the proper way to approach him. I made it to Second Avenue, in front of the Academy Diner, the place where every recruit has eaten since the academy was built. He stepped off the curb in front of PJ Clark's, a pub off-limits to rookies, then turned to look inside to see if any of the other bosses were bellied up to the bar for an evening nightcap. Zilch, empty. At this point, I decided to walk right at him. He saw me, looked at his watch, and returned my salute.

"What, did you miss your ride, Officer Cea?"

I checked my watch and lied, "My girl's running a little late, sir, so I was going to get some coffee."

He just nodded. "All right, see ya tomorrow afternoon." He gave me a quick salute and stepped off the curb again. I needed to stop him. After my experience that day, there was too much to talk about.

"Sir, do you mind if I ask you a couple of things? Won't take up more than a minute?"

He looked at me and then looked up to the sky. "Gonna rain, man." He again glanced at his watch, then glanced at me, sizing up the situation. "There's a place called Wanda Has Wings on Second Avenue and Thirty-second. I'm going to meet some people there. I'm walking. You can walk me halfway if you want. I'd invite ya', but you know the deal about fraternization with superiors and local gin mills, yes?"

As I kept pace with him, I felt inferior to this man. Maybe it was the war stories or the image that we'd all created in our heads about him, but I just did not feel that I was quite yet able to lead this man into battle. Though I certainly would have followed him. However, the objective of every instructor at the academy was to mold young recruits into leaders, not followers. After all, the public needed to be led, didn't it?

"What's on your mind, Officer Cea?"

"I just want you to know, sir, that that little mishap at the morgue wasn't the norm, I just—" He laughed and shook his head.

"C'mon, I don't know any instructor who hasn't had that happen to him at least once a trip to that house of horrors. It's a normal reaction. It's what was supposed to happen. You don't think that every one of your fellow PPOs wanted to puke? If they didn't, there would be something wrong with them. You need to know what you're going to see out there, and that wasn't nearly the tip of it, brother. Garbage in, garbage out, you know what that means, yes?"

"We're going to see a lot of nasty stuff out there, sir. Don't let it get to us?"

"That's right, Cea. Don't even think for a millisecond that you can take anything about this job home with you. I tell you this now because it is the most important thing that you should take out of here. If you carry what you saw tonight home with you, I guarantee you, you won't last a year on the job, simple as that. I've seen the sharpest of guys who were as hard as nails, they truly were meant to be on this job, real heroic animals in the street, you know what happened to them? They burned out that quick." He snapped his fingers. "Drinking, drug addiction, suicide."

The word "suicide" lingered. He paused. "Blew their brains out over some other poor schmuck's misery. Far as I'm concerned, no mope with bad wiring is going to accelerate what is too short a gift anyhow, anyway; you understand?"

This was hitting home in a big way. And it was clear the guy actually cared. I was emboldened, feeling that I had begun to search out a weakness and confront it. It was all going to be cool, really cool. But there was more that was on my mind.

We kept walking. Sergeant Tom never took his hand out of his pocket, and his eyes tracked his surroundings: the people walking across the street, the man exiting the cab two blocks away, the homeless guy sleeping in front of the church. I realized I was looking at the same people, that the training was working.

"Sir, that day that your partner, Conroy, came in?" He slowed; his gait was a little more guarded. "You mentioned something that I can't quite put my finger on; you said that if we don't fill out the UF250, we could be accused of being duplicitous on the job. What does duplicitous on the job mean?"

He was quick to answer. "It means that if you don't fill the paper out it shows that you don't want the job to know that you jumped the said individual; now why wouldn't you want to let the job know this? You could have other ulterior motives."

This was getting good. "Like?"

"Like you were looking to rip the cat off."

"Rip the cat off." I felt a rush of embarrassment, of absolute fear. Not once had the phrase "rip off" been used to any of the recruits, where we might actually be the perps. I guess the instructors and the powers that be did not want any of us to know that that dark part of street life, of street patrol, actually did exist. I didn't even want to hear those words, "rip off." Too fucking scary.

"Whether you were dirty or you weren't is not the job's concern. The fact that you didn't do what you were trained to do for six months wasn't carried out and they're certainly going to think the worst. That, my friend, is not the position you want to find yourself in, this I guarantee."

We got to the front of Wanda Has Wings. It was booming, a smoky place with loud music, men and woman huddled around the bar, dartboards and pinball machines. I did not see Sergeant Tom fitting in this place, at all. I was a little disappointed. Was he as mortal as the rest of us? He looked right into my eyes and I was sure not to look away. I wanted him to know that what he was giving me was bible. It might have well been written in the patrol guide, because it was sacred. "Listen to me, Rob; this is the greatest job in the world, by far. We are here for a reason"—he finally took his hand out of his pocket; he slowly waved it around the city almost gallantly as he continued—"to make this place habitable. That's it in a nutshell. In order to do this, we as cops have to remain on top, and if you don't take any of the nonsense home with you, you will remain on top. Remember, there are more than just the perps out there gunning for us, there are the scumbag defense attorneys. Staying on top means don't let them beat you in court, do all the paper, be so fucking correct with your story, and never, not once, change that story about how you encountered him and how you locked him up. Because the second you deviate from your truth, that's the day you lose credibility." He looked inside, then grinned. "This little after-school lesson stays here, right, Cea?"

"Absolutely, sir."

We shook hands and he disappeared into Wanda Has Wings. I stood there for a while, my head swimming. There was some traffic buildup in the street as cars were trying to make their way to the entrance to the Midtown Tunnel, not two hundred feet from where I was standing. *Deviate from your truth? Be so fucking correct with your story?* More questions, though I had the distinct feeling that these questions were not going to be answered by anyone but me. I felt like I was finally ready to start learning the true meaning of what it was to be a New York City police officer, on the inside.

I walked back slowly, trying to figure out the deeper meaning of what he'd said. A blast of thunder shook the avenue; car alarms started to scream. Then the rain came down. I barely noticed. I made it to Twenty-first Street, under the FDR Drive, and got to my car, which was the only one there. I'd never seen the area so abandoned, so scarily empty. I immediately rose up when I noticed movement behind one of the stanchions. I dropped my leather bag next to my car and slowly approached. Although I was unarmed, there was something really sexy about being there alone. I now heard someone behind the large green cement pole. My heart was pounding; did he want to rip *me* off? I was three feet from the pole when a drunken homeless man fell over, out from behind it. My tongue tasted like copper as my heart almost shot out of my chest. The homeless guy fell backward when he saw me. He backpeddled, then ran. My breathing slowed down, though I did not move; the feeling was terrifying, yet so fucking exhilarating. *What just happened?*

I started up the Plymouth and pulled out; I made a quick right onto First Avenue at Thirty-fourth Street. I was traveling in the opposite direction from the one I should have been going in to get home. Something was pulling me that way. I banged a left at Thirty-seventh Street, then another left onto Second Avenue. The rain was hammering the streets. I found myself parked across from Wanda's. I trained my field of vision onto the bar . . . and there he was, Sergeant Tom O'Lary. He was sitting at a booth next to the window, alone. There was no one there he was trading war stories with, no beautiful woman amazed by his vast knowledge about *the* life, no ghostwriter bleeding Tom's memoirs onto the page. It was just him, alone and seemingly so sad. It started to make some kind of sense to me. After all, he too had just witnessed the removal of a man's cranium. A body, a slab of meat with its brain scraped free of its container, then plopped onto a metal scale, weighed, bagged, and discarded with the rest of the city's garbage. *Garbage in, garbage out, Sarge.* He'd also just unloaded some deep truths to a young man he was hoping would not burn out and fade away. Who would understand him? After all, those happy people in the bar were discussing the stock market or their pay raises, their weekend in the Hamptons or the curtains they'd just purchased at the mall. How could they possibly understand Tom's language; that language that only a cop understands; the language of life and death? Was Sergeant Tom sitting there trying to be normal, trying to feel like he fit in, like he was part of the other world? Or was he trying to forget? *Is this what you meant when you said garbage out, Tom?*

"On the Outside"

It was one of those days that said God loves this city. New York's first real snowfall ended at around six in the morning and the snowplows and shovels had not yet blitzed the neighborhood, so everything was stark white. My shield was gleaming like cut Waterford crystal on my dress-blue coat. The gold double-breasted buttons that ran the length of the coat, up to my chin, made me feel like a soldier coming back from battle, victorious. My black leather shoes were so shiny I could actually make out the reflection of the fuses underneath my dashboard. The scent of my leather gun belt, of the clean, oiled, blue metal .38 revolver, the weight of it on my hip, it all moved me into an altered state of consciousness. I was through the training; now it was time to use it.

From this day forward, we were not supposed to salute anyone other than superior officers; we were equal to the vast majority of the cops on the NYPD. The uniform cops in the street who would jokingly haze us as we walked to the academy in our recruit uniforms were now on the same level as us. Now it was just a matter of fitting in, but where?

The graduation ceremony at Madison Square Garden went by quickly, though long enough to keep my attention from waning and to reflect on everything that I'd learned in the past six months. Mayor Koch did his best to entertain *his* police force and their families without trying to sound too condescending. All of the big brass on the job, from the chief of patrol to the police commissioner, gave dignified speeches. They made us feel we should be proud to have made it this far, and our altruistic efforts could only make this city a better place to live. My thoughts exactly.

Afterward Sergeant Tom gave us our assignments. He handed me a slip of paper, winked at me, and said quietly, in a thick Jamaican accent, "Fort Jah, fighting for the homeland."

Fort Jah was the unofficial name of the 6-7 precinct, located in Brooklyn's East Flatbush section. Every precinct is given a name by the rank and file, prefixed by Fort and then whatever the climate is there. For instance, the 6-6 was christened Fort Surrender. The story behind it: Back in the early eighties, the Hasidic community was outraged over the arrest of a very popular rabbi who was *allegedly* caught in a very compromising position with an *alleged* prostitute. So they collectively formed an angry mob of fur hats and long black wool coats and stormed the precinct, basically holding it hostage until the lucky cleric was released. Of course, the politically savvy Mayor Koch had the 6-6 precinct commander give in and release the prisoner before the NYPD sustained any more embarrassment. The 6-7 received its moniker because of its heavy Jamaican population. "Jah" in Jamaican means God. Now back in the day, the eighties, this area was number one in action in all of the city. It led in arrests, gun collars; ranked annually in the top ten in homicides, rapes, and robberies. You name it, this place had it, and I was heading right for it, like a hollow point ready to do some damage. This was also the place where Sergeant Tom and John Conroy had made their bones in the late seventies and early eighties, where most of their war stories had played out. I was thrilled to be going into such a busy house. My assignment was patrol in the 6-7 precinct at 0001 hours—midnight, in two days. Patty Pirelli was assigned to another nasty place on the other end of Brooklyn, the 7-6 precinct, in Red Hook. To my happy surprise, not only would Billy Devlin be joining me in Fort Jah, but he'd also be my partner.

• • •

Fort Jah was a Brooklyn I'd never seen before. It was affectionately known as the "Badlands," with burnt-out storefronts, jerk chicken, rotty houses, graffitied metal gates, barrel fires, and crackheads who moved through the dark streets like zombies. I had the very real feeling that I was not going to see daylight for a long, long time.

The precinct was apparently always short of manpower. If you were sent here and you had some pull, you'd get out ASAP, transferring to a cushier house that wasn't so miserable and dangerous. This was all part of the reason Billy and I were paired up. Generally, two rookies are never put in a car together as soon as they hit the streets, but as I quickly learned, nothing is normal in places like the Badlands. When they are short cops, the bosses on the desk will do whatever it takes, even turning out one-car units—one officer per car, another big no-no that was a given in the ghetto.

On our first tour of duty, we cruised the streets of East Flatbush touching the outskirts of East New York. Billy's body language and voice told me he was uneasy. He held on to his radio like it was another weapon.

"This is unbelievable." I was awed by my surroundings. I drove the RMP like a pilot ready to drop bombs on the thirty-third parallel. For some reason, I was like a kid in a candy store. I wanted to be a part of it, smell it, breathe it, be it.

"No shit!" Billy was not nearly as psyched as I was.

"I mean, Billy, can you believe this?" I laughed, the nervous energy getting the best of me.

"Hey, fuck this, in two years we take the sergeant's exam. After that the lieutenant's test, and by the time we're thirty, we can make captain." He was hoping to salvage for the future something out of where he was right at this instant. I was not having any of it, wanting to get the most out of where we were at this very instant, right here, right now.

"Then what, Billy, mayor?"

"You're fuck-A right, pal. You think I want to stay in this shithole, do you?"

"C'mon, Billy, you can't tell me that this isn't everything you thought it was going to be. This is friggin' amazing."

Before he could answer, the radio barked; central dispatch cut through the eerie silence the ghetto evenings are famous for: "Seven Adam, K."

"G'head, central." Seven-Adam was John Conroy's sector, or area of patrol, this evening. I'd seen him at roll call, standing in the back with some of the old-timers while the new guys were front and center. We didn't take our eyes from the sergeant during roll call, but I was aware that he was in the back. I'd wanted to talk to him since his classroom visit to the academy some three months before, so this was the moment I'd been waiting for.

Central gave Conroy the job. "Adam, ten-ten, foul odor. 4211 Rutland Road, apartment 5J."

Conroy's voice came back over the radio. "We'll check and advise, K."

"Adam. That's Conroy, Billy," I said.

"So?" Billy could care less. I began to think that radio runs and straight eight out of the box were what he'd be all about.*

"So c'mon. Let's go swing by." I was trying to be very nonchalant about it.

"What, are you nuts? 'Foul odor'—hello, it's probably a DOA, man. They don't need backup, Rob."

"I just want to say what's up, Billy. We met the guy in the academy. Let's tell him O'Lary sends his regards." He frowned, trying to decide what to do. "C'mon, Billy, the radio is dead. We get a job, we can pick it right up. He's in the next friggin' sector, for Christ sakes. Let's go!"

I didn't wait for his answer as I made a quick U-turn. I drove to the location at an easy pace since I wanted it to look as coincidental as possible. After all, this guy could smell shit underwater, and the last thing I wanted to do was start raising flags on day one.

I pulled the RMP down Ninety-second Street, one of those

---

* Meaning he wouldn't get out of the RMP unless directed to a job by central or a superior officer, and he only wanted to work the eight hours he was getting paid for. Straight eight was a company man's logic.

tight, one-way Brooklyn streets with rows of two-story railroad apartment houses on both sides. As we drove down the street, we could barely make out the addresses. The block seemed really dark; then it dawned on me—half the streetlights were blown out. Without any lights, it is harder to see what does not want to be seen. I also noticed movement on the stoops, though I could not get a clear picture of anyone. For all I knew, someone could have had an AK-47 trained at my head. Had they taken a shot at me, I would not have noticed anything other than muzzle flash and subsequently a *killer* headache, the kind you don't wake up from.

Down the street, we saw Conroy's RMP pull up with no lights, from the wrong end, to a prewar building. He double-parked, then got out of the car with another big uniform. They slowly made their way to the front. Conroy was casual in his demeanor, something I'd come to understand was part of his genius: Lull the bad guys into a state of calmness, then carpet-bomb the fuck out of them, into submission.

I could see Billy did not regard this man in the same way I did. I think he wanted to learn at his own pace, with zero input from anyone other than our immediate bosses. I also think that Billy saw John as an A-type renegade, a loose cannon. Me, I knew Conroy had seen it all, done it all. I could learn an enormous amount from this salty veteran.

We pulled in front of their RMP and got out. They both noticed us but kept on talking to a half-naked wire-thin Jamaican. Though it was barely thirty degrees out, the man only wore a pair of worn pajama pants and no top. He was sucking on what appeared to be a big, fat joint. Conroy and his partner stared at us blankly as we walked up; there was a very uncomfortable moment of silence. Billy just dropped his head in embarrassment. I smiled, then stuck out my hand. Conroy did not do the same.

"Who are you?" he asked coolly.

"We're in sector Charlie, right around the corner, and . . ."

Now the Jamaican cat was staring at us. He was definitely sucking on some of that serious Jamaican ganja we'd heard so much about. The Jamaican pulled back on it and smiled before he let out a monster smoke ring. "Is a Philly's blunt, mon," he laughed. It bothered me that the man was being overly disrespectful by smoking the weed right in front of us, four uniforms, but I instinctively realized that the Jamaican and Conroy must have had some sort of street give-and-take; they obviously knew each other. I could see that Billy didn't like being mocked, and then Conroy and his partner laughed as well. I felt as though we, the two rookies, were being tested. I began to feel the encounter going south very quickly. I decided to try and salvage what little pride we had left.

"We met you in O'Lary's class. He told us that when we ran into you to say hello." I thought I saw a glimmer of a smile.

"Couple a new guys huh?"

This was encouraging. "Yeah, this is our first midnight. You know, every time O'Lary gave us some wild scenario in class, your name came up."

He was sizing me up in much the way O'Lary had on the way to Wanda Has Wings, I thought. He then nodded his head, not looking at his partner, the Jamaican cat, or Billy, just me. He figured he's got the schmuck, why not use it to his advantage?

"Name came up in O'Lary's class?" he asked.

"Yeah, all good shit though. I mean, c'mon, two combat crosses, the medal of valor, yeah, your name came up a lot, right, Billy?" I turned to see that Billy was completely embarrassed by the encounter. Maybe I was gushing just a little too much, but I thought the guy deserved big ups. After all, he was the rightful owner of those awards and respect was the very least he should get. I was not going to be embarrassed about admiring him. Still, I am from the streets of Brooklyn and I know when a game is going to be played on me. I was waiting for the other shoe to drop, and then it did . . .

"Tell you what, guys . . . we're into our meal right now. Thought there was no units available, so as long as you fellows are here, why not let two of your older brothers get our KFC on? What's say you guys pick this job up for us, we owe you one. I mean, goddamn, we don't watch each other's backs, who's gonna watch it for us?" This made perfect sense to me. Before we could answer, he picked up the radio, put himself out to meal, and informed central that we were picking up the job. We heard a lot of units laughing over the radio. This was of course the worst job you could have, a likely DOA, and to give it away was like a dream come true, like hitting the patrolman's lottery.

I felt like a real schmuck as we entered the building. The heat was blasting from the radiators in the hallway; the cracked front window on the metal door was completely steamed over. It felt like it was a hundred degrees in there, like I'd just entered the gates of hell. I opened up my uniform coat, and already felt the sweat beading up on my forehead. I did not want to think about what lay ahead. Billy and I made our way up the stairs of the nasty apartment building with its stink of steam, burnt curry, and stale nicotine. When we reached the third floor of the building, it hit us, that putrid odor you never forget: the smell of death. Billy was pissed, to say the least. This was the last place he wanted to be, and I had placed him squarely in the middle of it.

"Why didn't you just pull down his pants and give him a blow job? I mean, are you fucking nuts?"

I covered my nose, though I didn't want Billy to see this. I kept walking up the stairs. "C'mon, Billy, guy wanted to go on meal. We didn't help him out, it would be all over the precinct that we scumbagged them. Then we'd be in worse shape. Besides, we did him a solid. Maybe he'll return the favor . . . hey, he's a good guy to have on our side out here."

He didn't say anything as the odor attacked us hard. I felt my throat starting to close; I stopped and gagged before I got to the landing.

"Billy, man, please . . . you go in. I'm no good at this." This of course went over like a lead balloon.

"Are you fucking kidding me? You got us involved in this bullshit. I'm no good at it either. What do you think, I'm the friggin' medical examiner?"

As we reached the door, I pulled out my nightstick and banged hard. I was praying that it was just some guy who wasn't very clean and maybe needed to take out the garbage. There was no answer. Billy pushed my shoulder. I turned the doorknob to find it unlocked, so I moved into the dark, quiet apartment. The smell was indescribable.

I whispered, "Fuck, Billy. Fuck."

When Billy clicked on his flashlight, I could see he didn't seem as repulsed as I was. For the life of me, I could not figure out how he could stomach the smell. He yelled out, "Police, anyone here?" I had to turn on him; my sarcastic look made the point.

"Hey, I have to check. There could be someone here." I would have laughed at his comment, but the shit I was wading in was knee deep. The apartment, through the thin beam of Billy's Maglite, looked as if it hadn't been cleaned in thirty years. There were pizza boxes with green moldy crust being eaten by an army of roaches, newspapers, overflowing ashtrays, feces. Maybe it's a dead dog, let it be a dead dog, please, I begged to the patrolman's God. The odor was too powerful though, all the markings of one very ripe dead person.

"Billy, this is way fuckin' foul, man," I said. Then I moved slowly into the back room. I pulled my Maglite out at this point; I guess I needed something to hold on to as I didn't think Billy would've appreciated me holding on to his arm. We shined the narrow beams around the room, and there it was, on the bed. I gagged, "Shit, Billy, shit!"

In the pale light, it didn't look real, which made it all the more horrific. He was a naked man, although it very well could've been a woman. The body was so distended, the only one who was going to solve that mystery was the medical examiner himself. A thick blue tongue was protruding from its mouth. The eyes were a dull yellow, and were so bulbous they hung out of their sockets. I never knew that an eyeball could hang down four inches out of its orbital. I tried not to fixate on any one thing. *Garbage in, garbage, fucking out, Rob,* I thought. My legs were so weak; I could not get another step closer. We noticed movement along its gray-and-black-splotched skin. *What in the fuck is moving,* I wondered. I inched closer though my legs at this point certainly had a mind of their own. I shined my light on one particular movement.

"Fucking maggots!" I yelled. Hundreds of them. Billy nudged his nightstick into one of the carcass's many folds. We heard a slight tearing noise and what sounded like a water balloon opening on impact. Billy shot back and screamed, "Fuckin' thing is exploding!" As I felt the room start to yaw, I charged out. The heat, the added ripe odors, and the fact that we were alone in this tomb of death forced everything to come up on me. Garbage out.

My first DOA was the defining moment in my very young career, and most definitely in my life. It taught me two very important lessons. One, this is what it really boils down to, this is where we are all going to end up, fodder for maggots. Doesn't matter what we did in life, no matter how great or miserable a life it was, we all end up as hatching pods for maggots. Whether it's in a temperature-maintained mausoleum, the basement of a prestigious hospital, or the comfort of your own bed, it's just a matter of time before you become a part of the unstoppable cycle of life and death, the transmigration from human to a viscous form of larvae. Within minutes I was stripped of any illusions I had of an idyllic afterlife awaiting me. This incident brought the simple brutality and inevitability of nature into focus. This thing in front of me stood out like a black dot on a white canvas. BOOM, end of story, last stop on the train; no matter what we do we will never beat the end. Finality at its fuck-you best.

Second lesson, I had to man-up on this weakness. Death would have to become a part of the rush for me, part of the jones that I needed to survive on these mean Brooklyn streets.

So a couple nights later, I went to discipline myself on the fine art of dealing with death.

On the way to my lesson, I bought a bottle of Jameson's to wet my old Brooklyn buddy Mickey Farrell's beak. I pulled onto First Avenue, threw my police-parking permit on the dashboard, and made my way to the side entrance, where I was met by a hospital security guard. He led me down the dreary halls to the medical examiner's office. Mickey was there waiting for me, just as we'd discussed when I had called him a day earlier. He smiled briefly, then his gaze quickly moved to the bag I was carrying. I hadn't seen him in over five years, yet that first encounter with him at the ME's office—when he seemed to thoroughly enjoy my spewing—told me he had developed a taste for the joy juice. His pasty face was starting to sag and crease, making him look like he was in his mid-thirties though he was probably younger than me. I immediately pulled the bottle of whiskey out and he actually licked his lips. He didn't look at me, didn't shake my hand, just took the bottle from me and turned away, saying "Yeah, that's what I'm talking about, Jameson's. Yeah, gonna be a good night, Cea. Follow me . . . By the way, meat wagon's on a run in the Bronx." He looked over his shoulder with a creepy smile as he walked. "They're bringin' in a nice decapitation. You wanna hang for that one?"

Job's perfect for him, a ghoul who likes to drink, I thought. I smiled back. "No, bro, just want to peek around for a half hour at the most. Thanks though, you're the king."

"Whatever," he said, fumbling with some keys. Then I saw a door open to a stairway that went one way, down. *How appropriate.* I went very fucking slowly.

He clicked a switch and the fluorescents jumped to life. I had to cover my eyes from the shock of white light, then kept them closed longer than I needed to. I took a deep breath and opened my eyes. The room was clean, white. White linoleum tiles, white walls, and a whole wall of gray metal, a grid of four-foot-square doors in rows of eight stacked three high.

His voice jolted me as it echoed through the room. "Take your pick, Cea. These are just the ones who were finished in the last twenty-four hours. There's way more next door, really fuckin' good ones . . ." I held up my hand to stop him from talking.

"You think I could get a few minutes alone?"

He smiled very broadly, as if he'd just figured out a math problem, then he snickered, "Yo, C, you ain't lookin' to tap any a these dead booties. I mean, you get caught fuckin' down here, that's the end a my career!" I had to blink a few times at the accusation. Later I could laugh about it, but at twenty-one the last thing I wanted to be thought of was a necrophiliac.

"No, no, man, it's got nothing to do with that, Mickey. I just wanna prep myself for when I run into this in the street. I mean, you saw what happened to me last time I was here."

He curled his lip and puckered up his face, "Oh shit yeah, C, I remember. Yeah, yeah, I'm digging it, Cea, do what ya gotta do, pal. I'll be back in fifteen minutes; that enough time?" He walked back up the stairs, and before he reached the top landing, he yelled back down, "There's condoms in the top-right desk drawer." His sinister laugh trailed off as he slammed the door closed. I heard him lock me in. *No way out, good.*

I pulled the first, then the second, third, an entire row of eight drawers. Each body was covered in a plain white hospital sheet. No frills; none could be expected. The atmosphere seemed a little less horrific than the last time I'd been in this building, though I felt my throat closing up. I didn't know what was underneath those sheets. *Fuck it.* I pulled each sheet off, one by one, careful not to *look* at what was underneath. I stepped back, staring up at the fluorescent lights, bit down hard on my back teeth, and looked down and studied the death in front of me. A black woman lay on the cold metal. Half her head was missing. I heard my pulse throb and felt the blood rushing through my ears. I avoided closing my eyes, forcing myself to take it all in. Next was a man with six tiny wounds in his lower extremities. I fought off the gag reflex, felt the tiny beads of sweat sweeping down my neck. Men, women, an infant, all naked, in various and strange forms of postmortem. The last drawer was a good one, a boy, no more than ten years old, white. *He could've been me.* He had baseball stitching running up his entire torso. *What must it be like to lose this gift so young?* I moved closer to the body, holding on, forcing myself to beat this. I extended my hand and finally laid it down on this kid's chest. I closed my eyes, felt the pinch of the thick thread that held him together. Moving my hand down the cold flesh, I felt his tiny ribs protruding through the skin. By the time my hand rested where his stomach had been, I opened my eyes. There was no more gagging. The sweat seemed to evaporate. I felt the waves of nausea leave my body.

I breathed in deeply, then out. I'd done it. This simple confrontation had exorcised the weakness within me. Dead bodies were now just that, dead bodies. Pieces of meat, much like what I'd seen a day earlier. *I walk into a DOA now, or gnarly crime scene, fuck it. It'll be like walking into any butcher shop to pick out the best cut of sirloin,* I thought. What I didn't realize at the time was the profound effect this would have on how I saw the living as well—that they were merely potential pieces of meat. Anyone, and most definitely everyone, was going to end up on these tables, or tables just like them, no doubt. From this day forward, anyone I met, talked to, ate with, or made love to, for that matter, was a slab of meat on those tables.

3

"Test-i-Lie"

It's hard to tell who's strapped. They all got fuckin' coats on, Rob." I wasn't really listening to Billy. I was ready to jump out of my skin with excitement. The moment we sat in the RMP, I told Billy I wanted a gun collar. I wanted to get in the game. I kept my hands tight on the steering wheel to keep from fidgeting. I did not want Billy to think I had some nervous condition or quite possibly a cocaine jones, but that's what I felt like. We'd been at the precinct a week already and I'd seen Conroy and his men bringing in gun after gun. I'd sit quietly pretending to read my patrol guide while I listened to every word they were saying about the collar they'd just brought in. I knew there was a way of seeing the perp carrying a gun. The slight twitch when he sees a cop, a stutter step, a shift of posture. It was subtle, but it was there. And I was sure I would see it.

There were so many Rastafarians out on the street, I felt like I was in a turkey shoot. They had really long dreads, and some wore jiffy-pop hats to hold in those "antennae's to Jah." I knew most of them were carrying, because this is where Conroy does his best work. I also knew they'd not seen Billy or me out here before, so we must be "puppies out the cage." They were right. I felt like I was losing the battle before it had even started. As I drove by them, they'd smile, taunting with their gold teeth and dark shades. Billy and I were fish in a large bowl and I did not like it, I wanted to turn the tables, bring the battle to them, see how they dug it. I really didn't know what to do, how to approach and which one to approach. Then I saw a group huddled around a storefront on Ninety-fifth Street and Rutland Road. It was in the middle of the block, so I figured if someone was carrying he could only run two ways, east or west. South would put him into the closed storefronts, north was where we were. I rolled up slowly, about thirty feet from the crowd of men, and all of them seemed to tighten up, meaning they either stood more erect or they got back on their haunches to see what *we* were going to do. I felt something strange vibrating through my body, the realization that there must be a runner here. Someone strapped who was going to take off like his dick was on fire. *How do I do this?*

Fuck it, gonna wing it. As I sped up the car, Billy slammed back into his seat. He was looking the other way, unaware of my intended prey. He held on to the door strap, screaming "Rob, fuck are you doing, man?" He raised his knees up instinctively to cover his chest and keep it from banging into the dashboard as I jumped the curb. Sure as shit three very large men took off, two west, one east. *Why is he going east, my car is facing east holy shit, this is going to be really fucking scary!* I was so G'd up about this first chase, I leaped out of the car without placing it in park. *Technically* I should have just gone after him with the RMP, but my mind only saw this dread moving like a deer and I needed to run as well. I heard the car skid to a stop as Billy jerked the gearbox, slamming it into park.

I'm sure he was screaming at me though, truthfully, I heard nothing. I saw this dread dart north on Ninety-fifth Street. *Two blocks and he hits Lincoln Terrace Park,* I thought. At the station house, I'd overheard Conroy say that once a runner made it into that park, whatever he was carrying was going to grow legs and he was going to lose his colorful hat and jacket, becoming just another dread in the park looking for some pay pussy. I hit Ninety-fifth Street, my legs feeling incredibly strong. I saw him jerk his head at me to see how far away I was. I realized that my gun wasn't out. *Rookie move,* I thought. I ripped it from my holster, and went into police-science mode, balling my right hand into a fist and placing it approximately where my heart would be. If he takes a shot at me and it's placed perfectly center mass, in that kill zone, the bullet just might ricochet off one of the many bones in my hand and miss the sweet spot, saving my life. Did it ever work? Don't know.

I was gaining on him. Fifteen feet away, I shouted, *"Police . . . Stop."* A car screeched up the block from behind, but I wanted to get to him before Billy did, so I pushed harder. By the time I was three feet from him, his hat had flown off and his long dreadlocks were whipping in the wind. Instinct took over as I dove forward and grabbed one of his dreadlocks. He screamed as it tore from his scalp, and he hit the ground hard, with me on top of him. I wrapped my right arm around his chest, pinning his arms so he could not move. It took a few seconds to get my gun into that soft spot just under his earlobe, but he certainly got the message.

"Yah, Officer, every-ting irie. Don't fuckin' wet me up, every-ting cool running." This he screamed so there would be no miscommunication between him, my trey-8, or Billy. I suddenly saw the blur of Billy's blue knee come crashing down onto the dread's neck, immediately rendering him helpless. I heard a bone or two crack under the enormous pressure. I knew at this point that Billy was going to be fabulous backup. Neutralize first: ask questions later," he'd say. As a crowd started to build, Billy helped me cuff him and I rolled him over, dug around his waistband, and felt a thin piece of metal. For a second I became very aware of my ass puckering, because I thought this very hurt individual was almost killed because of a slim jim or some other burglary tool. *This would not be a good first collar.* I frantically dug farther and felt the barrel of a gun. I pulled up his sweater and there it was: a stainless-steel .380 automatic. The weight of it, the smell of the metal, gave me an incredible rush, one that comes with absolute victory. The thin piece of metal was a cut-down coat hanger shaped like an S, with one end that hooked onto his elastic pants while the other end held the barrel in place. A Badlands holster for sweatpants.

I heard sirens getting closer. "You put this over?" I asked nervously.

"Fuckin' blow-job right I put it over! Why wouldn't I?"

Cars shot down the block like jet fighters, from the 6-7, 7-1, 7-3, and the 6-9. Four different precinct cops dropped everything to help another cop in need because in a flash they could be on the other end of that call for help. It was incredibly impressive, in less than a minute there were thirty men securing us and the perimeter. It was a rush to see all those turret lights, those blaring sirens, the guns drawn, the cops' backs to me, protecting us from the crowd. This was what it was all about. This was what I'd signed up for, and I wanted to do it again, right that instant, before the hot shot of adrenaline wore off.

Did we use excessive force? Don't know, but had "Nat E. Dread" gotten a shot off and punched a quarter-size hole through my windpipe, would that have been excessive on his part? *I am not getting paid to be shot. Last thing you do is sign out end of tour.* That little dictum suddenly made all the sense in the world to me. We were playing for keeps out here. Win, you live. Lose, you die, period.

I pulled the dazed and moaning dread off the ground, "Need a fuckin' doctor, mon, broke me fuckin' neck, mon, why dee's bumba-clots cuff me up like dis, why you terrorize me?" Then I noticed Conroy. He stepped closer and the Rasta started to wail. If he was looking for a friendly, familiar face, he found one. "Con, you see what this Rasta-clot did to me head bone, mon? Him fuck me up for a little biscuit, mon. Why dee's blood clots treatin' me like a dog, Con, why?"

Conroy's partner started to laugh. "What the fuck is a head bone?" That brought some of the cops to their knees. Another one said, "He didn't say head bone, he said ham bone." The sergeant on patrol started to laugh; he began to shuffle in the street and sing " 'The ham bone's connected to the neck bone, the neck bone's connected to the head bone . . . ' " I saw that Conroy really wasn't amused. He just studied the dread, Billy, and me as we placed him in the back of the RMP and drove him away.

In the car, Billy wasted no time before laying into me. "Don't do that again, Rob. Don't leave me hangin', not knowing where the fuck you went, okay? We can't protect each other if we don't know where the other is, yes?"

"Yeah, Billy, I'm sorry, bro. I don't know what it was . . . I just reacted; won't happen again." I felt uneasy as I drove, not about the chase or the capture, but the reaction of all the cops. This guy just had one of the worst days of his life and it was all about "the joke is on him." I actually felt bad for this guy, despite the fact that given the chance he'd probably shoot me point-blank in the face to get away. Catching a mope with a pistol didn't seem to matter to these guys. The importance of the collar meant nothing; Billy and I were simply the court jesters who'd brought them a warm ghetto body they could have a laugh at. I worried that I might become as cold and unsympathetic as all these salty veterans were.

Brooklyn Central Booking was the facility where every arrest made in Brooklyn was arraigned. It occupied the rear second floor of the 8-4 precinct at the base of the Manhattan Bridge. The precinct was located in the middle of Fort Greene, a very nasty place. As you approach it from the south end of Brooklyn, namely Flatbush Avenue, one thing always came to mind, "out of place." It seemed as if someone had lifted a slate-gray building up from midtown Manhattan and jammed it right in the middle of all these hideous brick buildings from hell. The Manhattan Bridge in the background made it feel that much more surreal, especially at night when it was lit and became the magic back-drop for the graffitied prison cells known as the Fort Greene housing projects.

The room upstairs in e-cab—the early case assessment bu-reau—where every Brooklyn cop arraigned his prisoners was a fifteen-by-fifteen office converted into a police holding area. It held a few wooden benches and one ratty easy chair with more tears in it than it had material; still, every cop wanted it, as it was the most comfortable seat in the house. There were rectangular windows that ran the length of the west wall of the room. They were sealed shut, locking in the mix of sweat, tobacco, dust, and paint. They were covered with torn black shades to keep the day-light out. I later realized that the room resembled a crack den.

You were up as long as any grinding pipe head, and when you left, felt just as dirty. This place was not built for comfort or cleanliness. It shouted to the cops upon entering, Don't even think about doing overtime up in here.

As I sat there, I couldn't help thinking about Conroy. How it seemed as though he was a part of everything and everyone in the streets. I'd had an odd, uneasy feeling since locking up the dread. It was the cold look that Conroy had given me. Did he think I was stealing his thunder? I could only hope he understood that I aspired to being as good a cop as he was. It was clear that he was evolutions ahead of any other cop out there. I wondered what it would be like to ride in an RMP with him, the incredible knowledge I'd gain was inconceivable to me at that time.

I heard my name called over the loudspeaker. *Thank God.* I'd only been sitting there for two hours, which in itself was a miracle, as some cops had to wait in e-cab three days before getting called by the ADA. This all depended on the computer system cooperating and how busy the streets were at any given time. I entered the ADA's room. Another office probably ten feet longer than the cop's waiting room except this room was cleaner, much cleaner. It held ten neat cubicles, windows that actually worked, a water fountain, even artwork on the walls.

I felt human again as I approached the desk of Archibald Waxman. He was a two-hundred-pound sausage in a hundred-pound Brooks Brothers bag wrapped with a polka dot bow tie. Under the bow tie it did not appear that Archibald had a neck. His head just sort of popped out of the striped designer shirt, like a pink bubble. He had large jowls and enormous cheeks. On his pinched and upturned nose sat round black glasses, the lenses so thick his eyes appeared as big as half dollars. *Pirelli would have a year's worth of material with this guy.* His head bald, with wispy strands combed over from first to third. He reminded me of a cartoon character. Then it hit me—Wimpy, the burger-eating guy from the Popeye cartoon! He didn't looked up at me once, just stared down at the paper in front of him. He waved his hand lazily at the chair in front of his desk. He then started to stroke his head, and closed his eyes. He said in a nasal voice, "G'head."

That was the clincher; I dropped my head and thought of anything I could to stop from laughing.

"I'm sorry, I'm not foll—"

He shot back quickly, trying to stay in the moment. "265.01.03. Yessss." He seemed slightly annoyed given the elongated es.

He still hadn't opened his eyes. "Uhh, yes, I made the gun arrest on Ninety-fifth Street, off Rutland Road."

"How did you make this"—he fluttered his fingers up in the air like he was shooing a butterfly away—"gun arrest?"

"I was driving eastbound on Rutland Road. I saw the individual tighten up, and he ran, so I chased him . . ."

"And why'd you chase him?"

Again I was stumped. "Because he got this terrified look and then he ran."

He unclasped his hands from his round belly, sat straight up in his chair, and opened his eyes. He smiled. "Let me make this easy for you"—he studied my nameplate—"Officer Ceeeeea. Did you see the gun before you chased him?"

I just shook my head no. He tilted his head at me, then pouted. "I have to 343 it." He pulled a fat gold pen from his really nice shirt pocket and quickly scribbled on my arrest sheet.

"What does '343 it' mean?"

"I'm tossing the case. We're going to drop the charges."

I shot up in my chair. "Why are you dropping the charges?"

"You can't chase someone for looking scared." Another odd grin. "Unless they want to be."

"But I got the gun off the street; I did what I was supposed to do. You can't just throw it out. C'mon . . ."

He eased up in the chair, laid his tiny, puffy, manicured hands on the table. He moved them in small circles, gently, along the desk. "There is no probable cause to make the arrest because there was no reasonable suspicion to make the stop. You understand this? Probable cause, Officer Ceeeeea. Words to live by."

• • •

We were into the Badlands for a couple of months by this point and it was teeming with dangerous street cats—besides the Rastafarians, there were homegrown blacks and the occasional Puerto Rican—all out there with deadly agendas. I studied them and where they lived. There wasn't one street I did not drive or walk down. I learned back alleys, courtyards, abandoned buildings; ways out, ways in. I wanted to know escape routes, lookout points. I wanted to know the people and the geography as if I'd been conceived on one of these roofs and been born and raised in one of these buildings. I studied them moving through on foot, in cars, on bicycles, cataloging in my mind the neighborhood guys, their girlfriends who lived in the area, and who was a transient. I also came to know who slung drugs, and what types of drugs they were slinging. My job was not only answering the radio, but it was seeing what did not want to be seen. The PRs were generally in the area to buy, mostly heroin, or "boy" as it was called. The homegrowns, or American Blacks, were into slinging crack or coke, which was known as "girl." The Rastafarians, the Jews of the Caribbean, they were into everything: slinging crack, coke, heroin, and their biggest street crop—marijuana. They took special pride in the sale and distribution of this because it defined who they were. It was their culture, and they were the cumumba-jumba connoisseurs of weed.

They were also extremely smart. Getting caught with a couple of ounces, or O-Zs, of coke was a B felony which, put into simple street terms, carried the same type of sentencing as manslaughter or attempted murder. Getting caught with a couple of ounces of heroin carried the same sentence as if you'd shot and killed a cop, twenty to life. A perfect illustration of this kind of thinking came from a defense attorney hired by some Rastafari I had locked up with a little less than two O-Zs of boy. Only a month before, we'd pulled a car over for running a red light. The driver was high on coke; his nostrils had white residue from all the blow he'd been snorting. Of course he had his drug testicles on, so he took off on us, but we caught him and locked him up. A subsequent search of his car turned up the heroin, simple, by the numbers, a-b-c. A week or so later he apparently made bail because I saw him out in the Badlands. I had treated him well during the arrest processing; bought him a pack of Kools, or double Os as they're referred to; gotten him a meatball sandwich; allowed him to make a bunch of phone calls. I'd been watching how Conroy was treating all of his perps and saw how much respect they gave him. When I say respect I mean he'd get street *jugo,* or juice, from them—all of his perps would roll over on other perps wanted for serious crimes, bolstering Conroy's already staggering arrest record. *Treat them good, they'll treat you good.*

So this cat and I were cool with each other. He came over to the RMP, started to laugh. "Yo, Officer Cool, what up, check this, ya man, check this. My lawyer tell me, why you no shoot that bumba cop in the head, looking at the same time up north, man, same motherfuckin' time behind this punk-ass drug charge. Him actually tell me to wet you up, same fuckin' charge." Now I had to absorb exactly what was being broken down for me. A defense attorney had actually told his client he should've shot the cop, *me,* because an A felony is twenty to life any way you cut it. He had a better chance by clipping me and getting away as opposed to letting the "bumba cop" lock him up to face serious time. This put defense attorneys in a special category for me. I wonder how many of his clients actually took his advice and ended careers and lives.

Back on the streets, I was learning not only who the dealers were, but also the lookouts and enforcers—or street lieutenants—who worked for them. The whole street operation of selling drugs was as much a paramilitary operation as the one I was in except the pay scale was very different. The risks were very similar though: lots of jail time, serious injury or death for them; lots of jail time, serious injury or death for us. Billy and I started out slow, bringing in a gun a week off the street. I treated my perps well, and developed a reputation on the street as being cool, which translated into them feeling comfortable enough with me to trade street secrets—who was wanted, what their competition was up to, who was bringing in quantity drugs, all of the shit that I'd signed up for. I was learning how to talk to them, and, more important, how to listen to them, not seeming too anxious or too condescending. I was learning from Conroy that keeping your enemies close is a necessity, and to do this you pretty much had to breathe the same air, eat the same food, and speak the same language. When in Rome . . .

I started to really feel the vibe. And I started to understand something about myself: *I really hate losing.*

I was making collars almost instinctively. I'd see a cat tighten up or change his body language at the sight of me and I'd feel the adrenaline shoot through me; it was an uncontrollable burst of excitement or energy that would always lead to a chase that turned into a gun collar. A lot of them were like the first gun collar, some were much more brutal, some were easy. What was killing me though was that for all the gun collars I was making, they all ended up the same: 343'd at central booking. Not one of the arrests up to this point had made it out of stage-one arraignment. Every time I'd bring it in, the ADAs would ask the same question front and fucking center: "How'd you make the arrest, Officer Cea?" My answer was the same every time: "He got incredibly scared, took off, and was subsequently arrested carrying a pistol." Their response was to dump it and dismiss me like I was wasting everybody's time, including that of the perps I was arresting.

Now, I wasn't much of a drinker at this point, but I'd find that when I lost in central booking, a few shots of bourbon would always smooth out the roughness I was feeling. On one particular evening, I found my way to Alfredo's, a nasty little hole-in-the-wall in Red Hook, Brooklyn, at the base of the Brooklyn Battery Tunnel. My academy pal Patty Pirelli worked in the area and was particularly fond of this place because of the anything-goes Latinas who hung here. I'd been to a lot of bars all over the city that guys claimed were infamous for tons of beautiful woman who would do almost anything for any type of legit guy, and in the ghetto the most legit guys these chicks knew were either lawyers representing the men in their lives or the cops who put them away. Sad but true. So I was expecting much the same as

I'd encountered in these other bars: a bunch of whiskey-dicked cops at the bar trying to chat up the same three or four nurses. I'd been wrong.

Alfredo's sat below the Gowanus Expressway, and was situated between a ratty tire-repair shop to its left and to its right a secondhand furniture store. The furniture was anything but secondhand, more like third and fourthhand. Alfredo's looked like any other ghetto gin mill. A storefront-type facade with blacked-out windows and a red front door. Inside, a red velvet curtain in the vestibule, a twenty-foot bar, and across from the bar about fifteen tables that looked on to a small dance floor. The difference was that this thousand-square-foot hole-in-the-wall was everything that Pirelli had said it was; it was the shit, it smoked every other club and bar in the city. The music was a mix of old school R and B, disco, and Latin. The walls were wet with the sweat from the men and woman grinding and dancing. If you were into beautiful Latinas, this was the jammy jam. I had never seen so many beautiful women in one place in all of my young life.

Tonight Pirelli was in rare form on the dance floor, jammed between two half-naked, spectacular-looking women who were grinding him from the front and back. Not one of Alfredo's patrons even raised an eyebrow at the behavior, as this was considered tame in this place. Billy was already at the bar, half in the bag, talking to the bartender, Roxanne, another ghetto fabulous, sexy Latina. I entered and moved right to the bar. Billy was surprised to see me, obviously, because we'd just made a collar three hours prior.

"What the fuck happened?"

"Same bullshit, Billy. 'How'd you make the arrest, Officer?' 'Myself and my partner rolled up the guy gets incredibly nervous, he immediately takes off, we chase him, make the arrest, blah, blah, blah . . . ' I'm getting fucking tired of this, Billy, tired of . . . wasting everyone's time. Six gun arrests, not one time to court. This prick was out before I was. It's like, what the fuck are we doing wrong? I just don't know what to do."

I knew Roxanne the bartender had a thing for me; Pirelli had told me. She jumped in and poured me a double of Jack Daniel's.

"C'mon, Rob, have a shot of sunshine." I looked at the shot and swallowed it, put it down, and she refilled it again and then once again. I dropped some cash on the bar. She would not take it, just leaned in and kissed my lips gently. "It's on me, ya pretty moth-erfucker." It felt good, too good. Her kiss was hot, sexy, different from my girlfriend's. Streety, and I liked it. This was a different type of woman, just like the ones I was seeing and becoming so very familiar with every day at work, only Roxanne was all that and a big bag of wings.

The warmth of the bourbon and the very friendly bartender was the perfect ghetto antidote to what I thought were the wor-ries of the world. I looked around and felt very insulated, cared for. I felt as though everyone in this room had the same disease I had, and all the ghetto beauty that surrounded us, and the bottles filled with that warming liquid and the lights, and my partners, and the life and death that we faced every day, and the chicks get-ting high in the bathroom . . . well, this was it, the place we could all go with the same goal, to find the cure. And at Alfredo's, cured we fucking were.

Pirelli danced over, leaving his two hotties alone to grind each other. "Rob, I thought you collared up?" He swabbed the sweat from his head with a bar towel. Roxanne jumped in.

"Don't get him started again or I'm a have to pour him an-other three shooters. Tatico won't be able to take me home tonight." I knew what "Tatico" meant in the streets: boy-fuck-toy. I pretended I didn't hear it, though I saw Billy jerk his head at me and felt Pirelli's foot kick my ankle. He then leaned in and whispered in my ear, "Tatico? Kid, I swear to God, look at those two chochas on the dance floor. They're into whatever the fuck I want them to be into. You, me, the bartender, and them, think of the laughs." I knew Roxanne knew what was being said. I thought of my girlfriend, who I was just starting to get serious with, and felt a pang of guilt.

"Got another one tossed at BCB."

Pirelli looked at me like I had suddenly grown testicles for ears. He looked at Roxanne. "Baby, fuck him, give *me* the shot." He then turned to me with absolute disbelief. "Are you kidding me, you're pissed because you got a gun bounced from some schmuck ADA?"

"Not one gun, six guns, Patty, six!"

"C'mon, Rob, fuck all that nonsense. Make a gun collar, go to BCB, make some overtime, get your arrest numbers for the month, and write it up for a medal. All this while having some fun putting our foot up some ani-mule's ass who really deserves it. Who really gives a shit if it's thrown out? You get the excellent police duty award either way. I got five EPD medals, not one a them made it to the grand jury. Tossed before I was even able to take a decent dump at central booking, and guess what, I don't give a rat's cunt."

"Wait a minute, all your guns thrown out and you still write them up for medals?"

"Hell yes, and why not? I'm entitled. Scumbag gets a shot off, caps *me* in the head, I go out of the picture, am I getting something posthumously?" Billy and Pirelli high-fived each other. The booze, the women, the music—they were reaching Pirelli, I saw it in his eyes. There was no turning back for him once that fire was ignited. "Goddamn right I'm a get that medal of honor . . ."

Billy jumped in, "And a really nice funeral." Again they high-fived. Roxanne poured another round of shots, and we all drank, including her. I still did not understand the logic. I wanted to stay on a higher plain. I was sure my methods were beyond reproach.

"Fuck entitled Patty. It doesn't mean dick without a conviction."

"Personally I could give a fuck behind convictions. We write the shit up, get a bunch a medals, look like heroes for the chicks at parades"—he made a masturbating motion with his hand—"And that is fucking that, my friend. I guess you ain't figured it out yet, Rob, but we aren't doin' balls out there anyway. So I'm just playing the game like you should be doin', my man, and on that note I'm a head back to those two pretty PRs and work on tappin' them two tight asses." He high-fived Billy, Roxanne, me, and everyone else he passed as he jiggled his way back to those very tight wagons on the dance floor. He really did not give a fuck; from the beginning I knew that Patty was a survivor, he had to be given where he came from, which just reaffirmed his couldn't give a fuck attitude. One way or another, he was going to make this job work for him. Me, I still didn't get it. That's when I heard a familiar voice.

"They're right, Tatico, play the game." I turned around. There he was, three bar stools separating us. John Conroy. I sobered up quickly. *Did he just call me Tatico?*

"John, hey, man, I didn't know you were here."

His words were slow, thick, though his eyes were as focused, maybe more focused, than usual. "Well, here I am, drinking."

I looked at Roxanne, then pointed to John. She moved to him silently. She did not look in his eyes, just poured. "What are you doing here alone, John?"

"Only drink with the ones I trust." He raised his glass, we toasted. Before the glass reached his lips, I saw him look into the mirror behind the bar. Someone was walking in, a large Spanish dude wearing tons of silver. He seemed like he had some serious street *jugo* and presence—the small entourage of beauties he had draped on his long leather duster said as much. He had to have been a regular, as Roxanne gave him a big hello, so he had to know the place was wired with ghetto cops. He clearly had no fear of us. John slowly placed his glass on the bar, not taking his eyes off the cat. There was an electricity emanating from John, and I knew something was happening, something between two Brooklyn cats from very different sides of a dirty fence. It was at this point that this Spanish Lothario noticed John. His smile faded, and the color drained from my man's face. He quickly turned to Roxanne, whispered something in her ear, did an about-face, and walked out, girls in tow. John slowly turned back to the drink on the bar, and without missing a beat, smiled at it then shot it down his throat.

I did not want to let the drama go. "What was that all about?"

He blinked at me, so laid back, the liquor working its magic on him. He almost smiled, then looked at Roxanne and raised two fingers; he dropped money on the bar and she poured, then took his money. "Just another unhappy soon-to-be-collared, broke-down motherfucker," John said. We shot them down. I guess both of our guards were lowered behind the liquor because he slapped me on the back and laughed. "Tatico, I like that, yeah, Tatico." John Conroy liked me. He squinted his eyes at me and suddenly turned serious, as if he were now in full control of himself. I thought it was amazing how you can be lulled into thinking one thing is happening with John when really something completely different is taking place. *He should be an actor, he's always pretending, or is it lying?*

"You're doin' all right out there, Tatico, really impressive for a guy who's only been in the precinct less than two months. How much time you got on the job?" Roxanne poured another round for us. He lifted it to his lips.

"Came on in the summer," I said.

Before he was able to drink, he stopped and side-glanced me. He watched me for about five long seconds, then turned back to the drink and shot it down as well. He picked up a wad of wet bills, dropped a twenty on the bar, and without looking at me turned toward the door and said, "Let's go."

I pulled a deuce out of my pocket as well, dropped it on the bar, and followed him out without saying good-bye to anyone.

His car was so nondescript, I, to this day, still don't know what it was. The backseat was filled with job-related paperwork, beer cans strewn on the floor mats. A pad hung off the dash, and a pen was jammed into the air-conditioning vent for quick access. *Guy is always on point,* I thought.

We drove north on Hamilton Avenue, which separated Carroll Gardens from Red Hook: the good and the very bad. Once Hamilton Avenue ended, we swerved left, driving west briefly, making a quick right past the Brooklyn Battery Tunnel, heading west on Columbia Street. It was eleven o'clock in the evening though the streets were so crowded with people it might as well have been eleven in the A.M. My first impression of this long stretch of road was just how dark it was; it made the East

Flatbush Badlands seem like an amusement arcade. Although the street was wide enough for three car lanes on either side, it made me feel extremely claustrophobic; I had an incredible feeling, as if I were traveling in a tunnel. The street was framed on both sides by low, pockmarked redbrick buildings. There was garbage everywhere, on the streets, in the doorways, in the bare branches of the trees—hell, diapers and sanitary napkins hung like Christmas ornaments. This little stretch of land felt like another planet.

We drove quietly. John was cruising, seemingly very content with where he was. This was his environment. He was clocking everyone on the street, occasionally nodding at someone who'd recognized the fact that King Kong was on the block. More and more people saw us driving and quickly U-turned the fuck out of Dodge. This was exciting for me because when I noticed someone, John would notice the same person. We would laugh when the cat we both spied would drop his head and turn away quickly, into the dark recesses of the Red Hook projects. John and I were having a silent dialogue with each other. We were a good fit.

"How is it you know a lot of these guys out here, John? We're a long way from home."

He glanced at me, his eyes red slits; he smiled. " 'Cause we all speak the same language out here," he said.

Another riddle, though I knew what it meant. He may not have known them at first glance, but they certainly recognized that he was a cop. The car we were driving in might as well have been an RMP and we might as well have been wearing uniforms. But there were still guys out there who were calling him by his street name, Con. John knew everyone, and the smart ones, they knew him.

He lowered his window all the way down, inhaled deeply, then exhaled slowly. "Love the smell of that boned-up air." *Boned-up air: the smell of weed, car exhaust, and coconut oil, the ghetto bouquet,* I thought. Yes, it was good.

"This is where I belong, right here, right in the middle of it. Fuck all that train riding to the straight job, in the straight world, living in the straight burbs bullshit. This here, this is in the blood." He turned to me. "Been watching you, you got a dose for it too, yes? You understand the life; you know what has to be done, don't you?"

I nodded, half understanding. I looked back out into the intense urban landscape. I suddenly thought of Sergeant Tom. "You and O'Lary, how come he ended up in the academy?"

He hesitated. This again raised me up. Whenever the past relationship between these two guys was brought up, there was always that slight blip on the screen.

"Tommy boy was going to get made sergeant and he wanted to . . . calm down a little."

"Calm down?"

"He didn't want any complaints pending that could hold up his promotion, so he put in for a transfer to the academy, easiest place *not* to get jammed up in."

"What kind of complaints?"

He smiled again. "You know, everyday Negroid nonsense."

I'd been on the job long enough to know what "Negroid nonsense" meant. Most if not all of the perps who were being locked up in the 6-7 were male blacks who'd resisted getting collared, which would mean they were physically subdued by the officer. Negroid nonsense referred to these perps dropping a complaint against the arresting officer for brutality. Each complaint was taken seriously by the job's Civilian Complaint Review Board, CCRB. Even though most of them were unfounded, the complaint stayed in your folder for the duration of your career. If you had enough of these nonsensical complaints, you could be held up for transfers or even promotions. These complaints had held down many a good cop. O'Lary did not want to be one of them. I got the feeling that John Conroy did not give a fuck.

"How much time you got on, John?"

"Fourteen years of kicking ass and taking names."

"How come you're still in the bag?"

"You ask a lot a fuckin' questions there, Tatico." He laughed. "Was in a robbery unit, three months from my shield, some mope I locked up claimed I *coerced* information out of him with my gun." He turned to me, suddenly very serious. "I ain't never coerced anything out of anyone with any kind of physical threat. The threat of twenty to life was always enough of a lubricant to make any animal roll. Prick rolled, his people heard, and he lied to save his own scumbag ass. Job took the word of a six-time-convicted mope over mine. I was given a choice of where I wanted to go, the contract was set up by my bosses, and that's how I ended up in the six-seven, back in uniform. Now, I'm on the move again."

I wasn't sure what he meant, "On the move?" I asked.

He pointed to an atrium that led to the entrances of eight buildings; in the middle of the atrium stood an empty flagpole. "Last year that place right there was the scene of twenty homicides. This whole area, there were sixty homicides. This precinct is one of the smallest in the city, but per capita it has the most homicides. You know why?" I was rapt, shook my head. "Because the best heroin in six states is sold right here, eighty-five percent pure when it hits the vein. You know how potent a hit that is?" He tapped on his forearm with his hand. "It's quite the motherfucking dose. Easy access into this shithole with the tunnel and bridges close by. The cops here are fucking morons or they just don't give a fuck, and the people who live in this toilet go along to get along. That is, till one of the"—he made quotation marks with his fingers—"community activists' kids took a hot one in the ass. Now there is a crusade to stop the drug crimes, and killings in Red Hook. So now 'the Job' is doing its little dog-and-pony nonsense to show it really cares for little Tommy Hill-nigger who was probably slinging anyway, which is why he took one in the ass in the first place. So I, because of my infinite wisdom of most a the players out here, am going into this plainclothes detail to clean up the out-of-control mess between the *local businessmen.*" He smiled; so did I; "local businessmen" sounded very proper.

"That's great, John, when is it effective?"

"Orders came down today. My old robbery boss is in charge of the initiative, so I get to more or less run the show." He glanced at me, grinned. "You can't make a move till you have about a year in a precinct, but tell you what, stay in touch. Lots a people still owe me a solid or two on the Job."

The thought of working in plainclothes with one of the city's best cops was inconceivable to me at the time. I thought it was just boozed-up small talk, but I would not forget what he said.

"I had five young guys like you, fuck, we could really do some damage out here. You know, give it back to the animals, something those stuffed shirts at the precincts and at One Police Plaza are afraid to do. Sh-i-i-it, you remember all the lessons you learned in the academy?"

I thought about Tom O'Lary, his impassioned speech to me on Second Avenue. "Yeah."

"Good, now throw it all away. None of it means a fucking thing out here. All that horseshit's fine for the classroom, but when you're out here alone, it's a fight to the death. The day you forget that is the day you take two in the head. Before, your buddy boy there at the bar, the cat with the two mommies, he was right. These ADAs don't have the slightest conception of what it's really like out here—no one does—so you have to tell them what they want to hear. I make a gun collar, I become fuckin' De Niro: 'Yes, sir, me and my partner approached the car to write a summons, and there on the dashboard under the newspaper is a loaded gun, right in plain view.' "

"They don't buy that, John, c'mon—"

He jumped all over me, much more animated than I had ever seen him. This was another John Conroy, John Conroy the teacher, the preacher.

"They buy what you sell them; they don't have and don't want a choice. By the time there is a suppression hearing, the mope usually will plea out and there's the ADA's conviction. They *want* us to bullshit them, makes their job a hell of a lot easier. They *need* us to bullshit them. *We* want the collars, *they* want the convictions. Don't really matter how it's done as long as it gets done. It is a tool just like this booty trey-eight they give us, only this is more powerful. Tell you something else; on the streets, scumbags ain't our only enemy, it's the jerkoffs who hide behind the desks and quarterback our every move, and sit on the benches in the courtroom . . . You'll see, the only way to get the job done is to tell them what they want to hear. Follow?"

I nodded, sucking it all in. I was learning something I knew anyway, deep in the back of my mind. I knew that every collar I had brought in was one word away from *not* getting tossed or 343'd at central booking. I just wanted to try doing it the right way. But the truth was and still is: The laws are built to protect the guilty. The cops are just the fall guys for when the shit hits the fan. I, of course, did not fully realize the latter until much later in my career, but guess what, it's so fucking true. That night in John's car was worth three years on the streets and lost cases in court.

I saw John's eyes light up from what I thought was the headlight reflection in the mirror. He slowed the car down and waited at the light. That same look crossed his face that it had in the bar.

A maxed-out Benz rolled up next to us. The smoked windows revealed nothing but John's reflection. John didn't care that he could not see the driver. He pointed his finger with very little effort toward the curb. The Benz slowly pulled in front of our car and parked. John pulled behind and wrote the name "SHAH" and the license number down on the pad he had stuck to the dash. I was really confused. *We can't do a car stop, we're not working.* I nervously blurted out, "What's all this . . ."

John did not look at me, did not utter a word. He unclipped his five shot in his belt and moved stealthily out of the car. The driver's door opened on the Benz. Out stepped the man known as Shah King. He was in his mid-thirties, about John's height, though he had long, thin muscles that flexed under the colorful tracksuit he was wearing. He wore a thick, gold, braided chain around his neck, a six-inch diamond-studded cross hanging from it. Around his wrist was a thick gold-nugget watchband that held a presidential Rolex. I immediately assumed he was clean. Nobody, not even the dumbest of dumb criminals, would drive around with anything on them while they were wearing the flags that Shah King was wearing. John obviously didn't think like the average cop or the average perp.

The Shah was all smiles as he stepped from the car. He opened up his arms as if they were long-lost buddies hooking up at some tailgate party. "Con, what up, kid? Long time."

I would later learn that Shah was the biggest and baddest dealer not only in the Red Hook projects but also in many other jail-cell projects around the city. His street-business acumen had made him rich, so rich, in fact, it was said that he had legitimate money managers inquiring about purchasing the New York Knicks basketball team. This was long before the Puff Daddies of the city had the sense to mainstream their own street talents into legit gold. The Shah was one of the originals. He was handsome, played both sides of the street fence very well, and was an organized street thug. He came up in Red Hook, but had long since removed his entire clan from its nastiness. Only John knew where Shah's main residence was, a secret they'd both take to the grave with them if need be. Shah sold TKO-brand heroin—technical knock out—the purest in the city. It was the same heroin that Conroy said fed into all the shootings and homicides in the area. Cars would line up with plates from as far west as Indiana and as far south as Virginia, and that is some serious play. Reason being, a street dealer could step on, or water down, the boy three times and still have a great product. The junkies would only have to purchase a few bags, stepping on it themselves or using less of the boy, cutting their trips to the street pharmacies in half, thus minimizing the risk of getting locked up by narcotics teams doing buy-and-bust raids. The Shah understood this: Sell a good product, the people will come and buy.

John did not hug the Shah, but peeked into the car. "All alone tonight, Shah?"

"Just dropped my aunt off, she love that bingo hall, yo, play that bingo long as the days ma'fuckin' long, son." He laughed nervously. "Yo, Con, what's with all the drama now, we ain't got a thing no more?"

John bent down and squinted at something in the front seat of the car, leaned in. At this point I got out of the car. I absolutely did not know what to expect. My heart racing, I unconsciously slid my windbreaker behind my holster. Upon seeing this, the

Shah sucked his teeth slowly, then made an extremely sour face at me that told me there were miles between the two of us. I was slightly intimidated, definitely out of my league, but I was fuck sure not going to show either of these men this. I just tilted my head at him trying to give as imposing a look as the one I was receiving. He countered by shaking his head, raising his eyebrows, and turning back to John, annoyed. "C'mon, Con, you know a nigga's clean now, what's all this?"

John slowly came out of the front seat holding on to a book. "Are you fucking kidding me?" he said. The book was an abbreviated version of the Koran.

Shah held out his hands, palms up. "So, you gonna lock me up for reading verse five from surah number six? What, you low on collars this month, Con?"

John did not smile, did not frown, he was robotic. He leaned back in the car and I heard the trunk pop. He stood in front of Shah, not looking at me. "Check the trunk, Tatico."

I wasn't sure that I liked the name, though in hindsight I don't think John really knew my first name, and now it was carved in the asphalt since the biggest dealer in the city knew me as Tatico. I noticed the sheen bouncing off the sixty-thousand-dollar Benz; I was almost afraid to touch it for fear of smudging it. The trunk was the cleanest I had ever seen; it was empty except for a GRAYCO diaper bag. It was zipped up, and bulging with its contents. I unzipped it and out popped some diapers, a thin box of Wet Ones, and underneath a plastic baby bottle were seven neatly stacked bricks of hundred-dollar bills wrapped in thick purple rubber bands, the kind guys like me never get in banks. Up to this point, my only collars were guns and the occasional assault second degree, or domestic bullshit off the radio. I had never seen this much cash in my life. I lifted up one of the bricks; John looked at it and was still unemotional.

"How many bundles you move for that?"

"C'mon, Con, you know me better than that, I'm holding that for my boy. Told you, yo, dropped my aunt off from the bingo hall." The word "aunt" was pronounced distinctly southern black, auwwwnt; this guy was about as southern as I was black.

"Is there a strap in the car, Shah?"

"Hell no, Con. Shit's beyond me, son." Shah looked down at his manicure, then adjusted the twenty pounds of gold around his wrist. He seemed appalled that the question would even be asked.

John, with the same blank expression, slowly walked to the driver's side of his car. He opened the door, pulled a set of handcuffs from his waistband, hooked one end to the steering wheel, then nodded for Shah to come to him. The Shah complied, though if a man's head could actually spin off and shoot into space, it would have happened right then. John clicked the cuff gently on his wrist. "Have a seat, Shah."

The Shah looked into the messy car. "Think I'm a motherfuckin' stand."

"Watch him, Tatico."

The Shah lifted his cuffed wrist up, repulsed. "Fuck am I gonna go?"

John went into automatic pilot. With intense speed and precision, he meticulously started to remove every item from the inside of the car, checking the contents thoroughly. When he was satisfied, he then went to work on all the interior parts: the door panels, front and backseats; he dug around in the speaker wells, he moved under the dash pulling at wires, in the trunk he pulled the spare and jack out. He laid the contents of the car neatly on the sidewalk. It resembled an illustration from a car manual. He then got on his back and went to work under the car. This I thought was a little obsessive. I actually believed Shah, but Shah was Conroy's job. The Shah was what Conroy did for a living, period.

It was at this point that I noticed an RMP moving slowly down the street. I realized two things. One, there were no crowds watching us. I assumed that the Shah owned these blocks, and nobody was about to show face in this uncomfortable moment, further embarrassing him. Two, in all the time we were on Columbia Street, this was the first RMP to cruise down the block. John was right; the cops did not give a fuck. When the RMP saw us, it slowed. John stood up, glanced at it briefly, then went back to work on the vehicle. The RMP made a quick U-turn and proceeded out of the area. Shah laughed at this sarcastically. I then heard the hood pop open; John moved to it and dug around. He checked the fan belt, and then I heard the spinning of a wing nut and the top of the air filter was removed. I had to breathe in deeply. *This guy is out of control,* I thought. I heard the movement from under the hood suddenly stop. I caught the Shah dip his head slightly; all the piss and vinegar in him seemed to evaporate before my eyes. John slowly walked around the car, not taking his eyes off his target. He was carrying a .45-caliber automatic. It looked big and clean, like everything else in the Shah's car. John just stood in front of Shah, who was looking at the ground. I was supremely impressed, shocked and awed.

"I'm never wrong about these things, am I, Shah?" he said quietly, slipping the gun into his waistband.

The Shah slowly looked at the gun. He didn't even try to feign disbelief, though he did not answer. He suddenly looked like the little boy who got caught with his hand in the cookie jar. John's hand lashed out across the Shah's face like a cold, wet towel. I jumped at the sound. The Shah just looked at him. John's fingers left thick red marks on Shah's smooth chocolate skin. "Am I?" Again the Shah did not answer, though the sting of the slap deflated any residual belligerence that he might've had left. Again without warning John slapped him; this time a welt was starting to rise above his brow. "Say it." Before the Shah answered, John hit him again. I saw a glob of spit shoot out of his mouth; I also heard a whimper of pain. I was sure he was beaten down by this point. Like a dog who was being trained by its owner, the Shah stepped up to the program.

"You're never wrong, Con." He was now as docile as a poodle. This did not sit well with John. During the whole encounter, it seemed, he had the Shah walking three steps forward, only now to have him walk six steps behind. He hit him once more for good measure, drawing blood from his ear. John didn't look twice at the blood on his hand. He pulled the .45 from his waistband, felt the weight of it, then pulled the slide back slightly, checking the load. There was one in the pipe. John placed the barrel on the Shah's temple. I had to catch my breath. This was not in the playbook that O'Lary had so explicitly laid out for us. What was I going to do if John put a hole in this guy's head? I'm sure I grabbed hold of my gun, for protection. *Please, John, fucking chill. Don't let this get out of control!* John pulled the hammer back. He leaned in, whispering in the Shah's ear. The Shah nodded his head many times. John then put the gun back in his waistband, unclicked the cuff, and Shah King briskly walked back to the safety of the Benz's hand-sewn leather seats. *Maybe crime does pay,* I thought. After all, he had just been given a pass, and after collecting his car parts was going to drive away in that very sweet ride, with a lot of cash in the trunk. I was sure that was not the last I was going to see of Shah King.

John got into the car and I followed suit. I was scared and amazed, all at once. This was a high-stakes game that I wasn't aware even existed. This was the major leagues. John tossed the gun in the backseat, looked at me, and smiled. "That boy is my best snitch, he is why I own these bitches out here, all a' them."

"He's your best snitch? Thought you were going to kill him . . . Why didn't you collar him?"

John went off. "That little twat will bend over or lay down for me or get on all fours behind my shit while I fuck him dry, you understand? He don't have but one simple choice either, I own him. These punks think they own *you,* like they got some sort of entitlement to these streets because they came up in this fuckin' toilet here. They think they got you right up under their arm, BULLSHIT! Every once in a while you got to show them that we are the Babylon bosses, you have to remind them that they need us a fuck lot more than we need them. By not collaring him, he realizes just how close he can come to getting collared, you understand?" I nodded, though I was completely unnerved by the street lesson I had just borne witness to. Many things crossed my mind: the brutality that had occurred, the fact that I'd believed Shah King was clean and would've fallen for his street shit and let him go. Was I that gullible? I decided at that moment that everyone out here was fair game, and the game was getting really interesting. John swung the car in a wide U. "I'm hungry. You wanna go to Nathan's?"

The next night had started out with a bang. Two cops from the precinct had been involved in a shooting earlier in the day. When I arrived for the four to twelve, I saw the looks on the cops' faces. They had lit up some animal carrying a MAC10 machine pistol, and now seemed distant, worn out by questioning from the bosses, internal affairs, the ADA. The mope actually shot at the two cops as he was running away from them. Unlucky for him because one of the cops was a crack shot and took part of the Rastafarian's jaw off with a perfectly placed head shot. So upon entering the station house, there was a vibe, as there is in any precinct when a brother officer has faced death toe-to-toe and won: It is us against them. No matter how hard they try to drill into a cop's head in the academy that that is the wrong approach to take, the truth is, it really is us against them, no matter how you cut it. We are not the individuals carrying guns illegally, we're just the poor schmucks who are paid, poorly, I must add, to go out and retrieve them. What we are not paid to do, however, is to get shot at by them, and a certain message must always be branded into the psyche of every street thug or potential animal: This fucked-up behavior will not be tolerated without brutal retaliation.

So Billy and I set out to collar another bad guy carrying heavy armament. I wanted the two veteran cops who were involved in the shooting to know that they were not alone, that no street thug can feel that it is "kool and the gang" to bust a shot at any one of us. I think that every cop who went out that tour felt the same thing, because it was a record-breaking day for gun collars in the precinct—in one four-to-twelve tour, eleven guns were brought in. Now that is one serious display of blue-wall solidarity. My friends who still work in statistics at One Police Plaza tell me that record still stands, and I was the four-to-twelve cop to bring in the first gun.

Billy was driving; the sun had not yet set, so visibility in the

Badlands was good. We turned onto Rockaway Parkway, a block west of the dividing line, Ninety-eighth Street separating the 6-7 from the 7-3, or Brooklyn South from Brooklyn North, bad to worse. Rockaway Parkway is a wide four-lane street that traverses East New York, East Flatbush, and deep into the southeastern end of Canarsie to Jamaica Bay. The roughest area was certainly the section of road we were traveling on right then. The moment we turned the corner, I saw him crossing the street. He was squat, with short, thick arms and a large, round head to match. He wore Day-Glow sunglasses that made him stand out like a crackhead at a Weight Watchers meeting. Billy and I hadn't said more than two words to each other since we'd pulled out of the precinct lot. We were keyed and ready to do some damage, as Conroy put it. Without saying a word, I pointed to Day-Glow. His jail-house antennae must've been up because the second I pointed at him, BOOM, he took off.

I jumped from the moving car, gun drawn, and gave chase. He was about fifty feet ahead, but had nowhere to go except into an abandoned building, because all the apartment houses on the street were connected to one another. He hit the metal door and disappeared into the darkness of the tenement. I heard Billy screaming into the radio that we were "in pursuit, man with a gun." As I hit the door, everything left my body—thoughts, fear, anxiety at the unknown. I didn't even think that he might be on the other side of that door in combat position, ready to shoot the first white guy in a blue uniform to come through. I just moved on adrenaline and instinct; my target was acquired and I was going to get me some. Did I see the gun? Absolutely not. Did I know he had a gun? 99.9 percent absolute. Was I thinking about the ADA, the medals, the high stakes we were now playing for? Nope. All I was thinking about was collaring a man who was running from the police because we both knew he was filthy dirty.

I heard him hit a back door. I knew I was close because the door was still swinging shut when I got there. I jumped out into the courtyard; the light hurt my eyes, but I wasn't in the dark long enough to have been blinded. He was now very close to me, screaming, "I'm clean, Officer, why you chase me!"

I could not see his right arm, he was running like a fullback carrying a football, and I knew he was holding on to something heavy. My gun was pointing straight at the back of his head. We were now in a narrow alley where there was a line of metal garbage cans he started to pull down to slow me, all that little flurry of action did was slow him down and make me run with much more ferocity. I wanted to put an end to this chase immediately. I hurdled three cans; my foot came down hard and hit him just below his ankle. I heard a loud crack and then I heard him wail. He was determined though, because he kept running, despite the limp and the pain he must've been in. I was now focused on two things, his head and his right arm; the second I saw metal or something even remotely resembling anything other than a hand, I was shooting him, and not to stop, but to kill. I was now less than a foot away; I lifted my left hand, lunged forward, and came down with my gun onto the back of his head. A solid hit, it sounded and felt like a watermelon had been split open. He went down immediately. Blood flow, in any head injury, is going to be heavy, but this seemed like a river gushing freely. It covered my face and I tasted that distinct coppery flavor. He still moved on the ground, so I hit him with the butt of my gun again to stop him. He laid flat and started to gag. I knew he had a concussion, so he would not be able to fight back or resist any longer. I cuffed him and turned him over. In his sweatpants was a trusty Badlands wire holster that was securing a beautiful Taurus .9-millimeter defaced automatic handgun, defaced because its serial numbers were scratched off. I grabbed my Motorola and screamed into it, giving my approximate location. I also called for an ambulance, or "bus," as it's referred to over the radio. Billy skidded the RMP to the front of the alley. When he saw me he screamed, "Rob, you're hit, motherfucker, you're hit!" He ran to me and checked my head, neck, and torso for holes because I was covered in blood. I wasn't sure what was happening, if in fact the mope was able to get a shot off and had hit me. Of course he hadn't, but when you're caught in an insane moment, when the difference between life and death is just an arm movement away, your mind gets fucked, so much so, you don't know if you've been shot or not.

He doesn't realize how close he came to dying in a very hor-rific way that day. If he is alive today and he is reading this—and by this description he certainly will know who he is—you can thank God, or Jah, or Allah, or whatever supreme being it is you pray to that you did not die in that dirty, abandoned courtyard, because, brother, you were as close as you can come to finality.

The paperwork was processed, and Day-Glow had a bedside arraignment at Kings County Hospital. I was off to central booking to process the arrest, and lo and behold, I met my old pal ADA Archibald "Wimpy" Waxman. I just described the ar-rest exactly the way it wasn't, the way that they wanted to hear it, the way the judges wanted to hear it so their calendars were cleared when the mopes pled out, and the way I wanted to tell it to keep the animals in the cages where they belonged. "My part-ner and I were driving southbound on Rockaway Parkway when we noticed the defendant checking what appeared to be a firearm between two parked cars. He sees us and takes off; I briefly chased him and after a struggle placed him under arrest for 265.01.03."

Wimpy sat up slowly, pulled the fat gold Mont Blanc from his shirt pocket as slowly as he could. He leaned in, puckered his pink lips at me, and said, "That's my boy. Grand jury in three days."

Test-i-lied. My second felony within the first couple of months on the job. Number one was letting Shah King go. There is no such thing as proper discretion when a felony arrest can be made, and the perjury I'd just committed, well that "tool" *was* the most powerful weapon I had on my gun belt, just like Con-roy had said. Thank God for it, because there were many bad men who deservedly were put away behind it, including this mope. He was wanted for a double homicide with the very gun I'd caught him with.

There was a nasty dive bar not far from central booking. After finishing the arrest process at e-cab, I headed right for it. I or-dered a double of Jack Daniel's. I wanted to be alone. I didn't want to feel the comfort of my partners or any of the ghetto beauty that Alfredo's offered. I needed to be alone with my thoughts about what I had just done. I noticed my hand was shaking as I shot the liquid back. I noticed the blood of Day-Glow caked under my nails. I didn't bother to wash it off. I just ordered two more doubles, shot them back, and suddenly the magnitude of the lie I had just told didn't seem to matter. I smiled at the fact that Day-Glow would not be able to hurt anyone, and I realized that I was now in the game for keeps.

4

Bully of the Badlands

With Conroy gone to Red Hook, I was pretty much on my own in the Badlands. There was no one as good as John in the precinct. There were some excellent street cops in the 6-7, probably the best in the city, absolutely, but they just did not have what John Conroy had. I hadn't met anyone else who had the ability to develop and cultivate snitches, to bullshit the bullshitters—and the streets were loaded with them. I now had to develop this talent on my own, without Conroy's guidance. I needed to mature as a street cop, especially if I was to achieve my next goal: hooking up with John in Red Hook.

The first step toward that goal involved a neighborhood cat named Bully. He was an impossibly huge man, probably close to four hundred pounds, though he did not seem fat, just big—big hands, big legs, big head, big dreads, big everything. He also had a big personality. He was a gentle giant who wore a continuous smile, constantly surrounded by his people, friends and family. He would always go out of his way to say hello, walk to the RMP and offer us coffee or free rotty at his jerk-chicken restaurant. He was always quick with a joke, but you had to listen very closely because his thick Kingston accent made it impossible to decipher the punch line. Yes, he was a "local businessman" with a popular Jamaican bistro and a comical personality, and he also had a very successful sideline in purveying weed.

We knew why he'd buddied up to us: Keep your friends close and your enemies closer. And in this sector, Mike-Nancy, we were his enemies. This was the heart of the Badlands, and it was also Bully's domain, his real estate, *his* sector. Now, the cops in ghetto precincts generally look the other way when any kind of weed is found, say, during a car stop or on someone's person. It's at the bottom of the food chain for arrestable offenses, no matter how much weight is found. The paperwork is long and tedious, and with manpower low in the 6-7, cops from the closest sector would have to pick up all the radio runs in the now-vacant Mike-Nancy sector, and for what? A charge that's only going to get tossed or dropped down to a lowly misdemeanor anyway, probably at e-cab, garnering no overtime and just pissing off the ADA who has to write it up. So not only do the cops know this and practice this street discretion regularly, but the street cats know as well that it's practiced.

Now if you pull some mope over and he's belligerent to you or your partner, you certainly have every right to lock Nat E. Dread up and quite possibly tack on the oldie but goodie discon charge as well. The discon, or disorderly conduct, charge guarantees every cop who makes an arrest that the mope will go through the system. How's that? Anyone can be charged with discon. If you are drinking an alcoholic beverage in the street, a cop stops you, you can go through the system for discon. You don't have any ID and are standing in a drug-prone location, or just look suspicious—BANG, you're sleeping in some smelly precinct for three days. Take this as an inside FYI: The next time a cop stops you and you are not 100 percent proper, smile and kiss ass, because the cop has that fabulous discretionary power. This the perps, and street hustlers, and dealers, and users, and bum rushers don't know, though many of them found out the hard way. Three days in the system, eating bologna sandwiches and drinking watered-down Kool-Aid, has got to suck for smoking a spliff with your boys. Bully didn't care about any of this because he was Bully, friend to cop, friend to all. But things were about to change. Bully was about to get played and then replayed, Conroy style. I thought about how every street perp knew only what Conroy wanted them to know. He was making moves on them without them even knowing it. He bullshitted the bullshitters and now it was my turn.

Bully never drove a car; he was always driven or he walked, as his world was the eight-square-block area in the heart of Badland territory that he called home. So on a rainy four-to-twelve tour when Billy saw he was driving a piece-of-shit nondescript Monte Carlo, we knew some serious shit was going down. Billy banged a sharp U and came up behind the Chevy. I turned on the turrets and then turned them off quickly so as not to raise up the neighborhood to the car stop. I gave Bully that kind of respect. I was learning. Billy turned on the side spotlight and pointed the halogen beam through the Chevy's rear window. We saw that Bully had placed his hands on the steering wheel, an attribute the smart perps in the street know all too well, compliance. By doing that, he was telling us he was cool, everything was irie, he was with the program. I wrote his name and license-plate number down on a pad, just like the one Conroy had in his car. I then put over the radio that we had a car stop for a traffic violation. Billy looked at me oddly because I was never one to talk into that radio for anything other than putting over that I had "one under arrest." I just winked at him. I had a good feeling about this. The fact that he was driving raised me up big time, and, more telling, he was driving out in the rain. Why would he do that unless he figured that no cop was going to do a car stop and get soaked in the process. It was thin, but then most of what I did in the beginning was thin. Sometimes you get lucky, sometimes you're the cock, and sometimes you're the anus. Today Bully was the anus.

"Turn the light off, Billy." He did, and I moved out of the RMP and up to the driver's side of the Chevy.

Bully wore his jiffy-pop hat as usual and was all smiles when I reached him. The rain was pounding. "Officer C, what up, get in the car, man, get out the rain, man, every-ting irie boss, it just me, Bully." He laughed, and when Bully laughed, all four hundred pounds of him laughed; the car bounced up and down gently with each guffaw.

I just smiled. Billy walked up to the passenger side and

tapped gently on his window to let Bully know he was there. Bully rolled the passenger window down with much effort, as they were not electric. He then looked at me, very concerned, and almost whispered, "Every-ting okay, Officer C; is there some-ting wrong, boss?"

"Bully, there's nothing in the car, is there?"

He looked at me and then just dropped his head, feigning embarrassment. Bully was too smart to play the angry militant. He also knew about the street warnings and admonishments doled out for weed transport. "Ya, C, me not gonna lie to the boss man. Got some ganja in the car, just a little, C, bringing it to me friends for personal." He brought his thumb and forefinger up to his lips, puckering them as if he were taking a hit.

"Where is it, Bully?"

"Did not want to disrespect you, boss, it in the trunk." He looked me directly in the eyes, trying to gauge what I was up to. He had no idea what he was in for.

"Open it, Bully." This I said with the least amount of authority possible. I wanted him to feel as if it was something that I was obliged to do; I wanted him to think that *he* had placed me in this uncomfortable situation, and it worked because he apologized to me before he opened the trunk. It clicked open, I walked to the back, and what I saw was nothing less than amazing. Monte Carlos have notoriously large trunk spaces, which would account for Bully's choice of wheels. Inside the trunk were five bales of marijuana wrapped in large black construction bags. At first I didn't know what it was because I just couldn't fathom that much weed, but the odor that wafted out of the car was unmistakable. It smelled really good too. Growing up, I wasn't into weed, but I certainly knew what quality weed smelled like. I tried to reach behind the bags to check further to see if there were any guns or cash, but the bales were jammed so tightly in the trunk that it was impossible to check. It was an empty gesture anyway, as Bully was too smart for that. He knew he quite possibly could ride this out in the event he got stopped, and, quite frankly, had it been any other time and John Conroy had not raised that flag of plainclothes up the pole, Bully would have made it to his overworked bong. I needed to make an outstanding collar to get into that plainclothes unit, and all that weed in the trunk was just the start of it.

I closed the trunk and slowly walked back. I placed my hands on the door. He was getting wet, and I must've looked like a wet rat because I was not wearing my raincoat; this was good for the drama of it all. I spoke quietly. "Bully, I'm going to go back to the RMP for a couple. I wanna talk this over with my partner. Shut your window so you don't get wet, just gonna be a few." He rolled up the window quickly; I tilted my head to Billy to follow me back to the car. He got in and we discussed my plan of action. Billy didn't think I could get away with it, but knowing Bully's culture and what occurs regularly between cops and bad guys in Kingston, Jamaica, I felt I had a better-than-good chance of pulling this off.

I got out of the RMP alone and moved to the passenger side of his car. I opened the door and got in. We didn't look at each other; he was waiting for the other shoe to drop.

"I fucked up, Bully; I put this over the radio, so central knows that I stopped the car, and when I went back to the RMP, Billy had already put it over that we had one under for possession." Bully made a hissing sound, like a teakettle just before it starts to whistle. "But I have an idea." His giant head turned slowly, and he glanced at me through half-closed eyes, resigned to the fact that something big was about to occur. "Now, there is an awful lot of fucking ganja in that trunk, my brother. I mean, goddamn, that is a big fuckin' load, Bull, big fucking load." He dropped his head and shook it slowly. Now I knew I had him. He was playing the game with me, knew it was time to pay a tax, and to Bully a street tax, or getting hit with a vig payment while on his way to make a delivery, well, that was just the price of doing business. It was good business as far as he was concerned. Fuck, this was Kingston, he'd get taxed, beaten, *and* collared, but this was America, home of free enterprise, and everybody understood how the grease game was played here.

"Whatcha need, boss man, what can Bully do?"

"Well, because my partner put it over, we have to make a play that we're bringing you in, so we bring you in. I'm going to say that we got you with a small bag of weed, write you a summons for smoke, and you're on your way."

Bully let out a big sigh of relief, dropping his big head on the steering wheel. Without looking at me he placed his hand on my wet shoulder and said, "Everybody said you was Officer Cool. Now I'm a let them know they was right. You Jah, child, you the Buffalo Soldier C, you irie, boss man."

"Now, Bully, c'mon, this is a major solid I'm doing here. I get caught I'm gonna lose my job and go to jail, you know this, yes?" He looked up at me quickly; now he was all ears. He knew this was tax time and that a number was going to be exacted, but once a criminal feels like he is dealing with another criminal, there is a bond that is developed, and even though Bully was going to have to pay, he was more into this now than before. He was so happy at the prospect that he was going to pay Officer *Cool* off, in blocks of *cool* hundred-dollar bills, that he was going to own me.

I laid it out for him, told him that I was going to keep half the weed in my car and that it was mine. I also told him he was going to have to pay me twenty thousand dollars. How I came up with that number is beyond me, but he didn't even flinch and agreed to have one of his boys bring it to the precinct within the hour. I wasn't making top pay yet, only $27,000 a year. *I am going to have to work a year to bring that money home,* I thought with much bewilderment. The money out on the street is fucking phenomenal. If I had asked him for two hundred large, I'm sure Bully could've gotten it brought right to the RMP on this rainy night, a drive-through cash transaction, time served and fine paid. But as it was, twenty grand was all that was needed for my purposes this evening.

I got him out of the car and walked him over to the RMP quickly. We placed him in the backseat, and here is where the fun began. I wanted to keep his guard down, let him know that we were primarily *his* bitches. We didn't want him to get wet, we didn't want the neighborhood lokes seeing him in this embarrassing predicament. We sold him lots of wet dreams and whatnot. And us being very cool, we would cuff him inside the car. I got into the front seat, and he, with much trouble, squeezed his way into the backseat. He tried to reach the door but could not grab the handle to close it. I got back out of the RMP and slammed it closed, though it must've hit his leg because all I heard was him scream, like his balls were on fire. I had to stifle my laugh. I got into the front seat and made him maneuver so I could get his hands cuffed. Now, this was virtually impossible because backseats were not designed for four-hundred-pound cats built like Bully. Cuffs weren't even designed for guys like Bully. I was trying my hardest to get one cuff on his wrist, and then he screamed in pain as I accidentally pinched his giant wrist. He was trying so hard to bring his arms around that he slid off the bench and sort of got jammed between the back of the front seat and the floor. He tried to get up, but the harder he tried the more he got jammed in between the seats. I was covered in sweat. "Fuck it, Bully, we can't do this in the car. Let's put the cuffs on in the street, then we'll work on getting you back in the car."

"Ya, man, but how you get Bully out the car?" His head was jammed into the floor, so it was muffled, which made it that much more hilarious. I know Bully started to laugh, because the car was gyrating as if we were in the beginning stages of an earthquake. If we laughed for five minutes straight it was a second, just the sight of his huge ass sticking up high above the front seat. I realized that the rain was starting to let up and that my sergeant was off meal, so it was just a matter of time before he rolled up on us, blowing this whole caper, so Billy and I got out and not so gingerly pried Bully from the bowels of the RMP. Now we had to cuff him, another monumental task because Bully's wrists could not reach each other. Luckily, Billy had an extra set of cuffs in his briefcase, and we attached both of Billy's cuffs and my set of cuffs together and then hooked them to both of his wrists; they barely made the connection. We all looked into the small backseat and then decided against it, Bully fit snugly in the front seat of his Monte, so fuck it; we let him ride with me in his own car. This also gave me time to grease him up even more and let Billy get to the precinct first and make the proper notifications. So I drove very slowly.

When I arrived in the rear of the station house, Billy was waiting for me. His uniform jacket was off, tie open at the collar, so I knew that everything was set up for us inside. The sergeant on the desk was a guy named Bannerette. He loved the games that could be played in the streets if the cops were smart enough and the perps dumb enough; luckily, all of the planets were aligning this evening. We followed Billy into a back room of the precinct; he said it was all taken care of and that the sergeant was in on it with us. Bully was a little disappointed. "I got to pay 'im too, C?"

"No, no, Bully, he comes out of our end, that's how it done. C'mon, brother, you've done this before, yes?"

We got into the room, sat him down in front of a desk, cuffed him to a metal chair, and placed a phone in front of him. I noticed there was a brown paper bag at the edge of the desk, but I didn't think it was anything other than someone's lunch; it wasn't mine, so I did not look in it, and thank God I didn't, Bully was magic; this was the first time I'd done this, so I was feeling my way around, but I must say Bully made it all very easy. He'd obviously done this before.

He picked up the phone. Before he dialed he looked at us and said, "Twenty g's and I walk, ya, man? No hidden surprise?" Surprise was pronounced "soup-prizzze."

"Nah, Bully, we want to continue doing business with you; we ain't about that, brother, our word is good."

Billy jumped in with this for good measure, saying, "We get to keep the weed, though, don't forget."

Bully liked that. He was glad that he could turn on the men in blue, get them high with his good herb. He laughed. "Ya, man, that some good herb too, your dick is gonna grow so much, man, you be able to suck it youself, man." He started to dial but was laughing so hard he had to stop. Eventually he dialed the number and talked to his boy in dialect I could not understand. He hung up, then kicked back in the chair, looked at me, and smiled. "Yo, C, you could get us some a that herb to smoke now?" We just looked at each other and laughed.

"Bully, you mind if we do this once a week? This is fun," I

said through gritted teeth. More laughter and I realized that this friendship could have gone far beyond uniform and semi-bad guy. Bully's beeper started to pulse; he looked up at us. "Him here, in the back of the precinct. He won't come in, you have to go get it."

I went outside; there was no one in the rear of the lot, and then I saw someone peek out from behind a tree. I called out, "You here to drop something off for Bully?" A beautiful young woman stepped into the street. She was diminutive. She looked like a fragile doll, the ones with the painted lips and porcelain faces. She was light skinned, like heavily creamed coffee, big almond eyes, and had her hair tied up neatly in a pretty cornflower blue silk kerchief. I had never seen her in the neighborhood; I'd never seen anyone remotely as beautiful as this woman in the neighborhood. These are the girls who are immediately hustled out of the Badlands by guys like Bully before they get corrupted by the mean streets. She just stood there on the curb, holding out the bag. I almost didn't want to take it from her; then I made a battlefield decision. I took the bag from her, looked around, and said, "Get out of here as fast as you can, just go." This was another illegal maneuver, a felony, to be exact, but I felt she had no idea what was occurring and Bully would probably have made her pay dearly had she refused his request to be the bag *woman* on this trip. As it was, she looked terrified, so she handed me the bag and without saying a word took off like a bat out of hell.

Bully counted out the cash for us, two hundred crisp one-hundred-dollar bills. Again the thought of all the hours I would have to work to see this kind of money flashed before me; it was so much easier to find a mope like Bully and just place him on the pad. "On the pad" was a saying that came from the old days when cops had a list of store and bar owners and wire rooms and illegal card games written on a pad. They would go through the pad each week and collect money from them to allow them to continue with their not-so-aboveboard business transactions. Cops made more money from the pad than their entire salaries garnered them all year. This was one of the unwritten and unspoken perks of the NYPD back in the day.

Bully smiled at us as Billy and I took it all in: all that cash, all that weed. Bully then lifted his mammoth arm up and jiggled it lightly. "Let me get that ticket so I can go, C."

"There's just one more thing I have to do, Bully. We have to put you in the cage in front of the precinct to write you the summons. Cool?" I asked.

The prospect of being in a cage did not sit well with him, though he agreed. I put him in, then turned around to look at him sitting there behind those bars. His hat had long since disappeared during the debacle in the car, so his dreads hung down freely. As he sat on the wooden bench, he started to pick at his dreads and the sergeant on the desk whispered to me as I passed him, "You can take the monkey out of the jungle . . ." He just laughed at his own twisted humor and went back to the sports page of the *Post*.

I followed Billy back into the room where all that cash and weed was. Inside, there were two guys in suits waiting for us. They both had mustaches, looked to be in their late forties, and seemed to be put off that they had to come out to the 6-7 on a rainy night to enhance, or cover, a bribery collar. They did not introduce themselves, didn't smile, nothing. All they wanted was to get all the information on the arrest, and write up the UF49, the NYPD's unusual-occurrence report, and then get the fuck out of the military zone. The taller of the two asked in a clipped tone, "Where's the tape?" I had no idea what he was talking about, but Billy moved to that brown paper bag at the edge of the desk and pulled out a very old-fashioned tape recorder and clicked it off. *The NYPD spares no expense in its quest to remain high tech*, I sarcastically thought. The tall guy hit the rewind button and heard himself asking the same question; he then rewound it to the beginning. "We'll voucher this at the desk, the forty-nine will be forwarded to you and the DA's office; my name is Sergeant Lenahan. This is Detective Schlongo. We'll be in touch." Scholongo made sure he looked at Billy and me when his name was mentioned to see if his surname brought smiles to our faces. It didn't till after the IAB pricks left. The two self-loathing IAB guys walked to the cage with us in tow. I could see that Bully, on first seeing the four of us, knew that he had over-played his hand; he just dropped his head and didn't speak a word. They informed him that additional charges of bribery in the first degree were added to the original charge of possession of a controlled substance with intent to sell. They turned around and spoke briefly to the desk sergeant, who made an obvious point of not looking at either of them. They walked out quickly.

IAB guys are not welcomed in any precinct; they are pretty much the enemy. They know it, so when they have to walk into a precinct like the 6-7 where every cop is just an inch away from some bullshit accusation—"Negroid nonsense"—that will lead them to an interrogation by one of those empty, duplicitous suits, they adopt a false sense of bravado and fearlessness. You see, back in the day, most of those guys were caught being very bad in the street: stealing, whoring, creating their own pads. They were turned by IAB to roll over on other unwitting cops. They were usually wired for sound to entrap any one of their brother officers; the more cops they could get on the wire, the easier it would be for them not to lose their jobs and pensions. Once found out by the rank and file, they were blackballed, their cars usually spray-painted with the word "RAT," their lockers smeared with feces and then set on fire. Some cops even had posters of giant rats placed in front of their homes so their neigh-bors would get a clearer picture of just who was living next to them. So the only safe place they could work on the job became the internal affairs bureau, rat central.

The rat patrol was called in on this bribery collar because in the twisted minds of these IAB guys, if someone tried to bribe a cop once, he'd tried it and gotten away with it a hundred times. They weren't at the 6-7 to pat two young uniforms on the back for having exemplary integrity. No, they were there to let Bully know he was collared for the bribe and that he was to be briefed in central booking to find out what other scumbag cops he had bribed. They weren't after Bully; they were after the cops he had paid to turn a blind eye. As a matter of fact, we found out later that they offered Bully complete immunity to roll on other cops. We were called to the grand jury, and that was the last I heard of the case and of Bully. I assumed the case was dropped because he in fact gave them what they wanted. I could only hope that no cop would get entrapped by lovable Bully of the Badlands.

What was my motive behind this elaborate collar? It did nothing for the taxpayers or the flow of excellent Jamaican herb through the streets of East Flatbush. No, but it would get me closer to Conroy. You see, whenever a bribery collar is procured, you are automatically invited to go to the "integrity review board." This is the board of police bosses who convene every month to review bribery collars, and to decide if you are in fact as clean as a whistle and beyond the temptations of the street. They want only the finest young guys who won't steal a penny sent into details where illegal money, and a lot of it, is present in every collar or case, such as the narcotics bureau, or the public-morals division (PMD), the two big guns in the organized-crime divisions. At the interview they ask you a couple of questions about the collar and why you would not take cash, and assuming you are not a total imbecile, you'll give them all the answers they want to hear. Then—and this was what it was all about—you are asked which detail you'd like to transfer to as a career path on the job. Now Billy and I had discussed this in great length. Every cop who goes before this little tribunal asks for the same details: narc, auto crime, or PMD, details where after serving eighteen months you can get your gold detective's shield. Billy and I, having less than a year on the job, knew this was a tall order. We would not be able to get that detail for two more years, which is standard procedure in the NYPD; no investigate details with less than two and a half years on the job, period. So, we reached for something a little closer to home, but just as enticing . . . to me more than Billy. We asked to be put into the plainclothes detail with John Conroy in Red Hook. Billy was still a little gun shy about working with this animal cop, but I presented it to him as being the only move we'd have to get closer to one of those investigative details in organized crime. And it would also be a no-brainer for the bosses of the integrity review board. It was a lateral patrol move; we would not be eligible for the shield and we would make room at the review board for worthier cops with much more time on the job. We were granted our wish, and told that we would be notified through the personnel orders of the transfer. We walked out of the meeting jubilant, to say the least. We had pulled off an amazing coup on a very street-wise cat who had much more time in the streets then we did, and we were heading off to a place called Red Hook where we would be working with the king of kings, John Conroy. All within the first six months on the job.

It happened eventually, the move, but I still had plenty of time to cool my heels in the Badlands and learn some more about the intricacies of the streets. I had a strong footing on the job; now it was time to secure my other life, Mia.

5

Mia

I had met my fiancée, Mia Graziana, about two months prior to entering the police academy. On a lazy spring afternoon, I was walking my dog on Manhattan Beach and contemplating my future. She was there with some of her friends celebrating her early graduation, magna cum laude, from the NYU business school. She was also celebrating her first real job, financial analyst at the Solomon Brothers brokerage house. Though she was with five of her friends, all really attractive, Mia was the one I focused on. She was beautiful. Olive skin, light brown hair, piercing brown eyes and strikingly high cheekbones. The moment I saw her, as ridiculous as this sounds, I was in love. Mia was the total package—she was beautiful, brilliant, and made a lot of money. But most of all, Mia was all heart. We had a blood connection, some chemical thing that even we could not understand, but from that day on, we were inseparable. Within eight months we were engaged to be married, and for the very first time in my life, I felt complete.

I was supposed to meet Mia for dinner at Peter Luger's, a restaurant on Northern Boulevard in Manhasset, Long Island. I had made an arrest the night before, and with all the paperwork had grabbed only two hours of sleep that afternoon. I was spent but looked forward to spending time with my girl and having a good meal. I was running late, and I hoped she would not be too mad. The gun collar from the night before had beat the shit out of me and I was in no mood to apologize for the dicked-up traffic in this parking lot called Northern Boulevard. The sun hadn't set yet, and as I drove east on the boulevard, I felt like a vampire looking for my coffin. I was dehydrated and still felt really dirty from the thirteen hours I'd sat in that crack den called central booking. I'd showered and tried to cleanse off the nastiness of the place, but the deeper I drove into this bucolic, moneyed town, the dirtier and more out of place I felt. Here, on these bright, clean streets where happy families strolled, and store owners greeted them, and everyone was smiling, without a care in the world. They didn't have the slightest notion that there are places out there called the Badlands, and that these pretty people stroll here in heaven, and not there, in hell, only for the grace of God.

I pulled into the valet-parking area, left the shit-box Plymouth K car running, and just walked past the valet as if he wasn't even there. I was in such a daze and so out of my element that I just wanted to get into the restaurant, have a few big, fat drinks, eat something other than fast food, and go home to bed. I entered the famous steak house, and even though it was early for dinner on the North Shore, the place was packed, three deep at the bar. I tried not to read any of the people in the restaurant, but I couldn't help it. The black cat who looked like an accountant, sitting in the dark corner with his white date. She was probably his secretary, having a "business dinner." They were most definitely from the lower end, South Shore, as his shoes were Barney's knockoffs, the kind that can be purchased at Macy's, and his shirt screamed "off the rack." She occasionally touched his hand, letting me know there wasn't anyone she could know in this part of town. There was the manicured wanna-be wise guy sitting in the middle of the room for all to see; he had a diamond ring the size of a potato on his pinkie, probably a cubic because his watch was a Movado. There were the three waiters near the men's room quietly arguing over who was taking the table full of blue hair and diamonds. Then there was the bartender, probably a part-time bartender, part-time weight trainer, and part-time con artist/gigolo to all those old ladies of the North Shore who'd drop by for Bellinis after their spa visits on the miracle mile. He was definitely a full-time knucklehead, and right now he was out of his league, as he was just a hair too close to Mia at the bar.

She had prime real estate at the corner of the small bar, as she had probably been there waiting for forty minutes. She wore a form-fitting black Norma Kamali cocktail dress with a plunging neckline; over the stunning dress she wore a white Chanel cashmere jacket with tastefully monogrammed gold buttons. She wore a pearl necklace I had given her and a diamond tennis bracelet I was able to pay for with my yearly uniform allowance; her hair was loosely tied up over her ears, which revealed diamond studs, a gift to herself after graduation. Her diamond engagement ring should've been a beacon to the douche-bag, pretty-boy bartender, but I guess he just didn't give a rat's ass. In any case, I tried desperately to untwist my balls before I got to the bar. I was here to relax, not go to war. I moved behind Mia; she didn't realize I had come in. The bartender looked at me and lowered his eyes, back to Mia, leaning in really close on his elbows, talking in a very low, sexified tone. He had to have thought that there was no way in hell I could be with this fabulous-looking woman. He said something that made her giggle slightly. She leaned back and bumped into me, turned, and saw it was me. For a second, I thought I saw a flash of embarrassment, which further let me know that what I'd had my balls twisted for was in fact justified. When jerk-off realized who I was, he quickly tailed down and moved to the safety zone at the other end of the bar. Mia touched my face and kissed my cheek.

"Baby, why so late? Traffic?" she asked nervously.

I didn't return her kiss or answer her question; I just looked at the bartender. Now, at this point in my life, I felt I was not even on the same planet with a guy like this, even though had I not taken the NYPD test when I was sixteen, I just might be serving behind this very same bar. I saw him glance at me as he mixed a Rob Roy for one of his half-in-the-bag admirers, then he nervously grinned at me and walked over. "Hey, guy, can I get you something?" His voice was affected; it had an annoying cool and carefree ring to it. *"Heyyyy, guy," sounds like a game-show host. God, what in the fuck am I doing out here, this could only lead me somewhere bad.* I tried to chill, but his voice, his wormy smile, his fake tan and raised eyebrow; these were things that weren't computing. This guy just did not live in the real world, he lived in a netherworld. I would rather have been with fifty Bullys or a hundred of the animals I was locking up daily than actually have to sit and talk to this guy. He was a fake in life, a coward, a hustler, and I, at that point in my life, was not going to get hustled by him or the likes thereof.

After a long look into his eyes, which did not seem as bright as they had before, I said, without trying to hide the disdain I felt for this bartender, "Yes, get me a Jack Daniel's straight up, make it a double, and get yourself a vinegar and water, douche bag." Mia had not yet seen this darkness in me, and why should she have? She was not of that dark netherworld, nor did I want her to be a part of it. She was the color in my life, beyond that other life.

I felt Mia tighten up; she was too smart not to understand where this was headed. She was immediately embarrassed, and tugged at my arm.

"Rob, please, not here, please, baby." She whispered this to me so plaintively; I did not like hearing her ask me for anything with such a tone. The red I was seeing completely vanished. Suddenly douche bag was no longer standing in front of me wearing a target, he was just some knucklehead bartender who was trying to get over. *Hey, look at her, for Christ sakes, she's beautiful, man, can you blame him?* I thought. All the heat was suddenly cooled out in me; I looked at Mia, squeezed her hand, and smiled at her reassuringly that everything was going to be all right.

I reached in, kissed her cheek, and whispered, "I apologize, Mi, long day." I looked up to the bartender. "Just kidding, *guy.* Keep the change on that forty, but I'll take one more, make it a single."

We finished our drinks, and had a fabulous meal. The bourbon and the bottle of Châteauneuf-du-Pape had given me a second wind. One I was going to need. Mia had her eye on what she was sure would be our first home. A friend was a high-end real estate broker and had given her the keys to the property. Mia was incredibly happy and assured me I would be too; it was hard to say no to her. I had to go along.

I followed Mia in her fine, brand-new ride—a candy-apple-red Volvo station wagon. She looked very much the part she was trying to project: Wall Street executive/soccer mom. We traveled north down a road called Little Neck Boulevard. The streets were wide and well attended, and rightfully so, as this area had some of the highest property and school taxes in the country. I felt as though I was on a different planet, and considering where I had spent my last twenty-four hours, the Badlands, and then central booking, or crack central, as we referred to it, this place *was* a different planet. We drove past a signboard that read: "Welcome to Kings Point." She made a few quick turns and we pulled up to a highly manicured two-story colonial. It had large stone pillars at the front door, which was adorned with a hanging stained-glass lantern, and beveled leaded-glass panels on either side. I was impressed, but I did not expect anything less from Mia; she had extraordinary taste. She jumped out of the Volvo and opened her arms as if to say, *WELCOME HOME!* I could tell there was no talking her out of this.

"So, what do you think, tell me you can't see us sitting on this lawn sipping chardonnay, I absolutely love it."

I smiled; I liked her fired up. Though I did feel a pang of guilt about all of this opulence. I felt as though this wasn't really in the cards for me. I had never known that this world existed. After all, I was a cop from working-class Brooklyn. What I was familiar with was living check to check, hand to mouth. Hell, I would've been happy living on the beach fifteen minutes from the Badlands. Mia, however, had different plans, and right at that moment, her plans were my plans. She excitedly grabbed hold of my hand. I followed her to the yard, which really wasn't a yard at all. There was a little knoll of grass that led to two wooden boat slips, the Long Island Sound was the backyard. A screened-in gazebo made it seem like a location out of an F. Scott Fitzgerald novel. I was blown away. "I'm, I'm speechless, Mi, I mean, Jesus Christ, how can we afford this?" *Always work the money angle into the equation; she'll think I'm frugal when I tell her we shouldn't live here*, I thought.

She smiled and shook her head slowly. "I did the numbers. We can swing this."

"But how? We need a down payment, no?"

She was quick. "I can get a low-interest loan from work; the principle is deducted from my salary every week, we won't even feel it. My mother and father are paying for the wedding; the money we get from that, bang, we pay back the loan and uncork the chardonnay." I followed her to the back door. She keyed it opened and the opulence continued on the inside. She turned on a hallway light and I followed her to a dark, sunken living room where a stone fireplace was its centerpiece. She sat me down on the floor and started to unbutton my shirt; I tried to unbutton her Chanel jacket, but this wasn't about her, it was about me. Mia wanted to show me what our world was going to be like in front of that fireplace, on so many nights. I lay naked on the thick carpet, which felt like a fur coat. The place was completely empty, which added to the mystique of what it would look like after she was done designing our world. She'd make it a home, much the way she had with my apartment fifteen minutes from the Badlands. She stood in front of me, and slowly undressed. She was the most beautiful woman I had ever seen, and yes, if this was what she wanted, then this was what she should have. She sat down on top of me, held my face in her hands, and kissed it slowly.

"I love you, baby, I love you, baby, I love you, baby . . ." She repeated this to me slowly, over and over. She was now where she wanted to be, with the man she wanted to share this ecstasy with for the rest of her life. I rolled her over, wrapped my hands around her wrists, and closed my eyes as I moved deeply inside her. Our lovemaking was usually gentle, working for each other slowly, but tonight it was about exploration, learning something else about our bodies. I'm sure she enjoyed the danger of this, making love in someone else's home. The possibility of getting caught must've been exciting; I'm sure this also helped her to achieve what she wanted, that incredible climax.

I suddenly entered a zone, a dark place that I had never been to with Mia. I was no longer on that thick carpet, I was somewhere else, a netherworld where salsa music pulsed. I saw Roxanne, I saw women snorting cocaine in a tight bathroom with red walls and a bare bulb. I saw that beautiful Jamaican who'd dropped off a bag of cash for me, and I saw those bodies lying lifeless in steel metal drawers. I saw the boy, the one who could've been me. I squeezed my eyes shut, then opened them. Where was Mia? I grabbed hold of her face and she was screaming my name. I finally saw her, Mia, there underneath me, scared, scared to death.

We dressed quickly and walked out back without looking at the rest of this incredible home. We sat out on the boat finger; I didn't know how to explain what had happened. I'd left my body, someone else had entered and violated what was pure? The guilt I felt was insurmountable.

"It was like you were someone else. I couldn't stop you, even your face changed . . ."

"Mi, I'm sorry. I would never hurt you." I looked into her eyes; they were rimmed in red, but worst of all, they were confused. This was a woman who at all times had everything clocked to the nanosecond, but right now she was lost and all I wanted to do was get her back, allow her to gain control again. "Mi, you are the blood that runs through my veins; what happened in there had to be from the wine and weirdness of being in someone else's home, and I've had only an hour's sleep in two days." I held her in my arms, I cupped her face in my hands and kissed her gently as I told her the truth. "I'm just so scared, Mi, this is all so different for me, I am not from this world, I've never been a part of it. I'm afraid when you wake up from this dream and realize that I am not the guy you think I am, you'll leave me, and I could not live without you. I would not last a second Mi, not a second."

She pulled me to her and rocked me. She was back in control. "I know who I am marrying, I know who you are, and I am so proud of you. You are the only one for me."

We kissed, and I would have done anything for her at that moment, anything, and that was that. She held me in her arms, a foghorn gently tapped rhythmically in the distance; the tide was moving in, which allowed the water to soothingly pound the dock; I did not let her go. I turned and looked at that marvelous landscape and the beautiful colonial stonework and once again all I could think about was my next tour of duty in the Badlands.

6

"Escopeta Pequeña"

I didn't tell Billy about the episode with Mia. I very rarely let him into my personal world, although truth be known, Billy, the Badlands, my job, my career—that's all there was for me at that point. I was stuck somewhere in the middle of actually having a personal life: Which part of my life was the personal one, which one should be kept a closely guarded secret, and who was I keeping that secret from? When I was with Mia, I kept the streets and what I was doing in them away from her; when I was with Billy, Mia and the luminous light that she brought to me was off limits to him. I had now truly fractured my world in two. I guess I wanted to be able to create that perfect balance. Things don't always happen exactly the way you want though.

We were doing a day tour in sector Charlie, which wasn't the Badlands but was still in the 6-7 and a dangerous place, as dangerous as any in the city. A large section of sector Charlie was Church Avenue, the road that cut right through the middle of the precinct, running to the farthest points west, which actually was where the station house was situated, and it ran completely east into the Badlands. It was approximately five miles long, bordered on the east side by the 7-3, west by the 7-0, and in part, north by the 7-1 precinct; each of these precincts was among the top ten every year in brutal felony crime. If the 6-7 was the nucleus of these three precincts, then Church Avenue was the DNA strand that linked all of hell together.

The avenue was filled with rotty houses; jerk chicken restaurants; record stores that blasted Bob Marley and the Wailers, Jimmy Cliff, and an assortment of third-world tunes through the streets from speakers jerry-rigged above their doorways. There were storefront weed spots, hair extension salons; men would illegally park their vans, open the back doors, and out of the back sell sugar cane, hawk mangos and watermelon, intricately carved bongs and pipes, incense and oils. The avenue was rife with color, music, and a dangerous mix of men from different cultures who carried guns. The American blacks, or homegrowns as they're called, took over this area during the white flight of the early seventies, then the Jamaicans started to populate the area. Their smart business sense of selling weed in doorways and offering a variety of different smoke became a bone of contention with the homegrowns, who had made a good living up to that point by selling nickels and trey bags on the corners. The Jamaicans came in with their posses, and the homegrowns were pretty much shut down or had to work for the Jamaicans. Needless to say, there was never any love lost between the two cultures.

Most of the stores were on the ground floor of two-story buildings. Above these stores were railroad-type apartments, generally two to each building, one left and one right. The apartments were tight and dirty. I hated going on jobs in there because the stairways up to the apartments were so narrow you had to climb them almost sidling against the wall. If someone wanted to get the jump on two cops, these would be the buildings to do it in. The radio barked, "Six-seven Charlie, K."

Billy picked up the radio. "Go for Charlie, K."

"Charlie; fifty two, family dispute, 3207 Church Avenue, K."

"We'll check and advise, K."

I swung the car into a U-turn. I hated family disputes, as did most cops. By the time the police were called, the situation was usually way the fuck out of control, somewhere up in the ether, and most of the time someone had been assaulted, 99.9 percent of the time a woman, and badly. The emotional level in any family dispute was off the charts, to say the very least, so these jobs were never easy. I had already been to many of these jobs, and more than a few times the man of the house would turn on us, demeaned in front of his woman or children. We would have to, not so gently, subdue him and then place him under arrest for assaulting us. Suddenly, at the sight of seeing the breadwinner of the household exiting with cuffs on, the woman of the house, who'd made the call in the first place, would subsequently turn on us, leaving us with no choice other than to have to collar her as well. There were always young children in the house, so the bureau of child welfare would have to be notified and then the problems and paper just escalated beyond belief. Now, back in the day, when cops arrived at the scene and anyone was assaulted, these offenses were generally squashed simply by escorting the gentleman out of the home, then warning him not to come back for a few hours. That would most certainly be when the cops' tour of duty ended for the day, but since many of these "gentlemen" would worm their way back into the homes and subsequently murder their spouses, the days of shit-canning family disputes was a thing of the past. Today, however, this was one for the books.

We arrived at the scene having already been advised by central that there was a backlog on the radio, which meant that there weren't any units available for backup. Everyone was on other jobs, including the patrol sergeant, so we were on our own. Now, we felt salty enough not to think twice about needing a backup on such a garden-variety family dispute, but like rifling on a bullet slug, no two family disputes are ever the same. Billy responded nonchalantly that "no back up would be needed." We pulled up to one of those second-story apartments situated over a low-end liquor store whose primary business was definitely not the sale of liquor. A Hispanic woman, probably in her twenties, though she looked to be in her forties, was holding on to two crying children. This in itself was an anomaly because there were no Hispanics in this part of Brooklyn. This family was probably the last holdout from a time gone by. The woman's faded nightgown was torn at her shoulders, revealing deep scratches probably requiring stitches. Her face was wet with tears and she looked terrified.

A crowd was already gathered as we exited the RMP. The first thing I looked for was anyone in the crowd who looked suspicious, maybe cocky enough to be carrying a pistol. This was all I thought about, guns and more guns. This poor woman whose life was about to be turned upside down had become secondary to me, and that on my part was, and is, inexcusable. Billy and I walked to the woman, like two done-it-all, seen-it-all hair bags. Who we were was Mister Dumb and Mister Complacent, and the second you get cocky and allow your guard to drop, that is when reality, most def, will rear its ugliness.

I looked at Billy and coolly said, "I'm going to talk to this guy, Billy, you stay with the woman."

"My husband," she screamed in barely audible spurts of English and Spanish; she was also hyperventilating, which made it even harder to understand what she was saying or trying to say. Billy held on to her gently with both of his hands, trying to calm her. "He's got my baby, he's drunk, he's got my, my, baby, please, he got the baby."

I walked toward the apartment, still with an eye on the street, smiling, assuring the boys who eyed me that we'd definitely hook up again. One of the boys, who could not be any older than sixteen and who was wearing a colorful gym suit and short, nappy dreads, smiled a mouthful of gold at me, pointed an imaginary gun at me, and said, "Yeah, man, you the gun boy, you the gun boy, never get me with no strap." I smiled at the Rasta in training and moved to the entrance; the Spanish woman was screaming and crying louder. My gun was still holstered and I didn't even have a nightstick with me.

"Please, my baby, *escopeta pequeña!*"

I stopped short. *Escopeta pequeña.* My Spanish was poor, though there were certain words I was sure to remember and know, like *escopeta,* rifle; *pequeña,* small. She was saying that her husband had a small rifle. She'd also said when we arrived that he had her baby, *gun and a baby;* I turned to Billy, who already was on his way to me with his pistol out. He pulled the radio out of its holder and notified central that this was now a dispute with a gun, child involved. She advised us that there was still no one available, and yes, we were still on our own.

We moved up the stairs cautiously. The door to the railroad apartment was open, and as I neared it I yelled inside that we were the police, the good guys, and we wanted to talk; there was no answer back. I felt my hands start to shake. This wasn't like chasing someone right in front of you, someone you could take out in an instant if he made the wrong move. No, this was a different scenario. I did not know where the man with the baby and the gun was. He could've been hiding behind a couch or in a closet, just waiting for us to enter, and systematically taken all of us out. The fear of the unknown is always worse, trust me.

I edged my way into the apartment. The first room in off the tiny hall was a kitchen. I peeked in; it was empty. Billy was behind me, covering my front. I felt him low, which told me he was kneeling and moving on his haunches. However, the subject of this call was holding a baby. *What if he uses the baby as a shield, what if he uses the baby as a card to get out, what in the fuck do I do if he is holding the baby and starts shooting, what if we shoot the baby . . .* These thoughts ran through my mind as I nervously moved toward the next room. I was young and scared, no longer that cocky hair bag who'd exited the RMP minutes before, eyeing the street for a *real* collar. I was just a young cop in a really bad situation; but that was what I was getting paid to do.

Sweat from my brow started to drip into my eyes. They burned. My throat was dry, and Jesus, did my hands tremble. I moved into the living room, a mess—tables turned over, an ancient TV with a bottle thrown through the tube, broken glass everywhere, the shades torn and windows curtainless. The sun was still at a low angle in the sky and shot rays through the nicotine-colored glass washing the room in an ugly yellow. The thing that was really raising me up was that in all the time we were up there, we had not heard the baby cry. That, and knowing that the distraught woman's husband had a gun, was making me angry, angry because he was in control; he had the cards and it was his deck. I hated this feeling of being at another man's mercy, of not being able to see what was happening. That is when I started screaming.

"Police, we're here to talk, sir, please, we just want to talk." I was screaming through the open door of the last room in the apartment. Billy tapped my leg and I noticed a closet in the living room; we were on two sides of the doorjamb in the beginning of the room, and Billy moved slowly to the closet. Now I had to cover him, keeping an eye on the closet door and an eye on that back-bedroom door. He made his way to the closet, ripped it open to emptiness. My bladder was telling me it was full. The last thing I wanted was to pee my pants, but it was quite possible that that might occur. I shook off my nervousness. I now knew that he was in fact in the last room, as the bathroom was off to the side of the living room and it was open and empty. I moved to the doorjamb on the living room side, held my breath, and peeked in. I pulled my head back, squeezed my eyes tight, then looked at Billy and nodded to him that he was, in fact, in the room.

Now he was as nervous as I was, and Billy was the type of guy who would rather take the wall down than walk through the front door. He was a very physical guy, and this situation certainly wasn't something that he could just hit with his fist or a nightstick to resolve. This scenario needed finessing, the kind that neither one of us could do, or the kind that wasn't taught to us in the academy. He started screaming, "Sir, we need you to come out here where we can see you, please, sir."

No answer; I looked in once again and got a clearer picture of what was before me: An overweight Spanish man was sitting in a weathered rocking chair with a quiet infant in his lap. He was sipping rum from a Bacardi bottle, and across his and the child's lap was a cut-down shotgun, *escopeta pequeña.*

"Billy, he's got a cutoff and he's holding the kid." I said this loudly, loud enough for him to hear, though for no reason other than tremendous fear. Now we both screamed loudly at this man holding this blameless kid. The room was tight and dirty and hot. Our screams were echoing, bouncing off the walls and into our ears; it was a terrible situation to be in, as he was simply staring out the window, chugging rum, holding this baby. It seemed as if he didn't even know we were there, not eight feet from him. This made the situation all the scarier because he was so not of sound mind. I remember thinking how in trouble we were, how in trouble this guy must've been, how he just stared out into those miserable streets and how they must've sapped him of his pride and dignity. I knew at that early stage of the game that the streets had those capabilities, could tear down even the strongest of wills.

The radio was squawking, central trying to raise us, but neither Billy nor I could respond. We were gripped by white-knuckled fear. We eventually heard sirens in the distance, but again, what good would they do? He was in control; as long as he held on to that infant, he was the cumumba-jumba. For all the screaming we were doing, all the pleading to at least let the little guy crawl to us, it did absolutely no good, he just stared out that window, drinking that rum. And then, as if it were an act of God, he turned to us, his eyes not as vacant. *This is a good thing, he is back on the planet,* I thought. *Oh thank you, God, thank you, there will not be blood here today.* Before that thought was completed, he smiled at us. This was promising.

He said, "Take care a the baby."

I didn't understand what he said; I was trying to gauge him—was he still smiling, where was the baby—and then suddenly he lifted the shotgun, I could not get a shot in, I dropped to my knees. *Oh no, the baby, God, no . . .*

He quickly placed the gun under his own chin and pulled the trigger. I felt the concussed explosion as my eyes closed, I felt my knees giving out, and I heard the baby screaming. *He's alive!* I thought. I opened my eyes and charged into the room. The air was filled with smoke and a fine mist of blood. The baby was in the man's death grip. I did not want to look at the body, but I had no choice. His head was completely ripped off at the neck, split in two behind the powerful blast, and the face mask of the man slid down the wall and rested in a smoky and bloody heap. Blood cascaded down the walls, from the ceiling and every corner of the room. His carotid artery was still pumping the remaining blood out of the gaping hole where his head once was. Suddenly there was no sound in the room, just that echoing and ringing in my ears. I charged for the baby, pulled at him with such ferocity that I dislocated the poor infant's shoulder; I knew this the second it occurred. The baby just wailed, then he started to cough and turn blue, choking on his own vomit. He was also covered in blood. I was terrified; I checked him for bullet holes. He was clean, the blood was his father's; I wasn't aware of anything that was happening around me, everything was moving, strobelike. I wasn't sure of what had just occurred. I was shaking, and I knew I was working on the baby, I saw him below me, I saw the blood and viscous he was covered in, I saw him coughing, turning bluer; I turned him over; his diaper was soiled, feces erupted out of the sides and onto my legs and uniform shirt. I balled up my fist, reached under his tiny belly, found where the diaphragm should be, and pulled my fist up and out to where his thin chest bone started. I did this four times, until he coughed; he then threw up. I turned him over and cleaned out his mouth; I then cradled him in my arms. I tried desperately not to cry, I felt my mouth jittering, I felt the tears rolling down my face, and I just sat in a bloody corner rocking this baby, only feet from a gruesome reality that was this child's life. I wanted to rip my eyes from my head, tear my teeth out, I wanted to stand up and stomp on that bloody, twitching body, I wanted to scream, but I could not. I was helpless. Billy might have been right next to me, I don't know. I was all alone in a bloody cocoon trying to protect that blameless infant from a sad reality.

Cops started to fill the apartment. This was a good crime scene for the ghetto ghouls, so everyone showed up. Most cops carried instamatic cameras in their RMPs just for occasions like this, so they all entered the apartment with cameras in hand, snapping away at the headless body; they then snapped away at the head. Once the sergeant left the room, one of them actually slipped rubber gloves on and placed what was left of the head in the corpse's lap and took more pictures. All this while I sat huddled in a corner with the crying infant.

My sergeant came back in the room and tried to remove the baby from my arms. I would not let him go, but after a struggle they got him from me. Everything came rushing back—where I was, what had occurred, the dead body, and all that blood and excrement from both father and baby; I was covered in it. I charged out of the apartment ripping the sticky uniform shirt off my body. Billy followed me out.

We drove back to the station house in silence. I was angry with myself for allowing my feelings to get in the way, but I still felt sorrow for that little boy. I don't know if I cried. Billy never brought that moment up. When we pulled into the parking lot, I got my gas card out of my shield case, turned on the gas tanks, and doused my shirt with gasoline. I then dropped it in a barrel and set it on fire. I turned around, went into the precinct, and never looked back.

I thought that I could burn those images out of my mind, but really, all you can do is suppress them, tamp them down deep inside, hoping they will never surface again, but sadly, that isn't ever the case.

Mia took off from work early and was already home at the apartment making dinner when I arrived that evening. She was dressed in fabulous tailored silk pajamas, the kind starlets wore in those black-and-white movies from the forties. She said she'd had a long week at work and just needed to chill; chill for her meant to cook, eat, and make love. I did not say a word of my day, there was no need to. She was the last person I wanted to know of this life. I just needed her to be there for me. I just wanted to know that she was close by.

The table was set with crystal she had just purchased for our soon-to-be new home. There were candles lit and white linen everywhere. She would pass me and touch my neck gently. She'd put down the antipasto and pour me some more wine, then hum some pretty Italian song and move back into the kitchenette. I was there in body, but my mind was not. The ringing in my ears had not stopped once; the smell of that acrid, spent gunpowder was still so abundant that I looked around the table to see if it was the food. I just drank more of the wine to help soften the day. Mia stepped into the room carrying a large bowl of something red, probably pasta; I remember that it was a lighter color than the blood I had witnessed that day. Then I looked at the wine, more the color that was emitted from my man's neck. I heard a tremendous crash and saw Mia running to me. She grabbed hold of my hand; only then did I notice that the table was covered in blood; I was toying absently with a knife and had slit a three-inch gash in my hand. She walked me to the bathroom, and though she was talking to me, I heard nothing, saw nothing except my bloody hand, which now was the exact shade of crimson I'd witnessed in that tight apartment on Church Avenue. I definitely needed a hospital visit even though I refused. She wrapped my hand and we sat on the couch. She asked over and over what had happened that day. I wanted to tell her, I should have told her, maybe it would have absolved me of the nightmares that were sure to come, but I just sat next to her and cried silently. Sympathy was the last emotion I was trying to elicit from her. I knew that if I was going to last without imploding, I would need to find an unemotional road to work on. That day redefined me. I swore I would never again feel that out of control; those woeful, disgusting, pussy feelings that coursed through my being were to be a thing of the past. This was to be the last time I would ever cry about anyone or anything. I kept rethinking the day, all the blood, and I kept drinking the wine, then some bourbon; I drank until I passed out. When I woke the next afternoon, I vomited uncontrollably; the food, the wine, the bourbon, and those white-hot emotions were excised and purged from my body along with everything else.

My transfer did not come for approximately eight months. That was okay because where Conroy left off, I picked up. Gun collars became an everyday event, capped off by an obligatory Academy Award performance with the ADAs. The perps I was locking up did not have a chance in court. Most of the time they pled out at the suppression hearing after the evidence that had been procured during the arrest was admitted into the court proceedings. Now, as opposed to going to trial and facing maximum sentences, most of the arrestees would plea to lesser charges and generally do a quarter of the time they would have done had they gone to trial. This does not sit well with the perps, but the guys who really get pissed are the 18b lawyers, or the defense attorneys. Not that I could give a fuck about the scumbags who told one of my perps that he should have "just shot me in the head, as it would have been the same charge." The more I beat these jackals in court, the better I felt, and trust me, the safer the streets of New York were because these "gentlemen" I was locking up were the absolute worst animalistic underbelly this city had to offer.

In the time that I remained at the 6-7, I was not only honing my street skills, but also changing within myself. Compartmentalizing every emotion. I had become or was becoming a different person. As I look back now, I realize that it truly was a catch-22. You see, in order to thrive and excel in working environments like the Badlands, you have to become the monster that surrounds you. You have to be as cold and unforgiving as the people you are paid to protect, but more important, as the people you are paid to arrest. I realize that not everyone unfortunate enough to live in the Badlands is cold and unforgiving, but you see, once a man blows his head off with his infant in his arms in front of two cops just to get the last "fuck you" to a society that has balled him up and spit him out, well, you kind of lose trust in the human experience. The rub of all of this: It is almost impossible, once your tour of duty is over, to turn back on those loving, gentle emotions that we are all born with.

There is a profound verse in Latin that has always spoken to me: *"Quod me nutrit me destruit,"* which is translated as "That which nourishes me also destroys me."

"Welcome to the Jungle"

Our transfers finally came through. We had two full years on the job, and all of that, not counting academy time, was done in an A house, code for a very busy and dangerous precinct. The 7-6 precinct in Red Hook, Brooklyn, was also considered an A house, especially with the dangerous housing projects that bordered it. The 7-6 had two civilized pocket neighborhoods running through the middle of it, Cobble Hill and Carroll Gardens, an area inhabited by a mostly Italian population dating back to the turn of the twentieth century. Al Capone grew up and was married in the area, and lived there until he was exiled to the far reaches of the Windy City. I was rarely in these two neighborhoods though, except to eat or drink. Most of my time was spent in the outlying areas: where the animals lived.

Billy and I drove to the precinct together the night before our tour began. We needed to find lockers and we wanted Patty Pirelli, who was now in the plainclothes anticrime unit in the precinct, to show us the area from his perspective. Patty had moved into the unit quickly, within his first year. It was probably a no-brainer for the precinct commanding officer, as Patty was different from the other cops who were assigned there. Where the other cops had to learn the streets, Patty had an inherent sense of them. Patty had become the go-to guy in the area. He had already cultivated snitches and made dozens of quality ar-

rests. None of it meant anything to Patty though. He stayed assigned to the precinct because of the abundant ghetto pussy that
the area was famous for. We knew he wouldn't sugarcoat anything, and we also knew he would have the skinny on everything
going on in the precinct and on everyone inside and outside the
precinct. What we learned was nothing short of amazing.

Patty explained that the 7-6 was a dumping ground of sorts.
That meant, in simple terms, that if a cop fucked up on the job,
but was lucky enough to beat a judicial trial and subsequently a
departmental trial, the job would punish him, or her, with a
transfer into these "dumping ground" precincts, hopefully never
to be heard from again. Most of the time these places were in far-
off environs where you would not have the chance to deal with
real people or real cops ever again. Whether they were in indus-
trial areas, or hellhole armpits of the city, they guaranteed one
thing: You'd never have to be bothered with normalcy again.
Welcome to Red Hook and Gowanus.

Most of the cops in the precinct had gotten jammed up in one
way or another with the job, but not just your average, everyday
run-of-the-mill fuckups. No, these guys and girls fucked up in
monumental proportions. This precinct held every psycho and
loony tune on the job. There was the cop who unloaded at a bird
in a tree because the bird shit on his car after two hours of buffing
and waxing. There were guys who worked in sensitive details
and mysteriously lost thousands of dollars in buy money. There
was the lieutenant who completely fucked up a high-profile
triple-murder case while commanding a PDU and was now back
in uniform working the desk, surviving on massive doses of thorazine. He had no friends or family, so the conversations he had
at home were with a life-size cardboard cutout of the Budweiser-
beer girl. There were the cops who lost their driving privileges
because of excessive accidents on and off the job, even cops who
were not allowed to carry guns anymore. How they remained on
the job is far beyond any realm of comprehension.

There is more. A five-foot-seven cop who weighed three
hundred and some odd pounds was suing the city for weight dis-
crimination. Another got caught with a box of grenades, then

skirted a serious collar by saying he'd found them on his way to work and was bringing them into the precinct to voucher them. Word had it he *was* bringing them to the precinct, but certainly not to voucher them. A bona fide terror suspect, an alleged hit man caught on a federal wiretap; and then the guys who were just caught fucking their bosses' wives or girlfriends. The list goes on and on; the 7-6 had them all.

Banishment to these precincts does not exist on paper as a disciplinary type of action. You get sent to these places behind a late-night phone call from one captain to another, and that is that, never to be heard from again—hopefully. I had heard that these guys and girls existed on the job though I'd never met any. Now, I was to work side by side with them. Think of the great Steve McQueen, Dustin Hoffman movie *Papillon.* Their home was Devil's Island; my new home was the 7-6, and I had asked to be there. This worked to your benefit if you wanted to excel on the job as far as collars were concerned, because the last thing any banished cop wanted to do was police work. They were embittered cops who only wanted to sign in and sign out—fuck the job and the system. So for guys like me, Billy, and Conroy, who were here to clean an uncleanable mess, this was the place to be.

Billy and I were in a zone anticrime unit subdivided into three teams, covering three precincts. John Conroy was flip-flopped, doing opposite tours, so we never worked together, though when I made a collar late in the tour, I would see him on my way to central booking and vice versa. He welcomed us when we got settled in. It was tepid, though I got a real sense that he was happy to see me. He briefed us on all the guns he was bringing in, where the hot spots were, and what cops to stay away from in the precinct: all of them. Our meeting was maybe three minutes long. I was glad I wasn't working with him right away, though I would want to eventually. At that moment I was content with Billy, even if we did not see eye to eye on the ways of the streets.

We hit the streets running, making collar after collar in this new hellhole. My stories with the ADAs were getting more elaborate because a lot of our arrests were being made indoors. The big difference between the East Flatbush Badlands and the Badlands of Red Hook was that, in Red Hook almost all of the criminal activity was done inside the projects, either in the atriums or inside the lobbies and apartments. In East Flatbush 90 percent of the work was in the field: the street. So of course the legal stories in court had to be modified with the change of environment—why were we in the building, how did we get into the apartment, what were we doing on foot in plainclothes in the atrium? We were also starting to go to trial more and more, as the perps in Red Hook were much more organized and lawyered up. Though we never lost any suppression, Map, or Wade hearings—three primary judicial trials to see if evidence, arrests, or statements were obtained without duress or coercion—it was really pissing off defense attorneys who thought they knew what we were all about and developed gonz-magilla hard-ons for us. For Billy, these were all obstacles to climbing the ladder. He figured that we got into this detail by a stroke of luck, so why the fuck upset the apple cart? He just wanted to ride it out, and after we had our time in, we could apply to an investigative unit to get our detective shields. He also wanted desperately to study the patrol guide in hopes of passing the tests for higher rank and working his way up the chain of command to captain. I had no interest in that; last thing I wanted was to be an astronomer when I could be an astronaut.

I knew as soon as I got to this hellhole that I would have to follow Conroy's "business model" and cultivate someone who'd be my stool in the street, someone who'd be my eyes and ears. The trick was getting an informant I could trust who was going to give truthful and good information. Without good information, you could go for years without really knowing what was going on in your own backyard or your target area, and there was way too much going on in this jammy-jam to let slip by. Yes, you could make the occasional car stop and find a gun or get lucky enough to stop the ride with a wanted homicide suspect in it, but you absolutely had to rely on inside help to get to the core of the problem that Red Hook and Gowanus faced, and that was seriously organized criminals and drug dealers. These criminals went for years in this precinct basically owning the streets; it was all about to radically change.

The biggest, baddest, and I must say smartest cat in these streets was John Conroy's go-to guy, Shah King. In terms of drugs, the Shah ran the projects on both sides of the precincts as well as in other parts of the city, and he also had a great business pumping, with his extremely pure heroin counts and his organized crew of workers. He was off-limits, of course, but he was the type of informant I could definitely use to eradicate other dealers sprouting up, trying to take over spots and indiscriminately busting shots into crowded corners, killing innocent kids and not-so-innocent parents. I needed a cat like him, and since there was no one on his level, I would try to turn one of his own people, someone close enough to the Shah to have the same information, yet in the streets 24-7 to get me information on his competition. That guy was Cholito, or Cho.

Cholito was Shah's main street dealer, and he was amazing. He did the hand-to-hand dealings in the street, so fast that I actually clocked him slinging Shah's potent boy to twenty junkies in less than a minute. That is a hand-to-hand every three seconds, truly a godsend in a business that relied completely on stealth and quick turnover of the product. He was short and chubby; junkie chunky, overweight from the massive amounts of sugar consumed during any junkie's waking hours. Cholito had tattoos up and down his arms; some were good, from back in the day when he took care of himself, when he just had a couple-bag-a-day habit. Then he fell deeper and deeper into the opiate's loving clutches and his teeth and weight and tattoos all went south. He did, however, have a heart of gold and a contagious personality, one that I would grow to like, a lot. Cho's problem was that he'd grown up in the Badlands of Red Hook.

I'd watch him out there doing his hand-to-hands. He'd have his team assembled nicely. The lookouts were young boys ranging anywhere in age from ten to thirteen, stationed on rooftops at the four ends of the Red Hook houses with a bird's-eye view of anyone coming into or out of the projects. When someone suspicious would drive in, the kids would whistle; simple as that, and it worked. Next came the steerers, the cats who would send the business over to Cho for the actual hand-to-hand. They were usually about fifteen years old, and would have to be proficient in telling the difference between the real junkies and the undercovers looking to jack the spot on a buy and bust. They were the eyes and ears of the neighborhood; they knew who was developing a habit, and who had one. They knew a user's daily intake, and they would raise up if someone suddenly tripled his or her intake of junk for the day. That would send flags up, telling everyone that that junkie might have gotten turned by the police and was now working for them as a confidential informant, or a CI. The last on the playlist were the girls; they would be used to mule the boy from the bagging plants and drop the heroin to pre-arranged spots where Cho's steerers could deliver it to him on his spot when he needed to be re-upped. Everyone knew what their job was, and it was performed with the precision of an automotive production line in Detroit.

Cho was good to us, giving us primo collars. He led us to gun after gun and guys wanted for shootings and murders, but there is a price attached to those great collars and Cho was very clear on what that price would be. He wanted to keep his ever-growing heroin habit going without having to pay for it. That meant that I would have to supply him with it. Now the last thing I was about to do was keep another scumbag drug dealer's business going with my money paying for Cho's habit, which would in turn feed my habit of getting excellent collars. So here's how I created a nice streetwise balance. If I caught a person with nothing on him but a few bags of boy, I would adjudicate his menial crime on the spot. I'd fine him and give him a "time served" sentence. The fine would be to take half his junk; the time served would allow him to go free without a three-day sentence in central booking, which would accomplish nothing other than tying up the system and putting more of a strain on taxpayers like you and me. This, of course, is 100 percent illegal, but I was looking at the bigger picture. This junkie was still going to be a junkie when he got out of central booking, and he'd probably be completely jonesing, looking for smack as soon as he hit the street. He has no job, so what's the first thing he's going to do? He's going to rob the first old lady he sees to feed his smack habit.

Anyone can say how wrong or immoral this type of deal was, but guess what, that is the way it was in the Badlands. So I'd find Cholito at a predetermined area, give him the junk, let him slam it, and then he'd give us everyone and their mothers too. This went on month after month. Cho was the bomb for us, informing even on cops in the precinct who were fucking some project "skeezit," or playing both sides of the fence for their own financial gain, in other words, cops who were ripping street mopes off. This we were uninterested in, but it did alert us to the possibility that Cho would roll on us as quickly as he rolled on them. This worried Billy, but in my mind the reward far outweighed the risk. It was all about results. I knew these were crimes I was committing daily. But I'd do it again and again. I'd learned in those two years on the streets that it's the only way to get things done.

We knew all of the mopes working for Shah or Cho, so when we saw an unfamiliar character, we'd be "cocksure" curious. One was a short, light-skinned Hispanic, a chubby cat with lots of jailhouse tattoos, and he wore a stocking cap even though it was humid and in the eighties. He was obviously steering for Cholito, as he would nod to where Cho was hidden whenever a buyer for TKO—the very potent smack Shah King pumped through these projects—neared him. Cho had not yet fed us the fact that there was someone new on Shah's payroll, so we had to toss this one, let him know who we were and what we were about.

The second we opened the doors on the unmarked Chevy, he pulled off his stocking cap. Suddenly all the potential buyers quickly veered away, and the walls of passersby seemed to evaporate. This was a great way of seeing who was carrying out there; go for the one who was moving away the quickest, they were generally the dirtiest. We approached this short, dirty-looking street urchin, and to our surprise he did not run. His shoulders sagged and he waited for us, almost like he was expecting us.

I grabbed him by the arm and walked him out of sight, behind one of the buildings; he went right along with the program, as docile as a puppy. "Who you working for?" I asked.

He had a Newyorican accent, so I figured him to be an outsider from Brooklyn North somewhere. "Yo, Officer, I'm straight, not with that now, just chillin'."

"Are you fucking kidding? We been watching you steer for twenty minutes, so stop jerking us off. Who you working for?"

I could see Billy was in a pissy mood and I did not want to scare this guy into submission. I wanted to let him know we weren't looking to break his balls for steering, I just wanted to know who was who; however, I did want him to know that he certainly could be collared very easily if he did not comply. I also did not want him to think we were running some nonsense good cop–bad cop thing on him, which real perps think is a joke anyway. I wanted him to know we were of the same place he was. "We're cool, friend, but just so you know, we can collar you right now just for doing what you're doing." He tried to talk; I held my hand up calmly. "Trust me, we really don't give a fuck that you're steering, but we can. So please, let's just cable-cut right through the bullshit: Who you working for?"

He nodded his head softly and smiled in compliance. "You right, Officer, you right"—he tapped his heart with his fist three times—"thing is, yo, I just got out, you know what I'm sayin', and last motherfuckin' thing a nigga needs is some heat, yo, know what I'm sayin'" Truth is, I needed a job, son. Some cat I knew from back in the day offered me seventy-five to look out, yo, and that's it."

We knew the cat he was referring to. "When did you get out?" I asked.

He was quick. "Two weeks ago, did some hard ma'fuckin' time too, you can believe that." He laughed, I smiled, Billy stared. Our new friend pulled out a crushed cigarette. He was about to light it, then he offered it to us; we declined. I was amused by the jailhouse gesture.

"Where was that?" I asked calmly.

"Ahh shit, all ma'fuckin' over, son. Year in Danamora, nickel in Clinton, some up there in Fishkill."

"Hard time indeed, kid." I laughed, because those prisons were in fact maximum security; the hardest state criminals were residing up there in northern New York; it was filled with every bottom-feeder we could offer them, lifers on down.

"You damn right, had to cut ma'fuckers all day long there, some big nigga's looking for some pretty Spanish ass. I'm not about that, son." He slapped his ass and laughed. "This shit's an exit homey, not an entrance, you know what I'm sayin'?"

"How much time you owe?" I asked.

"Not gonna lie to you, cool, I owe a deuce."

"Bro, you get hooked up out here, you've gotta finish that up, fuck you doin'?" I asked. He nodded his head then dropped it, going back to that jailhouse game every perp plays when needed, compliance without really meaning it.

"Oh yeah, you right, but you know how this shit go out here, who gonna hire an ex-con behind my shit? C'mon now, I got some kids, just trying to provide properly for them, shit, you know what I'm saying?" He rolled up his arm sleeves in a sudden flurry of excitement, showing me his forearms. "And check it out, yo, clean for five years, son, clean as a ma'fuckin' whistle, yo!" "Whistle" sounded like "wis-oh," he was damn proud of the fact that he hadn't slammed any boy. I guess that is an accomplishment from where he was standing, so I understood. It was cool that he was proud of that.

I was curious as to why he'd done so much time; he definitely did not look like the murdering type. "What'd you get knocked for?"

"I was in a spot with a lot of, you know, material." He dropped his head when he said the word, which he split into two, "mah-terial."

I didn't feel like asking any more, because three quarters of what he was telling us was probably bullshit anyway. I knew we'd get more of the truth from Cholito, who was sitting on a bench smoking a Kool, enjoying his hiatus. Before we moved away, Billy asked, "What's your name?"

"Angel, yo. Angel Borges." He stuck out his hand to shake;

Billy just turned and moved to Cholito; I pounded his fist gently.

If I'd known then what a scumbag he would be, I would've capped him then and there. Instead, I just said, "See you around, Angel Borges." Billy and I turned our attention to Cholito. He saw us walking toward him and BOOM, he took off like a rabbit. We chased him across the atrium and into a building, burst through the rusted metal door, then slowed down, calmly walking to the elevator, catching our breath. We stepped into the elevator and were pulled up to the top floor in the urine-laden iron box. It always amazed me how every project in the city spawned some animals who didn't mind peeing in their own elevators; they had to know that the housing-authority janitors were certainly not going to mop it up. I figured they just liked living in piss. I had been in and out of these elevators for quite some time so, unfortunately, I'd gotten used to the smell.

We reached the top floor, got out of the nasty four-by-four box, and moved to the stairway. We opened the door and climbed one flight up, to the roof landing where Cholito was sitting casually, just starting to boot up some smack. He was tying off at his ankle. He tapped just below the ball of his foot to check for a vein. Billy looked away, but I was fascinated by it.

"Yo, Tatico, C, slow the fuck down, you almost caught my shit this time, poppa."

"Start working out." Billy said this without looking at him, disgusted. I could see that Billy's eyes were sad. It just didn't seem like this was where he wanted to be anymore.

Cholito didn't look at Billy. He didn't care for him much anyway. Not once did Billy hand him a glassine of boy; it was always me, and always me he talked to. "I work my dick out, poppa." He laughed, though it was a preoccupied snicker; he was intent on slamming some love, and that was what he was going to do.

He looked up at me after he pulled his hypodermic, or "works," out of his dirty sock. "Bro, I don't have anything for you today, I'm sorry," I said.

He sucked his teeth and dropped his head, "Shit, C, what the fuck, yo?" Then, as if nothing had occurred, he pulled a bundle of heroin from his pants pocket, slid one packet out from its rubber-band wrap, unfolded the tiny envelope, which was stamped "TKO," and poured it into a dirty forty-ounce beer cap. He climbed up the stairs toward the roof, moved one of the bags of garbage, pulled out a small container of cloudy water, squeezed it into the cap, and proceeded to cook up.

"All the comforts of home." Again Billy sneered. I looked at him and shook my head slightly; I wanted him to ease up on our prized CI. Billy just blinked at me slowly. This was a serious inconvenience, having to witness this, but he did because he knew it was a necessary means to an end. That didn't mean he was going to like it or embrace it, and I certainly was not asking for that.

"Who's this new cat you got working for you?" I asked.

"Old school ma'fucker, good people, we go way back."

That was good enough for us; Cholito never lied about his people. Why should he? It would garner him no more or no less favor with us unless of course the cat was wanted, then Cho would give him to us in good time, after he busted him out, or after the worker was no longer of any use to him. Everyone was using everyone for something out there; the trick was to use them before they used you. "How much you slinging an hour, Cho?" I wanted to know how high Shah's profits were.

An angry-looking dark vein popped on his ankle; it appeared ready to explode. I watched the needle push through his scabby skin and the plunger ease down, sending the warm liquid on its hunt. He pulled up on the plunger slightly, drawing some blood into the tube, then he pushed down gently on the plunger again. He shook his head slightly, his eyes closing and opening slowly, his nose dripping a clear fluid. He didn't even bother to wipe it. This was sex for him. He did not even pull the syringe out of his ankle, he just laid back on the stairs, then focused on us. Only now did he acknowledge Billy, all smiles, in a hazy sort of way. "My niggas, what you need today, son?" He smiled, then shook his head, remembering my last question. "Oh yeah, boss man, yeah, yeah, that nigga's makin' much money behind the fruit of my shit out there, yo."

I was getting impatient because Billy woke up impatient, and I knew it was just a matter of time before he was going to spit on Cholito, so I wanted to move this along. "How much, Cho, how many bags?"

"Shit. A hour? Let me get my calculator out." He laughed at his drug-induced attempt at humor. "I say in a good hour, hmmm, six bundles."

I was blown away; I knew he was doing great business, but, in every bundle there are fifty decks, or envelopes, of smack; that's three hundred bags an hour at roughly twenty a bag, which translates into six thousand an hour, and that's just Cholito. Shah had Cholitos all over the projects, shit, he had them all over the city. The numbers were astronomical.

"What, that's a lot, Tatico? You know how I do out here, C. I'm the slamminest motherfucker up in here, son, you know how I do." He reached out with his fist; I tapped it. "And how could he not, you ma'fucker's is lettin' him ride for free out here, 'cept that crazy ma'fucker Con, he gots to pay up to Con, yeah, and everybody know it too." He wasn't telling us anything we didn't already know. Shah had a pass because he was Conroy's bitch.

He started to nod but snapped out of it quickly; he pointed at the needle in his lower ankle. "Yeah, this shit here is off the chart, son, I'm down to twelve bags a day behind this TKO." What he was saying was that the smack was so potent, he was using less; what Shah and company were doing was selling Ferraris to car enthusiasts, and at a really fair price.

"You know what's going to happen he catches you dipping into his supply, Cho, yes?" He looked up at me; he knew that I now had something on him; he smiled, playing the game.

"C'mon, C, I'm just dippin' a little. I put it back, or I pay for it. No one know the difference. When you think you get me a little taste, Tatico?"

Billy started to walk down the stairs; this meeting was over as far as he was concerned, and Billy hated the fact that I traded him smack for info.

"Anybody out here with a strap today, Cho?"

"I ain't seen nothin' yet, C, but you know this motherfuck

out here, C, it like cell-block D, yo, I'm a hook you up, C, you know that." He tapped his ankle, which still held the syringe. "But you know, poppa, don't forget your main German out here. You roll up on some punks, you know, break me off a piece, son."

The homegrown Puerto Ricans proudly referred to themselves as Germans. Don't know why, I guess the reasoning was the same as homegrown blacks referring to themselves as niggas, but then again, we were in the Badlands and nothing made sense there. I smiled at him as he nodded off. For some reason, I liked him. He was harmless, and went far beyond the call of duty for us. I guess, at the time, I saw him as a survivor, surviving in unthinkable squalor. Maybe I saw a little of myself in Cho; how right I was. I turned and followed Billy out.

In the unmarked RMP, Billy's mood did not change. I knew exactly what was bothering him though, having known him long enough; I waited for the other shoe to drop. Sure enough, after a few minutes of absolute silence in the car, he slammed his fist on the steering wheel. He jerked the car down a deserted street, pulled over, and slammed it into park.

"Rob, I hate working with that little junkie. I hate what we're doing, I gotta tell ya, I hate who we're becoming."

The last thing I needed was for him to start whining, I would rather have settled this with a friendly stick fight than do what I now had to do, and that was coddle him. He was a good and trusted partner though, and I did not want to break up the team. I had to navigate this carefully.

"Billy, just calm down, bro, just relax." I said this in an even tone. "We're the same cops we were when we came on, just further educated. Listen, man, we didn't know that this was the way things were done, it wasn't required reading in the patrol guide, if you know what I'm saying. But out here, you and I both know it's the only way. Maybe in Midtown South it's different, or somewhere in Queens, but you know where we are, Billy, and we have to stay one step ahead of these mopes. If I have to throw them a couple of bucks—"

He snapped his head at me; there was fire in his eyes. "Bucks?"

"What, you want to stop throwing him some boy bags? Okay, we'll stop throwing him the bags, but let me ask you this, Billy: What do we do with the bags that we get on these junkies?" He shrugged his shoulders. I understood his dilemma, but it wasn't as black and white as he was painting it.

"Because I got news for you, pal, I ain't collaring some animal for a few bags of smack or coke, taking me off the streets for two days, and behind what? A misdemeanor drug collar? I don't think so. Do you wanna take the collar? Billy, we aren't here for drug collars, we're here to make gun arrests and bring the numbers of violent felonies down, bringing up the number of arrests, period. What do you think the captain is going to say if we go off the reservation on his dime? What do you think he'll say when we stop making quality collars? Tell you what he's gonna say: 'You guys had a nice run, but it's time you went back to patrol, in the bag.'" Billy did not answer. He had to know I was right. Back to patrol in uniform would've been a major setback for both of us. While I was willing to cross the bridge into the netherworld, though, he was not. I also was willing to swing for it; in my mind, the means justified the end. "Just answer me this, Billy, are you willing to collar some disgusting junkie for a few bags a dope?"

"No, I don't want to do that either, that's just tying up the system and keeping us down."

"So what do we do when we grab someone and that's all he's got?"

"We toss it down the sewer."

"Then what's the fucking difference between that felony and the felony that's being committed by throwing it into Cho's ankles? You know what, Billy, fuck this, stop with all this delusional bullshit and don't play high and mighty with me. We are here on my dime, and yeah, my duplicity, but you knew the game I played on Bully, you knew if I got away with it, we were out of uniform and off patrol, and that is exactly where we are today. You and me, we practice the same hypocrisy; difference is, I'm honest about it. It's okay to lie to me, just don't lie to yourself, bro." Billy did not answer; he was too smart to think there was an easy way to navigate these not-so-black-and-white issues that arose in the street every twenty minutes. Every aggressive cop worth his salt in New York City knew this was one of those job hazards that was never talked about but was practiced daily, "discretionary power." Collar him for nonsense or let him go and try to get the real bad guys. This was the way I saw things, and honestly, there was nothing that Billy could say that would change that fact; a crime would be committed any way you cut it, whether it was tossed down a sewer or tossed to Cho. Same crime, different outcome, but once that crime was committed, why not make something good come of it?

He stared at me and jerked the car back into drive. "Fuck you, Rob," he said in an even tone. I let it go, and that was the last we spoke about it. What I did do was, every time I met with Cho, Billy stayed behind; whenever we tossed some schmuck and he had drugs on him, I made Billy give it to me and I never told him what I did with it. I guess he thought by not actually seeing the crime being committed, though knowing full well it was being committed, that it really wasn't taking place. He needed to make it right in his mind, which I thought was immature and, honestly, made me feel like a cheap suit. I was good enough to do the bad stuff and take all the heat if I got caught, but he would share the credit after we made those great collars given to us by Cholito and all the other slugs in the community I had to deal with daily who were sucking me dry. It was at that moment that I totally lost respect for him, and knew that we didn't have much of a future together.

8

Thirst for the Darkness

She was wearing a fabulous Frette silk pajama top with a matching knee-length silk robe she'd purchased at Bergdorf's earlier that week. She was kicked back, drinking some chardonnay, reading some magazine I had never heard of, when I arrived home. Mia looked so pampered, and she fit so well in my apartment. I just looked at her and forgot about everything filthy that I had witnessed that day: the animals, the guns, the TKO, all of it, gone that quick. She was smiling at me as she dropped the magazine and tapped the bed for me to sit next to her. It was a work night for her, but she'd made me promise to call her about eleven P.M. every night to let her know if I was collaring up. If not, she would wait for me, so she could feed me and we could make love before turning in. Tonight, I was hoping, would be one of those nights. I wasn't in the mood for any conversation. I just wanted to decompress and, simply, not think. I took a quick shower; the last thing I wanted was to have any street odor on me when I was with her. I was wrapped in a towel and sitting at the table where she had put down various plates of food: antipasto, fried vegetables, and of course linguini Bolognese, my favorite. She sat with me and sipped her wine; she was a vision of beauty. I was tired, and so happy she was there. After every tour, on my way home, in the quiet of my car, there was always a humming or buzzing in my ears. It would last at least two hours; sometimes I would feel it undulating in my head till long after I was asleep. I never knew why it occurred; maybe it was due to my blood pressure spiking so often during the day, or maybe it was all the unseen noises that are a part of the ghetto and shoot through your subconscious all day and night long, but tonight, the ringing and humming and buzzing was not there. It was just her. She reached out to touch my hand and I saw the engagement ring. I loved the fact that she never took that ring off; it was one of those untold gestures that said how much she loved me.

"How was your day, Rob?"

Between mouthfuls I said, "Long, and I'm so glad to be home, just wanna chill."

She smiled. "I'm glad you're home. So we have an appointment at the bank on Friday."

"Friday's no good, Mi, I have to work a two to eleven." I knew what the appointment was for; the owners of the home in Kings Point had accepted her offer and now it was time to mortgage up. I had issues with this, things were just moving too quickly. I wanted to move a little slower, but I could not tell her this without upsetting her. I had to be smart, and being smarter than Mia was a task and a half.

"Rob, I think that us getting this mortgage takes precedence over either of our jobs, no?" she said. It was common sense, and had I been a Wall Streeter, or a college professor, or a garbageman, for that matter, this *would* have been common sense, but I was not any of those things. I, and what I did for a living, was much different from anything she could imagine.

I stopped eating, gently laid down the fine Christofle silverware she had purchased at Fortunoff's. I knew that this conversation was going to have to take place sooner or later. I swallowed a large amount of merlot before I began. "Mi, I don't think I want to be on the mortgage or the deed with you."

I immediately felt the temperature change in the room. She tilted her head at me slightly, doing what she did best, analyzing me, the statement. She was going to filter the information, process it through her mind, and only then would she respond; Mia never did anything spontaneously, she did not live by the seat of her pants. Everything was thought out, to the letter. Emotions were not a part of any business decisions, where her judgment might be clouded; emotions, they would come later.

"You feel something in your past might stop you from getting the mortgage—past credit problems?" I looked in her eyes, shook my head no; she blinked twice, slowly, trying to work this out, and remained unemotional. "Well then, if it's not a past problem, why wouldn't you want to be on the paper?"

"It's the job, Mi. I'm on paper as a co-owner on the property, something happens on the job, we could lose the house."

"Well, what could happen on your job that would cost us the house? The NYPD will indemnify you if something occurs accidentally; that's why you pay into your insurance fund."

She was right about that; we did have a good insurance plan that indemnified us on job-related accidents. We were covered with RMP accidents. If I got into a gunfight and a nonparticipant civilian was injured by me, I would be covered, but like everything else on this job, there was a gray area. I knew how we were working in the streets without a safety net, doing everything a little off-color, and this she was not privy to. For example, say I received info that there was someone wanted for a homicide and he was hiding out in some apartment, but was on the move all the time. Our only chance of capturing the perp would be to get the jump on him immediately, so we would hit the apartment without a warrant and with as little backup as possible because the fewer cops who knew about our practices, the fewer people there would be to test-i-lie or, worse, tell the truth. But what if in the course of getting into the apartment illegally, some civilian got hurt? Or what if the wanted man shot at us and hit a civilian? We were dead wrong because of how we'd gotten into the apartment and we could swing from a large tree behind it. That is the gray area where we could be sued personally, in civil court. Civil trials are different from criminal trials because the evidence does not have to be so overwhelming to gain a conviction, and with one sketchy witness to our practices, that in itself could sway a jury or a judge against us, and then any of my assets could be used as a settlement. I explained most of that to Mia. What I did not tell her was that the cornerstone of every one of my collars started out sketchy, that my methods of apprehensions in the streets could almost always go terribly wrong, and that at every turn I could be sued. I played it off like I was just being cautious, but the truth was, yes, I did not want some mope who deserved to *get gotten* anyway possibly beating me in court with a jury of sympathetic cop haters, allowing him to take what Mia and I both worked very hard for. But, really, that was just a half-truth. The other side of that coin was my wanting to know that if I decided to get up and walk away, I could do so without any red tape, that with a snap of my fingers, I could pack a bag and leave behind this life that was planned out for me to the letter. It was a sad way of starting our lives, but in this job, in which I was fully entrenched, it was the only way.

Mia was deflated slightly; it was the first time that my job had gotten in the way, compromising our plans and our future. She was all about becoming one entity with me: our souls, our lives, our blood, our money. But she was realizing that there was something else that demanded my time, attention, and commitment—the streets of the Badlands. After a few moments of allowing this to all sink in, she gently touched my hand, smiled sadly, and said, "I'm really tired, baby, I'm going to bed." She stood up, placed her wineglass in the sink, and closed the bedroom door softly behind her. I sat there in my damp towel, suddenly with no appetite. I poured the rest of the wine and drank it till the glass was empty. The exhaustion I'd felt prior to this conversation was gone. My urge to be inside this beautiful woman had disappeared. It was just me and something racing through my body, the compulsion that I would always get just before we started our tour, excitement that was roaring through me, the excitement of the unknown. I suddenly did not want to be in my beautiful Rockaway apartment only 150 feet from the Atlantic Ocean. I wanted to be back on the street. I had a quick shot of Jack Daniel's, put my clothes back on, and quietly closed the door behind me as I went back out to the world I loved so much, the Badlands.

Before I got there, I'd need to fuel up. That meant Alfredo's.

• • •

It was booming, as usual; there were some burnt-out denizens from the precinct, who I had met, their goomadas, and the string of sexed-up Bettes from the Badlands. Roxanne was behind the bar, and the second she saw me walk in, she pulled two glasses off the rack and poured four fingers for both of us. I moved right for her. She looked sexy, wearing a pair of daisy dukes and a tight red halter top that accentuated her perfect breasts and red lips. Her hair was pulled up librarian style and she wore nonprescription glasses to feed the image. She should have just worn a sandwich board that read: "I am built for fun and will rock your motherfucking world." Words cannot describe the sexuality this chick exuded. I was ready, mentally, to walk down that road. Maybe it was fear of the future—this thing of raw sex and beauty that could be mine for the taking would no longer be available to me after I was married. Maybe I was angry at having my future so perfectly laid out for me and I wanted to "man up" slightly, to show myself that I still had a modicum of control in my personal life. Or maybe I just wanted a secret that I could take to the grave with me. In any case, my heart jumped as I reached the bar and she open-mouth kissed me for a few hot moments.

"Tatico, where you been? You know what nights I work, why you ducking me?" She said this almost as a whisper; she held my face in her hands, very close to hers; she looked at my lips and wiped the lipstick off them softly.

I looked her up and down, but not disrespectfully; I wanted her to know that it was all about her, and I was available, and that she was "all that." "You are so fucking sexy. You know that?" I asked.

" 'Bout fucking time you noticed; we was startin' to wonder about you, Tatico." She laughed; it was cool and comfortable. She might have been from the streets, but goddamn, she was so at ease and happy with who she was, it made me want her more.

"When can we be alone?" I found myself asking.

Her left eyebrow lifted. "Ohhh, you wanna hang out." I saw

her nostrils flare; I knew this was not going to be a one-off, hit it, and move on. No, this I should take my time with, enjoy a little. Some drunken psycho from the 7-6 was making a racket at the end of the bar behind the slow service. Without removing her eyes from mine, she just lifted up her middle finger to the unseen, annoying cop and flipped him the bird. "I'm a take care a this asshole at the end of the bar, then I get a break for half an hour. We can go for a walk if you want to."

"I want." She kissed me again as I closed my eyes. I got aroused immediately, but this was different, there was more heat attached to this. This felt primal.

Alfredo, the owner, came behind the bar when Roxanne motioned to him. He was shortish, about thirty-five. He was thin, probably from a serious cocaine habit, but he was friendly and handsome enough to get over easily, and the cocaine he always had available would get him over in the fashion he liked so much, with multiple partners, all at once. He smiled at me when he stepped behind the bar. It was a guy thing, he was saying, Hit it hard, with his knowing eyes. He enjoyed having guys who could get over in his bar, especially cops. We were protection for him, and we also thought he was kind of a cop buff, but definitely enjoying his status as a civilian, enjoying his extracurricular activities—snorting up half of Bolivia with chicks who were no less than solid eights.

Roxanne grabbed hold of my hand and I followed her out, past the onlookers who all wished they were going to the same place I was. I knew there were cops in there who semi-knew my story. They knew that I had a really beautiful legit-type girlfriend, and that we were getting married. I knew the fact that I was walking out the door with Roxanne was going to be big news in the bar and the precinct. I didn't care, because I really did not associate with any of those cops in the precinct; at the time, I felt they were below me, and I had nothing in common with them. They were just trying to get over on the job while I was trying to get over on the ADAs, the scumbags in IAB, the vile defense attorneys, and most important, I was trying to get over on the animals in the street. Our views on police work could not be more different, however, if they needed me in the street; I was their brother, and a trusted one they could absolutely count on. They knew my reputation was that I was as crazy as they were, but in a different way. So this dirty little secret would—like all of the other secrets—most definitely stay right here, in the Badlands.

It was a nice night. At this time of the evening, the traffic above us was light. The expressway was like a giant canopy, offering shelter to the homeless, the degenerate, and the horny. She led me across Hamilton Avenue, west, toward Red Hook, without saying a word. Underneath the expressway, she seemed to know exactly where she was going. I followed her to the wall on the farthest south part of the underpass. It was dark, but if someone pulled up they would see whatever was happening. At that point, I didn't care, and clearly she didn't either. She leaned up against the wall, smiling as she pulled my hands to her. She closed her eyes and started to kiss me. I felt her heart pounding, she was sweating, and she was moaning as she thrust her tongue deep in my mouth. She lifted my hands up to her breasts; she was not wearing a bra. I felt her nipples, large and hard; she took my two fingers in her hand and forced me to pinch them, hard. She moaned loudly, "Ahh fuck, Tatico, fuck." Her eyes were half open as she whispered this. She took my hand in hers and placed my fingers in her mouth, then slid her shorts to one side and slid my fingers in. Her eyes rolled back in ecstasy. She pulled my fingers out and fed them to me. "I taste good, baby?" she asked. I could not talk, I just nodded, placing my fingers in her mouth and we both kissed them. She lifted up her halter, revealing her perfect breasts. She then started to rip at my pants, and very quickly unbuttoned them, my five-shot Smith & Wesson tumbling off my waist and hitting the ground; I didn't care. I unbuttoned and unzipped her shorts. Her breathing was labored and loud. Now, this was all about need. She wanted me, I wanted her, no pretense, zero bullshit. It was just about the primal urge we all have, it was a sex thing. "I'm a take care a you with my mouth and tongue later, Tatico, just want you inside me now, wanna feel you deep inside." She held me in her hand, she did not waste any time with foreplay and slid me right inside; I became animalistic.

Every inch of her was raised up, all of her emotions, her breathing, every piece of her was an exposed nerve ending. I knew this was going to happen fast for both of us. I thrust inside her, and she made no attempt to lower her voice; with each move she screamed and said something in Spanish, very throaty and sexy. This was truly one of my most intense sexual encounters ever. Not because of who she was, but because of where we were, the danger of it all, and that we really didn't give a fuck. This was as natural and raw as it can get. I heard the cars roaring, overhead, I had heard footsteps nearby, I knew my pistol was on the ground, behind me; we didn't give a fuck. It added to the fantasy. She had a violent orgasm; she grabbed hold of my back, I felt her nails dig in deep. She hiked up on the wall, feet off the ground, straddling me, and she came again; this time I joined her. I was covered in sweat and completely spent. She could not move. I had to hold her up as I felt the muscles inside her twitching uncontrollably.

As her breathing evened, I let her down gently. I pulled up my pants, sliding the gun in my lower back, and she leaned against the wall half naked and flushed, eyes glazed. She looked as if she'd just taken a hit of TKO. Then she slid her shorts back up and zippered them without buttoning them. "Why don't you button up, Roxanne?"

She smiled. "'Cause I don't wanna cut off any feeling down there, I can ride this shit out for at least another half hour." She then slid her hand down the front of her shorts, then pulled it up to her face and inhaled. "Plus I can smell you real easy now, Tatico." I felt myself getting hard again behind her honesty. She was as sexual as someone was ever going to get. We kissed and walked out from the dirty underpass, back across the avenue to Alfredo's bar. The whole encounter took less then ten minutes, but the bridge that I had crossed in those ten minutes could never be walked back over. *Can't undo the done,* I thought.

She moved back behind the bar, looked in the mirror and put on some lipstick, not caring who saw or what they thought, then started serving drinks like nothing had occured. She gave me a little wink as I turned and walked out. I can write this now, and I hate the fact that I fucked around on Mia, but at that time in my life, I didn't think it mattered. I was living in a place where a bullet could have ended it all. This nihilism was becoming a huge part of my mentality. Death was around every corner, so what the fuck? I'm not trying to justify my infidelities. Not every cop is going to fuck under some expressway in full view of the public, because of the possible pitfalls of our job—that tomorrow just may never come. I'm saying that is what *I* was feeling at the time, and that with every tour of duty, the law of averages was catching up with me, because I was truly over-the-top aggressive in my fieldwork. In hindsight, the thing that strikes me the most is how fatalistically I viewed my world, all at the ripe old age of twenty-four.

My thirst for the darkness did not end inside Roxanne. That was just the warm-up. I got in my car and headed straight for Red Hook. The zombies of the night passed me, knowing but uncaring. I rolled my window down, needed to breathe in that air, exhilarated to know that these were my streets, that I was making a difference. The cats who knew me all gave me respect and moved indoors, but I wasn't there to launch a late-night ambush. I just wanted to cruise; I felt like this was my kingdom, I wanted to survey my property, maybe catch something that I could use tomorrow, maybe meet someone ready to do some work for me. An open car door revealed one of Red Hook's two-dollar hos giving some guy head. Junkyard dogs roamed the dark streets in a pack, looking for food, or worse, no different from the animals who were bipedal. More hookers were standing in a row, topless; as I drove by, they called out my name, holding both breasts in their hands and jiggling them gently. I was now in the most abandoned part of the Hook, the waterfront. I could see the Statue of Liberty in the background; she was certainly not a voice of inspiration to anyone unlucky enough to have seen her from where I was at that moment. Farther on, the ancient and abandoned grain terminal moved up on me slowly. It was an indelible icon of what Red Hook had become: The closer you got to it, the easier it was to see the cracked mortar, and the gaping holes along its massive structure. It was dark and scary; it was the perfect symbol for the hell it bordered. In the foreground, I saw movement from a bench on the other side of a small, vacant, crater-filled park. I slowed down, popping my head out the window, listening carefully for any sounds of distress. There was a voice, pained. I pulled up and saw Cholito sitting on the ground, using the bench to hold himself up. I walked to him slowly. "Cho?" I called out. He was moaning, not crying, because that emotion is burned out of any junkie or ghetto cat at a very young age. I got a frontal view; it was not good. He'd been beaten, badly, his head swollen, bulbous almost, his forehead protruding out, dark blue, almost black. His eyes had swelled shut beneath some huge gashes. The person who'd done this to him made sure that Cho's arms and legs were not touched, assuring that he would be back slinging when his tour of duty began the next morning. This told me the perpetrator was the Shah or one of his lieutenants. Cho used his fingers to pry open the skin around his eyes so he could see who was calling him; he just leaned back when he realized it was me.

"C, you caught me at a bad time, yo." I think he laughed, but it was hard to distinguish any noise that escaped from his bloody mouth. His nose was spread across his face; I ran back to my car and pulled out a rag and an Evian bottle. I doused the rag and handed it to him. He accepted it and tried to wipe away the blood.

"Can't wipe away the pain, Tatico . . . ma'fuckers took my stash . . . I'm sick, C."

"C'mon, I'll take you to the hospital, brother, let's—"

He was pissed. "Not the beat down, C. I'm motherfuckin' sick . . . I need a boost." He started to throw up, and he was shaking. The horrific beat down he'd so violently received ran a distant second to the pain of not being able to boot up some smack. "Please, poppa, you holdin' for me?" He was almost in tears at this point; he was starting to shake violently and I could not imagine the pain he was feeling.

"I'll be right back," I said as I ran back to my car.

"Hurry, C, I'm gonna . . ." He moaned some more as I jumped into the car and drove three short blocks. I knew some Panamanian upstarts were out there this evening slinging, so after I parked my car in one of the housing-employee lots, I used the cover of darkness to spy the Pano who was pumping this late in the evening. Boy is a twenty-four-hour business. Once someone starts jonesing for a hit of smack, they will do anything, suck anyone, fuck anyone, or sell anything for that syringe of liquid love. I had witnessed a broken-down junkie chick who at one time was supposed to have been a beauty contestant in Puerto Rico; she actually gave a dog head for a dime bag of heroin. The Shah made us watch because he thought it would bond us; I must say that I was curious. I did not think that any jones could be so powerful that it would allow a person to sink that low, but he was right, and he had all of his boys out there watching, taking pictures and filming it. The Badlands were motherfucking perverse and TKO could corrupt anyone's soul and humanity.

The Panos were smart. They not only knew when our hours ended, but also when the narcotics teams' tours ended, at about one A.M. So they felt relatively safe; their guard was lowered, there were no rooftop lookouts. In short, they were extremely vulnerable. The street lookout was a big kid, about eighteen years old. He had jailhouse muscles, but his back was to me and he was seated on a bench looking at the Pano sling. The slinger was wiry; he looked like he could run, but so could I: I had my head down as I walked out of the shadows to the asshole on the bench. He was not even aware of my presence, that is, until I had my gun and shield out in his face. He was about to say something, but I had no time for bullshit. I clocked him over his left eye with the butt of my gun. He went down like a box of rocks, then got up and ran away. The dealer saw what had happened and took off. He did not disappoint me, as he was quick, but I caught him between two buildings. I swung hard at the back of his head with my gun and he stopped running, hitting the ground hard. No words were exchanged. I jammed my gun with extreme prejudice into his ear; I saw blood drip down his neck and chin as he screamed in pain. I tossed his pocket, felt that familiar bulge of a package, and tore at it, ripping it off the pants leg.

"Don't move or I'll blow your fucking heart out." I said this calmly; I don't even think I was breathing hard. He had no idea who I was, but complied, probably happy to think he was getting ripped off as opposed to getting collared. I took about fifteen bags, rewrapped the remaining gack in the rubber band, and tossed it at his feet. "Have a nice night," I said as I trotted back to my car.

Cho looked worse than before, pale, unable to speak. "You got any works?" I asked as I pulled the decks out of my pocket. He kicked out his leg with great effort, revealing a syringe jammed into his sock. "Can you cook?" He shook his head no; he was a stone-cold junkie, so I knew that if I weren't there, and he had no arms or legs, he would have found a way to cook up, but I let it go. I searched for a bottle top, found one, used the Evian to clean it out. "How many you want?"

"Whose is it?" This he asked as he heaved some more.

"The Pano's."

"How many you got?"

"Fifteen."

"Put two in the cap, fill it halfway with the water, then light it up."

This was a first for me, but I had watched him and others like him do this hundreds of time, so it felt natural. "Cho, I'll cook, but I ain't gonna feed you, brother, you're on your own with that, *sabe*?" He nodded through a ferocious bout of convulsed coughing. This truly looked worse than any torture imaginable; the Shah knew how to get Cho, deep up in his guts. He fucking owned Cho; he owned everyone up in the Badlands.

I sucked the brown liquid up into the dirty syringe and handed it off to Cho, who was shaking uncontrollably. *Let this be a hot shot, put this poor motherfucker out of his misery*, I thought. It was decent boy though, and the second he banged it in his foot, without even tying off, it was as if God had appeared, placed his hand on Cho's forehead, and released him from his wretched agony. The color came back into his face; he looked at peace, even happy. He drooled slightly, a sign that the chocolate gack had found its mark. I helped him up.

"You the motherfucker, Tatico. You everything they say, true that, C, true that!" he mumbled as he limped to my car.

We stopped at a bodega for some forties of Bud, then drove

to the pier at the tip end of Red Hook. He was flying and feeling no pain any longer. He pulled out his works again and was going to hit it once more. "You going deep tonight, Cho. Slow the fuck down, 'cause listen to me, you OD, you're on your own, hustler." He sucked his teeth, then spit out a wad of brownish fluid, traced with blood and phlegm.

"You think an oh' school ma'fucker like myself gonna play out on a few bags a this cheap Johnson? C'mon, son, I'm hittin' twelve bags a eighty pure a day, I'm a missile, son, I gots more love in my veins then all a these ma'fucker's put together. Shiiit!" To translate: His body was already immune to a hot shot of smack unless it was purer than the 80 percent he was banging all day long. It would take a deeper count, or more heroin, to lay him down, and dime bags were no more than what they were sold as, dime bags. He should have been a pharmacist, hell, he *was* a pharmacist.

I opened a forty, and drank as he booted another barrel. "He caught you dippin', yes?" I asked.

"Yeah, some white ma'fucker came back crying like a cunt, sayin' the bags were soft and weak on the count. Shah happened to be there, grabbed me aside, pulled my shit off me, and left. He must a tested the shit, 'cause I was waitin' to get re-upped, next ma'fuckin' thing I know, I'm dodging some big-ass Filas, and lots a them too!"

"I don't know why you don't just take the money you make in bags instead of cash."

"Why pay for it, Tatico, when I could get it for free? Man, fuck that, nigga', when you ready to bag that punk up you let me know, 'cause we can light his shit up, son. I know when all the play is played." I laughed; I liked him, and he liked me. He laid back on a piece of cracked and upturned asphalt, a ghetto beach chair, cooling the fuck out. I watched him and slugged from my forty; a couple of old buddies just chillin'. I noticed the lights across the river. Manhattan was so close in proximity that I probably could've taken some of the lights out with my five-shot, but like Rockaway, my home, it had become a different planet for me; I had no need or desire to ever step into that borough again. I was home and so content right there, on that rat-infested pier, with my number one cumumba-jumba, Cholito. If he had the keys to the castle, we would loot the motherfucker dry.

He scratched at his nose slightly; it bled a little but he just let it drip, then wiped it off. "What you doin' out here, Tatico? Lookin' for some a that ghetto pussy?"

"Couldn't sleep. Needed to get out for a while."

"Right." He laughed. "Everyone come to the Badland when they can't sleep, 'cept if they lookin' to get high." He focused on me, and smiled deliberately. "You lookin' to get high, Tatico?"

I tilted my head at him and grinned. "I like you, you little German, but I will place a cap up in your ass."

"You so full a shit, C. I gots eyes, I see right through you."

"Only thing you see are bottle caps, tie-off belts, dirty works, and bags a TKO, which is gonna get you got, sooner than later. So just sit back and enjoy that Pano's gack. Which, by the way, is brought to you from the *fruits of my hard labor.*"

He laughed, liked the fact that I was stealing his line; he had always said he got half of Brooklyn high "behind the fruits a his shit." "Yo, you ain't like the rest a these 'my name is Joe' ma'fucker's out here, that's for damn sure. Why you become a cop?"

"So I can keep crazy lokes like you on your end a Brooklyn, far the fuck away from my end a Brooklyn."

"You keep feedin' yourself that shit, maybe someday you actually believe it." He laughed again; he liked playing with me.

"Why? Why else would someone come on this job? The perks? Like all those fabulous and interesting cats we meet shuttling from restaurant to restaurant sippin' martinis and spending all the cash we make?" I looked at him this time without smiling. I guess I wasn't that hard to read; Cholito may not have been schooled with books, but in the street, and his judgment of the people who played the street for good or bad, well, he was an Einstein. There was no getting over on this fated little junkie.

"What you think, Cholito is stupid, yo? You out here like the rest a us, you lookin' to tool up, feel the juice, pumpin' it hard right there on the edge." He jerked his fist up and down, as if he were masturbating. "You lookin' a ride up in here with the rest a us, do the same ma'fuckin' thing we doin' 'cept you wanna get medals for it 'stead a gettin' collared for it." He laughed, leaned forward for some ghetto dramatics. "Gots the four-eleven on you, Tatico, there ain't no difference 'tween you and me 'cept you's got ambition."

"And I ain't got a habit, son."

He eyed me knowingly for a moment, then he looked out into that expanse called the East River. "Yes you do, C, yes you do."

That was the first time that someone else had acknowledged what I thought was known only to me. I'd wondered if I'd be able to cover up my track marks the same way that junkies covered theirs, but I did not have long sleeves or pants legs to cover my telling eyes. I sipped the forty, and watched Cho nod comfortably, surrounded by dirt, garbage, and weeds. I kicked back, and those moments of worry and angst disappeared as quickly as they'd come, because I might have had a jones for the Badlands, but from where I was sitting, I was as comfortable as that little junkie, who was now sleeping peacefully.

9

"Shots Fired! 10-13, K!"

My resolve to move on and away from Billy Devlin grew every day. I had told Conroy about the potential breakup and he was glad. He thought Devlin was soft in the street and he didn't trust the fact that Devlin would be in a 100 percent test-i-lie mode at court; he didn't trust him. He thought Devlin would be a better fit with the crew of guys he had working for him on his team. Those cops just weren't on the same page as Conroy. Yeah, they would do what needed to be done, but they just did not understand the darkness as we did. They could not communicate with a lot of the perps in the street, and that is 90 percent of the game, being able to get down on their level, so we could all speak and understand the same language. John and I were just biding our time till the hookup would occur. And the more I enjoyed the darkness that the streets afforded me, the quicker that was going to happen. Especially after the Tuff Gong incident.

It all started when Sergeant Mahoney called us over the point-to-point radio band to see if we would pick up a job, man down, for the precinct commander. There had been a major backlog within the confines of the 7-6 he said, and they needed backup at the Tuff Gong Bar and Grill. Mahoney was one of the good ones; he was squat in size but had incredible strength, as he worked out in the precinct gym every chance he got. He had a streak of white hair that he desperately tried to blend into his orange hair as he headed toward the wrong end of middle age quicker than he had ever anticipated. He had twenty-five years on the job, and at his age he should have been long retired and working toward a second pension, but this job, he felt, was a young man's job, and by his remaining on the job, in these nasty streets, he was going to stay young forever.

The Tuff Gong was a Jamaican hangout that was located on Smith Street, at the ass end of the precinct. It was a transient bar, located close to the Brooklyn and Manhattan Bridges, bringing in blood from that other borough. It was right off the corner of Atlantic Avenue, which ran the entire northern part of Brooklyn from west to east, bringing in its own denizens from every nasty section that Brooklyn had to offer. There was always a gunfight between Jamaican posses, the occasional stabbing, or really fun-to-watch catfights that would erupt outside the place every Friday night. Riding with Mahoney one night we picked up a half dozen eggs (a six-pack of Bud) and sat in our unmarked across the street from the Tuff Gong. We watched the chicks fight, just tear into each other, ripping the clothes off their backs; someone would always end up naked. Many a night we'd get out of the car, identify ourselves, and transport a three-quarters-naked girl home in the back of our ride.

Billy and I rolled up to the storefront bar, where we noticed Conroy's unmarked parked up on the sidewalk.

"What the fuck is he doing here?" Billy asked. He didn't know Conroy had done a tour change and that we were working the same chart that night. I did not feel like getting into an argument with Billy about Conroy's motives, but I assumed they were good ones, otherwise this would be the last place he'd be.

The outside of the bar was small, about twenty-five feet across, but upon entering the garish bar I saw it was three times the size of the outside. Walls had been removed on both sides, and the club had picked up the extra space from two adjacent stores. It was completely empty except for Conroy, Mahoney, Pirelli, the DJ who was still spinning third-world tunes, and a very nervous-looking bartender biting his nails behind the bar. Conroy, Pirelli, and Sergeant Mahoney were sitting at the bar nursing three Heinekens. In the middle of the now-empty dance floor lay a man, obviously dead. With the music playing and the disco ball shooting shards of light over the dead guy's bloody body, the comical juxtaposition of the situation was not lost on any of us. This was as surreal as it was going to get.

"He was just dyin' to dance." Pirelli said this with absolute deadpan humor, which he was by now famous for. Mahoney coughed out some of the beer and Conroy had to hold himself up on the bar to keep from laughing. I figured Pirelli must've been on fire with this scene since they'd walked into the place. They all touched their bottles in a toast and drank.

"What we have here is an alleged misunderstanding between two of the local businessmen," Conroy mocked.

Again Pirelli jumped in with deadpan delivery. "Over drugs we're told, and the bad man who did this . . . black!" Everyone laughed except Billy, though he did smile to show that he was with the program. I knew the truth though. He was definitely *not* with the program.

"We picked up the job boss. What are you guys doing here?" Billy asked. I was annoyed by his lack of spontaneity on crime scenes like this one. He knew they were there because it would bring a laugh in horrible situations. He was taking everything way too seriously. What I did not realize was how right Billy was to look at this murder scene for exactly what it was: a guy just out to meet some people, drink a little, blow off a little steam; instead, he came out to dance and ended up murdered.

The rest of us looked at this differently. In situations like this, most cops try to find the humor somehow. You have to, otherwise you will eventually become so battle fatigued you'll end up sucking the barrel of your gun. What you have to do is try to balance the humor without running away from the reality of it. You can't shy away from the truth, as I'd tried to do after the man blew his head off in front of me in the 6-7; I'd learned my lesson, or so I thought. What Billy was able to do was process the truth, confront the feelings he had, and then move on. What we were doing there on that scene was just tamping it down with humor and booze. We never looked at the plain facts, that this guy was a child once, with a mother and a father, and maybe he did have a family who cared for him. At that moment, he was a performer in a twisted ghetto comedy.

"We're just taking in the ambience . . . plus, we hear the rotty is spectacular." This time I laughed out loud at Pirelli's humor. He started to dance to the music. "Hey, DJ, you got any good salsa or Latin tango? We need to get this party started right." He danced his way over to the dead man; he was immersed in the music. Conroy looked at me with a jolt of excitement.

"Tatico, go in my car and get my camera."

I ran outside to retrieve the Polaroid camera. I did not look at Billy when I passed him. I knew what his eyes were going to say. When I returned, Pirelli, Conroy, and Mahoney were dragging the bloody body toward the bar. "Jesus Christ, this guy is dead, fucking weight," Pirelli said, to much laughter.

"Fucking bumba-clot devil's work." The unamused bartender poured himself a double, then just sat back and watched.

"Hey, Nat E. Dread, we ask for any shit, we'll pull on your dreads; in the meantime, you shut the fuck up. This is an important crime scene," Pirelli said as he placed the dead man's red, black, and green knit Rasta hat over his own head. Conroy grabbed the camera and shot Pirelli wearing the Rasta hat. The camera spit out the picture. Conroy bent down and helped Mahoney and Pirelli lift the man up to a bar stool. At that point, the bartender ran out from the bar and into a back room. The DJ, however, was enjoying the show.

"Ya, man, you the Babylon bosses, man, you some crazy motherfuckers, hey, Officers, you mind if I . . ." The DJ, holding up a giant joint, said this from the microphone hooked up to the speakers. "Can I smoke up some ganja, boss?"

Mahoney laughed. "Yeah, just don't Bogart all of it though, with them big lips a yours." Even the DJ laughed at that one as he lit up the giant splif. While I helped hold the dead man up on the chair, Conroy ran behind the bar and popped open some more beers. He swiped a pair of Ray-Ban glasses off the speed rack. He handed us each a beer, slid a bottle in the dead man's hand, and placed the glasses on his half-closed eyes. Then he looked at Billy.

"Devlin, c'mon, take the shot."

Billy just smiled and played it off really cool. "I'm gonna wait out front in case the patrol supervisor comes; I'll come in if I see him rolling up."

He turned to walk out. Conroy asked him again, "C'mon, at least take one picture."

"Nah, I'll let you guys catch the Kodak moment."

The DJ sucking on that bazooka joint appeared in a cloud of smoke. "I take the picture, man." He laughed as he snapped and pulled each picture out. Billy ducked his head back into the club.

"Lieutenant's rolling up."

"Which one?" Mahoney asked.

"Rosenberg." This time Billy had a slight smile on his face because he knew to what extent every cop in the precinct would go to play practical jokes on Lieutenant Marvin Rosenberg. Marvin was the boss in the precinct who got jammed up for botching a major triple homicide in the Midtown South precinct. He was the same lieutenant who, while driving home every night, talked to a cardboard cutout of the Budweiser girl, and the same man who was whacked on thorazine 24-7. When he was young he'd found his father with his head blown off from a self-inflicted shotgun blast, and clearly had never recovered. Marvin was kind of squeamish around any DOAs. He had no idea what he was walking into.

He was totally bald, so he always wore his police hat cocked at an odd angle. He was also overweight, and a chain-smoker who wore huge wire-rimmed glasses, the kind that David Berkowitz was wearing upon his capture. As a matter of fact, that is exactly who Rosenberg resembled, a fatter, older, and balder version of the famed serial murderer. Cigarette dangling from his lips, he ambled up to Mahoney, who pretended to be busy with his memo book. Mahoney saluted the visibly nervous lieutenant. "How ya doin', Lieu."

"How are you, Sarge? Thought this was a DOA?" He was puffing hard on the Virginia Slims cigarette. He toked hard whenever he was nervous, which was 99 percent of the time.

"Yeah, Lieu, you know what, you need to talk to the bartender, he's a little upset, sitting behind the bar; he apparently knew the DOA."

"Yeah, okay, but where's the DOA?"

"He's in the basement, Lieu. You need to take a statement from this guy, he saw the whole thing."

There was absolute silence as Rosenberg walked carefully behind the bar to the corpse we'd arranged on the bar stool. We had made the DJ cut the music for supreme effect. I had to bite my lip to stop from laughing as the lieutenant approached, as shaky as a torch on a crack stem. On the bar's wooden platform was the corpse, with his head between his legs, holding a beer. He must've appeared to be crying, because the lieutenant, who could definitely understand the man's grief, walked up to him. "Hey, fella, sorry for your loss, but I need to . . ." The man did not acknowledge Marvin and it was then that Marvin noticed a photograph in his hand. He lifted it up and recognized us four cops and this man now sitting behind the bar. He looked at us and shrugged his shoulders. He looked back down to the man and nudged him gently with his knee. "Guy, c'mon, I need to . . ." The man tipped over and kept tipping; at this point, the DJ blasted the music to an eardrum-splitting decibel, and Marvin saw the man's bloody innards hanging out of his now-open shirt. Coupled with the jolt of the music, he jumped back and with the highest pitch I had ever heard erupt from a man's mouth, he screamed and kept on screaming. He backed out of the bar holding his genitalia, then headed straight for the door. He was not amused, but he knew where he was working and that these things were everyday occurrences in the loony bin that was now his home. As he passed Mahoney, who was doubled over in laughter, he yelled, "This ain't fuckin' funny! You handle this mess till PDU gets here, ya fuckin' moron. You're a lucky cocksucker you ain't assigned to the precinct, a lucky son of a bitch!"

I could not stop laughing; the only person who was not laughing was Billy Devlin. I had completely lost sight of the trees in the forest.

• • •

holito was apparently put on wavers behind his bag-dipping episode and the beat down he'd received, so he was not seen in the street for a couple of days. I knew the one person who would have information on the DOA and the shooter in the Tuff Gong club was Shah King. Now, John Conroy had swung out, so we would get to the Shah before John did. I was driving and saw him sitting on a bench in front of Flag Pole* on Columbia Street. He walked over to our car without a care in the world. He didn't like us; we were the schmucks who were working for the white man's welfare paychecks, pretending to believe that we were actually making a difference, that we mattered out there. Only thing we were doing was costing him extra money to place lookouts all over the city. He ducked his head into the passenger window, and with much effort, shook Billy's hand and mine.

"Wassup, dawg?" he asked with an aloof, velvety voice laced with the slightest bit of contempt. He was king shit and he knew it. He figured he had us in his pocket because he went way back with Conroy. Billy disliked him, and so did I; the difference was that I knew I had to work with this scumbag until he could be played. I was going to kill him with kindness, and then kill him for real.

I handed him the picture of the dead man from Tuff Gong. The corpse was surrounded by the four of us, five homies having a beer. Pirelli was wearing the Rasta's hat and the Ray-Bans, Conroy and Mahoney were using their thumbs to pull up his eyelids, which did nothing other than show the whites of the dead man's eyes. This gave him the eerie look of a dread-locked Zulu zombie. I was toasting my beer with the corpse's beer. Billy could not stand to look at the picture. His contempt for all of us, and everything we were doing and becoming, was building.

The Shah forced a laugh. "Oh, shit, the dude's dead?" I nodded and he continued laughing. "Damn, remind me not to die around you crazy motherfuckers." He handed me back the picture. His forced laughter ended abruptly as he looked away and

* Flag Pole is the center point in the atrium of the Red Hook housing projects.

waited. He knew why I'd given him the Polaroid and he knew what we were there for. Without looking at us, and with the seriousness of cancer, he asked, "Where Con at, Tatico?"

"Vacation." I smiled; I didn't want to raise him up because he did not have to give me shit. He was the property of Conroy and Conroy was the property of the Shah. So I playfully tapped his arm as he looked intensely down the street. "We kind of inherited you till he gets back, you cool with that?"

He did not like having to deal with another set of cops who clearly weren't anywhere near the vicinity of his universe. After a long and quiet pause, he said, "Eddie Griffin, Rasta ma'fucker, from downtown Flatbush. He hang over at Gowanus, got that weed spot off of Baltic. Gots some bass-head ho he fuckin' at 227. You catch that motherfucking island nigga' right now in all probability you were to drive by. He wearing one a them matching shorts and shirt things that the bitches wear. Can't miss him, yellow on yellow." He turned to walk away; over his shoulder, with much distaste, he said, "You owe me behind this one, Tatico, yeah you do."

No wonder Conroy's top-dog collar man in all of the city, I thought. Shah King had a direct line jacked into everything that happened and was about to happen, not just there, but all over the city, and by default that meant that John Conroy did as well. I saw how easy life on the street would be if I had the Shah in my pocket like Conroy did, and I thought how unbelievably fast my career was going to change once I started working with King Kong of the Badlands; that was a premonition I should have analyzed very carefully. Had I been more like Mia—analytical, rational in my reasoning—things would have been very different.

We drove to Baltic Street where the Gowanus Houses stood like giant gray cell blocks in the southeasternmost part of the precinct. These projects had been built much later than the Red Hook Houses, so they were taller, and that was the only difference I could see between the two. They both bred animals, they both were rancid and smelled like urine, and they both were home to the Shah's burgeoning dope spots. Technically, this was what we'd been brought from the 6-7 for, to collar shooters like

Eddie Griffin. *This was going to get us another commendation for sure,* I thought.

My eyes were all over the street. I was looking for yellow on yellow. The tour was ending and I wasn't able to find my soft target, as there were just too many people in the streets. Occasionally I'd spot something yellow, key on it, but lose it quickly in the many tiny walkways that connected the twelve or so buildings with each other. Our tour was an eleven to seven, so the late summer sun was dropping westward, toward Red Hook and beyond. It was at the angle that told me not to chase this cat west, I'd be blinded by the sun, giving him the advantage. *But what good would it do without finding this murderous fuck?* I thought. I was like a dog without his bone. I just drove and drove and drove, swooping back and forth from one side of the street to the other. The Gowanus Houses were situated in a tight eight-square-block radius, west on Hoyt Street, south on Baltic to east on Bond Street, then north up Warren Street, then swing back around and do it all over again. Billy was getting impatient and started whining about turning the car in.

"Rob. Guy just clipped somebody. He ain't gonna stick around waiting to get collared. He's in the wind."

"Bullshit, Billy, you think Shah just gave us that heads-up to make us drive the fuck around in circles? He knows who the fuck we are. He wouldn't have told us just anything or fed us disinformation."

"Well, then somebody tipped off this Griffin dude, 'cause I don't see no yellow on yellow." He tapped the LED clock on the dash, "Seven-oh-five, Rob, let's go back in. Common sense says if he is stupid enough to be out here today, then guess what, he's gonna be out here tomorrow."

"Common sense" told me different, which is why Billy was no longer flying in my air space. The shooting was fresh, day old. I felt the shooter was going to stick around, collect some money from this weed spot of his, reason being that the word on the street would take a little time to filter back to the cops as to who the shooter was. Griffin figured he had a day, two at the very most. I figured we only had tonight to grab him before he busted out of his spot and headed to another part of Brooklyn to kill again. I was as impatient with Billy as he was with me. He had been with me for almost three years by this point; he knew what I was all about, what my street mind-set had developed into. I would never lose in these streets, under no circumstances would I go home empty-handed, beat by some street animal, some murderer who thought he could do whatever the fuck he wanted to do whenever the whim arose, just pull out and start blasting at some mope on a dance floor, no regard for anyone or anything. This was a Jamaican trait—shoot first, don't ask any questions later, and don't leave anyone to answer any questions later, period. The more I thought about this perp, the more I hated him and what he stood for, and the longer it took me to find him, the more I wanted to get him. The further Billy twisted my balls, the longer I was staying out there. I was ready to pistol-whip Billy, the frenzy that was playing havoc in my head was going to manifest itself on Billy if he *didn't shut the fuck up*, I thought. I knew this was going to end up rather badly. If we were splitting up, it was going to be a DefCon One–type divorce, and tonight, with the lights dimming over the Gowanus Houses, that scenario might occur sooner rather than later.

I drove some more. Billy's leg was tapping furiously up and down, one of his nervous habits that would occur during the questioning of some street animal who was just feeding us bullshit line after bullshit line. His leg would gyrate like a nuclear-fueled piston when he could no longer take the insolence and lies we were being fed; he would just swing around in the seat and hook off with a solid right hand to the unsuspecting man's temple. One shot would feed his need for the truth. I understood this anger, which could erupt in a nanosecond. Most every street cat working the streets knows exactly what is going on: who's selling, dealing, slinging, carrying; who's wanted for crimes all the way up to multiple murders. But when they are caught dirty, the way of the street is straightforward. Give us the info we want or go to jail. You fuck up the food chain, you don't fuck down, but some of these street guys just hated giving the cops anything and they were stupid enough to take a collar behind it. We of course could care less about some bullshit narc collar, so the last thing we wanted was to actually collar the mope. The more we'd try to reason this out with the perp, the less he'd give us and the more incensed we'd get. This went back and forth till we could not take any more of the jailhouse nonsense and the perp would end up with his pride lost and quite the knot on his head. This of course after Billy's leg started to twitch just the way it was twitching at that very moment.

Time was running out; I just wanted another half an hour to look for the perp. In my bones I knew he was still there, and I did not think that anyone had tipped him, that was the stuffed shirt in Billy's unconscious talking to him. I believed different. I *was* different. Our detail was not on the same frequency as the precinct's was; we were on a city-wide band, so we would not get called in by the 7-6 dispatcher. We were on our own, though we still had to account for where we were and why we were not end of tour by now. I had an idea; I picked up the radio and said, "Zone crime, K."

Central responded, "Go crime."

"Central put us out sixty-two mechanical, flat tire." Billy slammed his hand into the dash. I just stared at him; he knew this was a battle he'd have to win in the parking lot after the tour was over.

"I know he's out here, Billy."

"This is so fucked, Rob. You are out of control."

He might have been talking to me, but I did not hear anything except my heart pounding. I wanted this man so badly, this feeling of wanting to catch him eclipsed all others; I wanted to show Devlin that we were on two different planes. He was taking the easy road, just like the rest of the cops who worked in this godforsaken place. He was willing to give up, and in my mind, it was the coward's way out—and then I saw him, about two hundred yards due east. The perp stepped out of one of the buildings and walked the atrium north, heading toward Hoyt Street. His pot spot, as well as his girl's apartment, was in the other direction. He was walking casual, though he seemed to have purpose in his step. There was a bodega on the corner of Hoyt and Warren, so I figured he was going to buy cigarettes or a forty of something, then he'd walk back to the weed spot or his bass-head girl's spot to tap that box for a while. We needed to get him now, while he was aboveground.

I pointed him out to Billy. This wasn't about telling Billy told you so. I had none of that playing off in my head. I had eyes and heart only for the killer who was two football fields away from me at that moment.

I can only try to explain the feeling that we as cops get when we are so dogged in our work and then the intense determination pans out. It would place me in a state of euphoria. Just like TKO did for so many junkies—we were all getting high out there. I knew I was making a difference regardless of what the Shah thought and regardless of what my partner thought. This was one of those quiet victories, the one no one was ever going to hear or read about; it was one of those rare moments in life that tells you, you are exactly where you're supposed to be.

I swung a quick U-turn after I watched Eddie Griffin walk into the bodega that sold low-end cigarettes at inflated prices and charcoal-brewed forties that told you you were in the ghetto. There was a billboard, an ad for a cheap wine cooler, on the side of the bodega and it showed a handsome black cat and a half-naked black woman staring at each other in front of a four-poster bed. Every billboard in the ghetto had all these handsome minority men and beautiful minority women slinging cigarettes, really cheap liquor, or ads for AIDS or pregnancy testing. *These are great images for an eight-year-old to see on his way to school,* I thought. And now to see the white devil roll up and take out one of the neighborhood's finest, well, what hope would my predecessors have on the job? Young Johnny was being schooled at a very early age to worship all things that were bad in society and to turn away from the good. Every day on the job I knew that we were just tamping down the problem, there were just too many billboards, too many Eddie Griffins, and so many Johnnys learning how to worship and to hate.

I drove east on Hoyt the wrong way on the one-way block. I accelerated, ducking one car after another until a truck pulled up the block. He had to have known we were cops, but the two brothas in the front cab were laughing as they continued driving forward, making it impossible for me to cut around them. I slammed my hand on the roof of my ride, Billy lifted the cherry light, turning it on and off quickly to make them move or back up and to reaffirm who we were. The scumbag driver knew we were going after someone, so he wanted to fuck the cop before we could fuck one of the upstanding neighborhood citizens. He smiled and lifted his hands up as if to say, Sorry, boss, didn't see ya. At that moment, Griffin walked out of the store and saw my car pointing the wrong way. I knew he was going to take off, so I leaped from the car, leaving it in the middle of the street so the truck driver could not go any farther either. I had a subplot devised for this prick when I got back. If I got back.

Griffin dropped the bag he was carrying. It exploded into glass and foam when it hit the ground as he took off. He was fast. I knew this was not going to be easy. Billy jumped from the car as well. He was as fast as I was, so I knew if Griffin got me, Billy was going to get Griffin, or the other way around. Whatever my differences with Billy—he may have been overly cautious and shaky at times—when push came to shove, he was no coward, not in this situation.

Both our guns were out. I heard the radio crackle as Billy screamed into it. I was cool with that because I knew for sure that this was the shooter, and in all probability he was carrying the large gun that had done much damage to some poor cat on a dance floor just a few blocks away. We were on the east side of Warren Street, where most of the nonproject buildings stood— old, attached two-story brownstones, which meant that Griffin could not go left and disappear into the maze of walkways, alleys, and buildings that the projects would afford him. No, to get back to the projects he'd have to make a hard right, crossing our paths, and if he was holding on to anything that even remotely resembled a gun, I was going to shoot first and not ask any questions later, much the same way he had.

He chose the cover of the projects and was now maybe thirty feet ahead. By the time I noticed his hand, it was too late. I saw the muzzle flash first and then heard the explosion and felt a concussed ping fly right next to my ear. It was almost a simultaneous occurrence, but there was enough of a gap in time between the two for me to take notice. I only say this because during a gunfight, you become aware of the oddest things. You're not thinking of your loved ones at home, or what your demise would do to them. No, your long-term memory is no longer a functioning sense. The only thing you see is what is right there in front of you, what is happening in that instant. You are more aware of life at that moment than you could ever be, or would ever be again. You are so focused and in the moment that the air in front of you no longer becomes a transparent gas, it is a particle-filled mass, *you can actually see air.* The everyday sounds of the street are magnified and filtered, and at that moment I actually felt more alive than I had ever felt before. Maybe it was because I became so aware of death that these doors within me were unlocked and flung open? In any case, as horrible an experience as a gunfight is, it brings you that much closer to the meaning of life, to the beauty that we all take for granted every day, just walking in the street.

I squeezed the trigger and dispensed six .38 rounds, probably in less than two seconds. In all my time shooting at the range, I had never noticed that the gun actually explodes from the bullet chamber. I saw the brilliant flashes of light erupt from the side of the gun, even though I never took my eyes off Griffin. The gun jerked up and down furiously, then it jerked down at the ground and there were no more explosions or pretty streams of light. I heard tinny clicking as I continued to fire even though my gun was empty. I ran furiously, holstering the six-shot while simultaneously pulling out my five-shot backup. I let those rounds go even quicker until I heard that same dull metallic click, click, click. I was empty, both guns useless. I kept running though, and trying to gun.

"Rob, fucking reload. Rob, you're hit!"

It was at that moment that the cold reality of the situation invaded my stream of thought. I heard Billy's gun explode furiously. I looked down and saw my hand bleeding. I checked myself for other wounds, but there were none. I continued on, after Griffin. I did not bother to reload, I don't know why. I heard sirens in the distance. Billy had given excellent coordinates when he'd called the 10-13, and there must've been an RMP close by, because I heard the tires screeching inside the project atrium. An RMP jumped the curb and was moving fast, toward us, and more important, to Griffin. He made the left hoping to get into the first building he could, but he was trapped. He launched his gun toward the street, then got on his knees with his hands up. Tossing the gun was smart. He was clearly a seasoned perp, because he knew we were keyed on capturing him. The gun was secondary at that moment. In these situations, the gun would usually be picked up by some street mope watching the excitement, never to be seen again. This was called "the gun grew legs" in ghetto precincts. Now once we'd get to trial, if there was no gun found at the scene, it would be our word against the perp's that he in fact was carrying and did fire on us. This, of course, was the cloud the jury of Brooklyn imbeciles would need to acquit said scumbag, allowing him to skate on the attempted murder and assault one of a police-officer charge. This happens all too often, but the public never hears about these cases. A perfect example of this occurred back in the early eighties. An animal named Larry Davis shot seven dedicated ESU cops, some seriously. He escaped and was later captured. The scumbag defense attorney, William Kunstler, had the jury buying his completely fabricated story that the cops were a part of a major drug ring and were going to kill Davis. The poor young man was protecting himself. Just another reason to despise defense attorneys and what they're really all about.

I stopped running. In a zone of extreme focus, all I saw was Griffin kneeling comfortably on the ground waiting for his hands to be cuffed. I felt my feet pounding, one in front of the other, with immense determination. If Griffin was in the same mind-set I was, he would have to be feeling the sidewalk shake and rumble as I neared him, because with every step, that is what I felt. All sound disappeared except the drumming of my heart, my labored breathing, my footsteps, my teeth grinding together, the skin on my thumb and middle finger rubbing tightly together as I gripped the five-shot. I got within an inch of Griffin and all I saw was my hand raise high above and come down with a tremendous thud on the back of his head. Now, I knew Billy was right next to me, and the uniform cops were in front of Griffin with their guns pointed at him, but all I could do was hit him over and over. I did not take notice of when he fell, or for how long I hit him; I knew it felt good though to give him some of the payback that he absolutely deserved. Some might say that's not the cop's job, that it's up to a judge and jury to decide his punishment, and they'd be 100 percent right, but until you have actually been in the situation I've just described, you really can't understand the fury that explodes from within you at that moment. The knowledge that it could've been you on the ground with a bullet hole in *your* head distorts any normal reasoning. I can quarterback that situation now and say damn, that was fucked, I should've just cuffed him and let the Brooklyn jury decide his fate, but I did not, and that is a fact.

I felt sets of hands wrap around my middle section. I was being pulled off him. I saw my feet kick out, trying to stomp his head. I did connect with his face, but it didn't matter. He was out cold by that point.

I was not through. Before the bosses arrived on the scene, I had one more collar to make. Without missing a beat, I stood up and pulled away from the cop's grip. I walked back out onto Warren Street, made my way to Hoyt, and spotted the prick truck driver who, had it not been for, Eddie Griffin in all probability would have been caught without a struggle, as we would have gotten the jump on him without a chase. He would never have known we were there till the cuffs were on him. I walked up to the driver, grabbed him by his shirt collar, spun him around, and arrested him for obstruction of justice. I can guarantee you two things: He would not play chicky with the police again, and he was definitely no longer taunting us and smiling.

• • •

The attending physician checked my hand at the hospital. It was swollen, though there was not a bullet or even a bullet hole in it. One of the shots blew up a bottle, sending shards of glass up into my hand, opening it up.

After all the interviews from the riding ADA, and the precinct detectives, Billy and I sat quietly on two resin chairs just outside the ER.

"We shouldn't have been there, Rob. We were end of tour, our workday was over." There was no anger or any emotion in his voice other than sadness. He spoke in an even, quiet tone.

"Billy, we solved a body, took another animal out of the game, fairy squary. That's what we're here for, Billy, that's what our job is." I truly did believe what I was saying.

"No, Rob, my job is to go home at the end of my tour. You knew who he was, we had a name, you could have given it to homicide, end of story, but no, you had to ride it out till the very end and then some."

"C'mon, Billy, had I given the info to homicide, he would have fallen through the cracks. You know how that shit goes, we been on long enough to know that. We did good and we'll get the combat cross behind it—"

He turned to make sure I saw his eyes; he was more determined now, though did not raise his voice. "Fuck the cross. Don't you understand how close we came?" I didn't answer him; those words were meaningless to me. As far as I was concerned, it was all part of the game. He studied me for emotion; I gave him nothing. I wasn't condescending, but I also wasn't running away from my belief that what had occurred was for the greater good, that the end justified the means. I saw him look away, to watch a woman violently puking onto the dirty linoleum. He turned back to me. "This isn't working out, Rob. I am going to work with Pirelli. You can hook into Conroy's team. It's what you always wanted anyway. I need to slow down a little." The words hit me like a sledgehammer. I remembered O'Lary from the academy. He was there because he needed to "slow down a little" before he got made. It was becoming clearer to me, but I did not want to face the truth. I was moving inexorably out of control, into the same path as my hero John Conroy, though I was too blinded by ambition to care. I had set unreachable goals; the only way I was to attain them, I mistakenly thought, was to allow this intelligent cop sitting next to me do exactly what O'Lary had done to Conroy: leave. That was the biggest mistake I ever made.

10

The Slow Decline

The breakup was smoother than I had anticipated. Billy started working with Patty Pirelli, since Pirelli had been invited to work in our detail, out of his plainclothes anticrime unit. Patty was as aggressive as I was, though he knew when to back off. He had a very go-with-the-flow attitude toward work and the job. He got his arrest numbers, made some impressive collars, and chilled in the time in between; that, I was sure, was how Billy wanted it, to make arrests when need be, and to work completely aboveboard. It was going to be interesting to see how the two fared, but I wasn't going to obsess about it. Cops split up every day on the job for many reasons; mine was no different from a lot of others that occurred.

My wedding was in two weeks; Mia had planned everything, right up to the limo ride back from our honeymoon in Mexico. I did not have to do a thing, which was fine by me. She'd even gone alone to the closing of the house in Kings Point. All I had to do was show up, which I did with very little enthusiasm. When I was home I wanted to be there, back in the Badlands. I was always at work earlier than I was supposed to be, reading 61s, which were the complaint reports of robberies, shootings, and murders, all the stuff that cops should be keying on, the crimes that I became a cop to solve. My personal life had been completely eclipsed by work and I was happy; my beautiful wife was not, though she put on a hell of a charade, which would come to an end like everything else.

I was assigned to my new team, with John Conroy; our first weeks together we did quite well, gun collar after gun collar. Each arrest was brought to the ADA with the perp willing to do a video confession. Why? Because John Conroy had every perp in his pocket and they took his advice to the letter. This was a new trick I learned from John—lie to the perps, allowing them to think that confessing on camera would lead to an extremely light sentence, probably time served would be all, meaning that the time they served during their arrest, processing, and arraignment would be enough of a punishment served because of their willingness to come clean. I would never have believed that anyone could fall for this tactic, but John showed me how wrong I was and how the power of persuasion sent many bad guys away for many years. Once they did a video confession, there was nothing that a court-appointed attorney could do except to plead with the judge that the confession was given under duress, which basically meant that we'd placed our guns to the perp's head to get the confession. After viewing the tape and seeing how relaxed and happy the perps were, they were promptly sentenced to jail terms in upstate New York. We did not know it, but we became the number one archenemies of every defense attorney working within the public defender's office in New York City. And we were about to find this out.

The wedding went off without any problems; Mia led me from the photographer to the dance floor, then to greet our guests, then back to the dance floor, then to the dais. She would find me in between each of these necessary wedding tasks sitting with John Conroy, strategizing on who was to get collared upon my return as he schooled me on who was who out there. I thought I knew all the players, but there was a list of guys in the streets who were smart enough to run much of the drug operations from behind fortified doors in and around the projects. These were the money players, and they mostly dealt in coke since the Shah had cornered the heroin trade in the area.

The wedding ended, and the next morning we flew to the

west coast of Mexico for ten days. By the third day, I wanted to get back. I started to realize that I could no longer talk to Mia about the simplest of things. She just did not see things the way I did, and how could she? She wasn't privy to the darkness, and anyway, I didn't want her to bear witness to that filth. So I pushed her out of that part of my life, and she slowly started to understand that that was the way it was going to be and accepted it. It was still wonderful to be in her presence and to make love to her, but it was the in-between time that wasn't the same. We just didn't have that much to say to each other. She tried, but I just wasn't that interested in anything other than who was strapped, or wanted. It was that plain and simple.

My tour for the day was a six P.M. to two in the morning; I arrived at the office at four in the afternoon. I was sitting with the PDU detectives, drinking coffee and studying wanted posters of perps from all over the country. I had a superb memory for faces, and I figured that these projects were a great place to hide if you were wanted by the law; I had already made collars off these very helpful wanted posters, so this time in the office allowed me to focus, to sear these faces into my memory.

Tommy Mahoney was doing the day tour and was just banging out when I entered the PDU. He tilted his head at me, indicating that I should follow him, never a good sign. We moved to a back stairway. The four-to-twelve tour was downstairs in the muster room doing roll call, so we would not be bothered. Knowing the cops who operated in this place, I assumed that these covert little meetings took place here quite often through the years.

Mahoney was sweating; he looked like he'd had a shitty tour and was unable to collar up for his cops. He leaned against a wall, lighting up a Macanudo Robusto. He blew out a thick ring of smoke and waved at it, clearing the air between us. I knew this conversation was going to be serious.

"Got a phone call from a friend a mine who works at IAB." He held up his hands to deflect my hatred and to defend his choice of friends. "Captains and above get assigned there, he's good people, trust me, that is the last place he wants to be, fuckin' scumbags . . . Anyway, he tells me there's something going on in zone eleven, doesn't know which precinct, or who is involved, but we are very fuckin' hot."

I didn't think that I was a target. After all, zone eleven encompassed many square miles of Brooklyn and housed three different precincts, including narcotics divisions and a handful of other organized-crime units. I didn't think anything of it. I grinned and said, "You know how we do, boss, we ain't ripping anyone off and we ain't using, so what could they possibly get from us? We're number one and two in violent arrests, Sarge. They'd be crazy to try and bust us out. I'm okay; you're okay." He slapped me on the shoulder, I went back to my work, and he went home. What I said I actually believed, but the truth was that everything I was involved in was dirty, right down to the video confessions we were getting from the perps that would lead to their ultimate demise. But I was believing my own lies.

John came in about an hour early to scan the arrest reports and 61s and wanted photos; to us, not only was knowledge power, but it also protected us in the street. I walked him to the back stairway and told him what Mahoney had relayed to me; he did not seem bothered by this information in the least, or if he was he put on a hell of a performance for me. We tooled up and began our tour.

I was fixated on how easily Cholito could find a vein and bang a powerful dose, all within a matter of seconds, though once that juice hit the spot, he would try and capture that first buzz by pulling back on the syringe's plunger, drawing blood, then he'd squirt what was left back into his arm or leg or foot. John found it, and him, distasteful. He thought that Cho was beneath him, though if he wanted to know something that the Shah might have been holding back, he'd try and worm it out of Cho, waiting of course till after Cho had slammed. This would reassure John that the lies would not be so overwhelming. I, on the other hand, thought it better to talk to him sober, because Cho had to know we were playing him, especially when we'd give him some bags to trade for the info we were seeking. He had to know that we thought he'd be more honest while he was high. I figured that this was an insult to his street smarts, so I generally took what he said high as half-truths, and when he was straight I'd get better street data. Any way you looked at it, it was always touch and go. We took what we could from everyone, then cross-referenced all of the street talk and tried to decipher which information matched. Tonight was no different.

Conroy turned to Cholito after the smack had reached its mark, blanketing Cho with velvety softness. He fell back in the rear seat as if he'd just had a powerful orgasm, drooling like he always did when the boy came home. "How was that?" Conroy asked, not caring that he sounded like he didn't really give a shit.

"Ahh shit, Con, now on, just bring me this TKO." He laughed, very slowly; his eyes remained closed. "Bring this ma'fucker to me, son, yeah, boy, bring it! Shit, everything else up in here don't even come close. Let them non-connoisseurin' white ma'fucker's from Manhattan shoot that rat mix these niggas be slingin'. I know my shit, and this shit got me down below twelve a day, you ma'fucker's performing a public service. You . . . what they call it . . . yeah, you weanin' me off the boy . . . yeah, you is." He opened his eyes. They were glassy, his pupils like pinpoints. "This is what you boys should be gettin' them medals for, all this good shit you be doin' up in here. You my niggas . . ."

Conroy had had enough of Cho's chatter. "Who got straps out here today?"

"Tell you what, yo, I'd love to do." He looked at Conroy and smiled. "Now I know this field nigga your boy and all, but fuck him, I'd love for you to bum-rush his spot, as long as your number one German is here to get me's mines. 'Cause like I said, this TKO is why ma'fuckers like me get high in the first place, you know what I'm sayin'." This was the second time that Cho had offered up the Shah to the cops. I knew that sooner or later he was going to roll hard on his boss, and that eventually someone was going to take him up on it, and why, I thought, shouldn't that be us? "But we can, you know, blow that bridge up, you know, when it's time to . . ." He started to nod again; Conroy hit the police siren, jolting Cho back awake; he laughed. "What you want . . . my attention? You got it, son . . . what you need, bodies—"

"Cho, quick and fuckin' easy, who's got a strap tonight?"

"That Rudy ma'fucker over there down Gowanus, he pulled out on me today, frontin' for them Aunt Jemimah–lookin' hos, you know, wearin' them hoops and what not in their—'

"When was the last time you saw him?" I asked.

"Hour ago, front of that Jamaican place . . ."

"Tuff Gong?" Conroy asked impatiently.

Cho tried to snap his fingers; he laughed when he could not. "See how this shit do, can't even . . ." He tried to snap his fingers again, could not, and just stared at us. He suddenly became melancholy; maybe there was just a glimmer of clarity left inside him, maybe he realized how fucked he was. Then another wave of "ope" rocked him and he was smiling again.

I wrote the names Rudy and Tuff Gong down in my book, and was expecting Conroy to send him on his way. Then, he asked in an even tone, "Cho, anyone out here asking you anything about us?"

I felt a cold shiver run up my spine. I now knew that this investigation was for real and that we very well could have been in some powerful gun sights. I didn't look at Conroy or at Cho, but I listened carefully.

"What you mean, like these niggas out here. Shit yeah, they wantin' to know whenever you's two is ridin', you know how it be out here, you the ma'fuckers . . ."

"No, Cho, not the workers, the buyers." I understood his logic. It wasn't a homegrown street snitch out here, they all knew our game. If it were the job, they'd send in a UC, pretending to buy, or they'd send in a UC from narcotics to collar everyone up and then debrief them all separately. We knew that Cho was collared along with most of the other workers out here. Conroy wanted to know if anyone had broadcast it to him that they were questioned.

"Nah, Con, not that I know of, but you know me, I'm a keep my shit down to the ground. I hear anything, I'm a give you the four 'leven." He reached over to shake Conroy's hand, but he just looked away. I quickly took his hand and shook it.

"You are the cumumba out here, Cho, you know that. You the number one German." He laughed at my atta-boy. Conroy blinked slowly. He reached behind him and opened the door for Cho to leave. I did not like the way Conroy treated him. He was my guy and did me many solids, but I don't think that John ever got over the fact that we got to his main cumumba, Shah King, before he could, to get the jump on Griffin. This I kept to myself, but I started to see cracks in John Conroy's armor: John did not like to share his King Kong stature with anyone. Cho took it all in stride, did what he did best, rolled with it.

Cho laughed, looked at the open car door. "Ahh, here's your hat, what's your rush, that how it is?"

Conroy just looked out into the dark night, and said, "Why should it be any other way?" Then he turned to Cho, his stare icy. Cho was afraid of Conroy. They all were afraid of John Conroy. Cho didn't say another word; he slid out of the car and disappeared into the night.

We parked on Pacific, just off Smith Street. Tuff Gong was a block east, so we walked with our heads down. Technically, we were not allowed to enter any establishment that served liquor unless we were in the presence of a boss. We also were aware that if we were being watched, this would be a ground ball for IAB to tag us with, so we used the cover of darkness, a back exit of one of the bodegas, and if we were tailed, we lost them easily. Our other motive was simply good street tactics; we didn't want to raise anyone up inside the bar. We wanted the element of surprise on our side, not the other way around.

The first person we saw when we walked in was Cholito's new steerer, Borges. Peculiar, because this place did not cater to Hispanics, it was a hard-core West Indian club. The occasional homegrown would stop in for a drink or to cop some weed, but this was strictly for Jamaicans. The second we walked in, the mood turned dark. The bartender from our past encounter at the bar was not happy to see us. *No one* inside the place was happy to see us, but we peacefully inched our way in between the throngs of dreads and gold. The room took on a whole different look with people in it. It seemed a smaller and a much more dangerous place. It was filled with thick clouds of reefer smoke; Conroy smiled as he inhaled deeply. "See now, that's some good weed, Rob." One of the dreads who knew Conroy stepped out from behind a pillar, holding a monster joint. He blew a thick ring at us; Conroy laughed and banged fists with the man. He then whispered something in his ear and the man discreetly raised his eyebrows at the bathroom door. I followed him in.

The lock was broken on the door. We entered quietly. It was the only bathroom in the place, so men and woman used it, and for more than just relieving themselves. You name it, it happened in that squalid little two-stalled room. A woman was applying makeup when we entered with our guns drawn. She didn't look at us twice. But she sucked her teeth at the inconvenience, picked up her makeup bag, and walked out. I smelled that familiar ghetto street smell. A combination of butane and crack; it always made my eyes water and my nostrils flare. Not a pleasant odor. I wanted to move this along quickly. We saw two sets of feet behind the closed stall door. John lifted his gun, head high, and pulled open the door, to reveal Rudy lighting the glass stem of the pipe for a tall, muscular bass head, or free baser, with pock-marked skin. Both of them looked like they'd been grinding for days. Rudy was one of the homegrowns from Gowanus who sold coke and crack and was good for the occasional info, but only if it worked to his benefit, like someone moving in on his real estate who he wanted taken out. We used Rudy more than he used us, and we would collar him in an instant if he were found dirty.

The pipe slipped from the tall, muscular man's hand, crashing to the ground. He first went to try and salvage what he could of the crack on the floor, but decided it was best to just raise his hands in the presence of two cops with their guns drawn. Rudy was pissed. He shook his head quickly, motored by the hits of crack he'd just inhaled. "Now where in the fuck I'm a get another stem, you clumsy ma'fucker?" He looked at Conroy, aggravated and speedy. "Damn, Con, this shit couldn't wait?"

"Shut up, Rudy, and put your hands up." He looked at the tall, ugly bass head, "You move once and I'm gonna open you up, you hear me?" The man dropped his head and nodded quickly. John holstered his gun and slid it toward his back so neither man could grab it when they were being tossed. He led Rudy out of the stall by his bicep and placed him up against the dirty sink. He was shaking, and Conroy just laughed. "Damn, Rudy, you need to start cutting that shit you smokin' with less speed, or are you just scared?"

"All of a sudden you gonna give me tips on how to cook up? You do what you do best, Con, and that's fuckin' up the party."

"Mind your Ps and Qs 'cause I will slap the candy out your ass." Conroy said this half joking, though it was full of menace. Rudy knew he could go only so far with us, so he allowed Conroy to frisk him. John looked at me; then at the tall cat. "Toss this animal."

"You got any needles on you? I get stuck, you in for a world of pain," I said as I moved to him. His body odor was the worst I had ever smelled, his hands were caked in dirt, and his fingernails and fingertips were chewed down to bloody stumps, caked in soot from working the butane lighter. He was almost in tears, shaking and moaning as I patted him down quickly. Rudy had no time for this.

"Oh, motherfucker, stop that squawking, you punk-ass bitch."

"I'm sorry . . . Got a problem with this shit, I know . . ." The tall guy's teeth were chattering from the come down, so we really couldn't understand what else he was saying. Rudy suddenly swung wildly at the man's face, connecting an open fist above his nose. The tall dude fell back against the wall and continued to cry; Conroy pulled Rudy back against the sink.

Rudy screamed, struggling against Conroy's grasp. "You's a cunt, punk-ass nigga. I see you out here again you gonna get got, you cryin' little bitch. Put you in a ma'fuckin' pair a panties and lipstick, do some knee work."

John had had it. "Rudy, shut the fuck up! Rob, he clean?"

"Yeah, John, he's good to go."

"Good." He looked at the man whose head was down. "So go, you fuckin' animal."

Oddly, the man turned off the tears. He still didn't look at us as he said, "Ahh, thank you, Officer, you know I got—"

Again Rudy tried to swing on the man. I pulled open the door and pushed him out, then slammed it shut and stood in front of it. Rudy started to laugh; he pulled six jumbo vials from his pocket. "Yo, thanks, Con, that dumb ma'fucker paid for the party that you almost fucked up."

Conroy slapped the vials out of his hand, pointed in Rudy's face, and said, "Motherfucker, I will flush that gack, then send you after it, you don't shut the fuck up, you hear me?"

"Cool, Con, you right, I gotta walk correctly, you right."

"Where's the gun, fuckhead?" Conroy was still in his face when he asked.

"What gun?"

He slapped Rudy so hard he was lifted off the floor and slammed into the tiled wall. Rudy took it in stride, like most street guys. This was just part of the game. "Oh, that gun."

"Yeah, that gun."

Rudy pointed to the door. "Sold it."

"To who?"

"To that squawkin' motherfucker you just let walk out a here."

Conroy looked at me in disbelief. I was embarrassed and pissed. "You saw me toss him, John."

Rudy laughed as he spit out some blood in the sink. "You didn't toss his balls, C."

We exited the bathroom; the bar was now almost empty. The bartender sneered at us and pointed around the empty room. "You the white bumba devils. Stay the fuck out, man."

Conroy was still reeling behind my fuck-up in the bathroom. He casually walked to the bar, picked up a Heineken, and launched it into the mirror above the bar, sending huge shards of broken glass everywhere. He then slowly raised his middle finger at the bartender. Before we reached the door, Borges was laughing at the whole episode he'd just witnessed. We walked past without acknowledging him, and out the door we went.

As I walked to the unmarked on Pacific Street, I started to get angrier and angrier; the last person I wanted to show any weakness to was Conroy. He needed to know I was as reliable a backup as anyone he worked with. "John, let's go to Gowanus, where Rudy deals. If the mope is gonna be looking to get his jumbos back from him, that's where he's gonna go."

He smiled at me. "You lookin' for a little redemption behind that abortion, Rob?"

He was half sarcastic, and I didn't like it, especially since it was at my expense.

"Let's just go and see if he's out there, okay?"

Before he could answer, central tried to raise us over the radio: "Zone crime, K."

I picked up the radio. "Go for crime, K."

"Ten-two the seven-six, K." That meant we were being summoned into the station house to do a face-to-face visit with whoever was summoning us. Whenever a cop was 10-2 to the station house, it was always an uneasy ride in. Guys that were about to be arrested were 10-2'd to the station house, or if they were to be suspended, or if they were to be questioned in regard to a major fuck-up in the field, they were 10-2'd to the station house. Needless to say, I started to feel the paranoia that was sure to come behind all of our street antics. We headed back to the house not speaking to each other. I think that neither one of us wanted to raise the other one up, that we actually were frightened of what was in store for us at the house.

As we approached the precinct, we looked around for any unusual and out-of-place sedans on the block. There were none, which gave us some comfort, but not much. We parked and walked in. Sitting in the muster room was the lieutenant of our detail, Nicky Tanner. He was younger than Conroy and young to be a lieutenant, twenty-eight. He was good-looking in a collegiate way. He was a detective by the time he was twenty-four, passed the sergeant's exam first shot, then passed the lieutenant's exam in the top twenty. He hit the tests right and was making the job work for him. He was on a fast track and this detail was good for him because most of the guys in it were salty and would only make him look good. It was win-win for him, so the last thing he was going to do was let anything get in the way of his greatness at the porcelain palace: One Police Plaza as a chief. John smiled at the boss when he saw him; he knew that if it were serious and about him, he would've been beeped to an untraceable phone booth; so he figured one of two things: I was the reason we were pulled in, or he just wanted to ride with us for the evening. He was right the first time—I was why we were pulled in. John and Tanner shook hands. He smiled at me and tilted his head toward the captain's office. "What's up, Bobby?" I hated the name Bobby, but I gave him the cushion of calling me it because it wasn't done with any animosity at all; he just thought that was my name. "I need a few with Bobby alone, John, like ten minutes. You cool with that?"

The walk to the captain's office felt like I was marching to the electric chair. So many things started to play off in my head. I suddenly saw every perp that I'd fucked over, ever dime bag of dope I'd given my snitches, I heard Conroy call after us before we entered the office, "Hey, Rob, don't forget to tell him about the little episode with Rudy." I heard him laugh as the door was closed behind me. The office was empty. It was the first room in the precinct, to the right of the desk, with a wall of windows that looked out onto the front of the precinct. *Captains have a lot of real estate to protect, just like the Shahs and Rudys of the world*, I thought. They wanted to see exactly what was going on in front of their territories.

We sat down in front of the big wooden desk with its pictures of children of various ages. It also held a large paperweight with the captain's four shields encased in glass. The room was city green with beige linoleum tiles. I felt as though I was about to get a rectal examination.

"So, Bobby, you put in for narcotics after your shooting, yes?"

I breathed a sigh of relief. This was about the request for

transfer that I'd applied for with the integrity review board. Much the same as the bribery collar, once you get into a shooting and it is deemed clean, the job feels obliged to reward you. I had forgotten about the transfer request because I did not have to be reinterviewed, as I had been there behind the bribery, so it was just a UF57, or a request for transfer to narcotics through the police mail. Tanner, being my immediate boss, had to okay the request, so he had to sign off on it, which is what he did. Here's what happened.

"I think you are an excellent street cop, Bobby. Mahoney gives you above standards every evaluation. Conroy swears by you, and all the other guys in the teams dig you. You make unbelievable collars, never had a complaint substantiated."

My breathing leveled off; I was so happy to be in that room, looking at this lieutenant who I'd probably be a few years down the road once I got the street out of my system. I smiled broadly. "Well, Nicky, I'm just working it, I love doing what we do—" He raised his hand quickly.

"Before you go any further, Bobby, I wanted to push the move for you, you're ready for your shield. This gun bullshit is good for bosses like me, but you guys in the street are an inch from getting jammed up, you understand that, yes? Last thing I want is to see a sharp young guy like yourself getting poled by some defense attorney and his drug-dealing client." I didn't understand why he just didn't tell me I was transferred. Was he trying to apologize for allowing it to happen that quickly? "So I made some calls to expedite the fifty-seven . . ." He slowly shook his head from side to side, as if he was trying to understand it. I now felt the room close in on me. "A flag came up in your folder, stated you could not be moved from the unit. There is some investigation going on, don't know who has it. Now, if it were field internal affairs, you'd be able to move, so it's got to be IAB or . . ."

"Or . . . ? " escaped from my mouth.

"Or higher up the ladder." He was studying me for emotion; I know my face was flushed from embarrassment, but mostly from fear, fear of the unknown, which is a way of life on this job.

"You know, Bobby, you screw up once on the job, you're pretty much out on your ass. There is the one-strike rule; they either fire you or you're back in the bag working in this shithole with these friggin' maniacs. Sometimes it's not fair, but it is what it is."

"Nicky, if this is about money, I never took a nickel."

"Cool; so if that's what they're looking for, let them look, and you don't have anything to worry about, yes?"

"I mean, I'm no angel, boss, but I am only doing what I'm paid to do, trying to get the pistols and the shooters off the street. That's what I'm all about."

"Bobby, listen to me, for what it's worth. I do believe two things. I believe there is a case someone has open on you, and I do believe you aren't rippin' anyone out there. But there are other ways of getting hammered by these guys; you understand? This thing blows over, I'll get you to wherever it is you want to go, but until then, watch what you do out there and be very, very careful. These guys are so crafty, they'll turn someone without them even knowing it. Or . . . they got someone in here."

"Someone in here" scared me as much if not more than had they turned someone on the outside. It was very clear to me at this point that the ways of the street were catching up with me. I was sure I was the target. I didn't know what collar it was that I'd gotten pinned for, maybe it was all of them, but I knew that it was time to regroup. It was the first time I was really scared for my future, and things would only get worse.

11

"Monster"

Even with all the bullshit that was going on, there was still the day-to-day job of putting animals away. One such animal was a pattern rapist. He'd struck in Flatbush, all the way deep into the 7-1, and into the northwestern sections of Brooklyn. Now he was hitting zone eleven—the Badlands. He was a brutal rapist with particular tastes. Number one, he would deface his victims' bodies post-rape by jamming a brick in a mouth or a metal pipe in a uterine canal or other orifices of the body, and he liked shit-holes like the Badlands. The garbage dumps, the forgotten docks, the burned-out and ruined factories, this was his canvas; and now he was very close to home. His victims were all found near the vast waterfronts of Brooklyn. My very first impression of the scene was that he liked the dichotomy of his chosen locations: a river separating all the beauty that Manhattan had to offer from all the hell that these parts of Brooklyn had to offer. He was given a name by the various units who had the unlucky duty of investigating these rapes: He was called the Monster. At the time, the crimes weren't on my radar. There was no picture, not even a sketch at this point, and he was careful in his methods, taking his four female victims down from behind. There was a tiny task force from the sex-crimes unit attached to it, so I figured they did what they did best and I didn't think about it again—until that warm spring morning.

Conroy and I had a tour change, so we were overlapping with Patty and Billy. We heard the job come over the radio as a 10-10, past assault. Billy jumped on the job, as he was around the corner from the scene; generally, the plainclothes units were not supposed to take calls from the precincts, but Billy must've been raised up by the job for a reason. Then he called for the PDU, sex crimes, and the precinct boss, so we knew that this was a victim of the Monster. Conroy swung the car in a U-turn, heading to the scene.

"Let's not go there," I said. "Everyone and their mothers are gonna be there, plus sex crimes has the case."

Conroy shot me a look. "All of a sudden rape isn't a collarable offense in this car? Wake up, Rob."

I was embarrassed. He had a way of making me feel less adequate, but in hindsight, he was so right. I was still blinded by the crimes that I knew: guns, robberies, shootings, murder. Rape was foreign to me, maybe because I didn't want to think about that type of human degradation, but I was going to get a firsthand look as Conroy sped to the scene.

We arrived at a sanitation truck depot just off Hamilton Avenue, between the 7-6 and the 7-2 precincts. It was stuck between the Red Hook Houses, the Gowanus Canal, and the hundreds of abandoned, broken-down lofts and factories that dotted the Brooklyn piers of Sunset Park. One of the sanitation workers had noticed the victim walking aimlessly in between the trucks, her clothes ripped, her face bloodied.

Billy and Pirelli's car was parked out front when we arrived, the radio chattering with transmissions, and sirens in the distance. I knew this was going to be a mob scene in minutes. Conroy walked to Pirelli, and I lagged behind. The woman was walking in small, tight circles, dazed and in shock. She would cry and then she'd stop, look at her bare wrist, and say that she had to pick up her children from school. Then she'd look into the sky and remind herself that the kids did not have an umbrella. It was heartbreaking to me. A beautiful woman, a mother, beaten, humiliated, and raped. Her hair was disheveled and matted with grime and dirt and her own blood, though I could tell that it was styled nicely, indicating that she wasn't a hooker and she had some sort of means. I watched as Billy gently talked to her. He wrapped a blanket around her, separating his body from hers so as not to place her in any more discomfort. He let her sip from a water bottle, then he doused a towel with the water and gently patted a bled-out gash on her chin. His face was full of genuine concern. *He's as real as it gets,* I thought. It suddenly struck me, out of the blue, that I'd lost my way. What Billy was doing, and the compassion and humanity that fueled it, were no longer a functioning part of me. I was mesmerized by the scene, proud of Billy and what we as cops do, but I felt like I was no longer on that team, the team that is out there to help. My idea of helping had gotten tainted somewhere along the way. I only saw guns and shooters, and pulling them off the streets was a way of helping, that is true, but there are other facets of this job that I turned away from, really heroic stuff that I took for granted. I realized I wanted to get it back, somehow, if it wasn't too late. I heard Conroy's voice break through my stream of thought.

"Rob . . ."

I focused. Conroy and Pirelli were right in front of me, talking.

"Tell him what Tanner said." Conroy was also watching the woman and looking around the area trying to decipher where she'd come from and how the rapist had pulled her in without any of the workers seeing. I was rocked right back into the miserable situation that I was trying so hard to block out in my head, every second, for the last forty-eight hours.

"Didn't know if it was IAB or bigger. No movement on my part, which tells him it's big." I said this with my eyes on Devlin; the only thing that mattered to him at that moment was this poor beaten-down woman, and I respected him greatly for it.

"I wonder if these cocksuckers are on to all of us?" Pirelli asked.

"Just me," I said.

"If they're watching you, then they're watching all of us." Conroy said this with condescension. He was treating me in much the same way he treated Cholito or the hundreds of other street mopes we dealt with every day, except he was subtler. *Not subtle enough,* I thought.

Pirelli turned on the coolness. "Only thing they could have is turning these little pricks on for info, and that's a factoid out here. No way they're into us for that, and if they are, fuck 'em, our word against theirs. They ain't got audio or a videotape, they got balls. What do they think, we can do straight eights out here without dealing with these scumbags? They could suck my dick . . . talk to me, John."

"Tell him what else he said." He seemed accusatory this time, like he was my guardian and the curfew I'd broken had to be explained to the headmaster. I looked at him, hoping that he'd see I was riding on a very thin nerve ending. I know he saw how that manifested itself in the street—a beat down. I just hoped that he understood that it could happen here as quickly.

"He said it could be on the inside as well, maybe a cop rolled."

Pirelli looked slowly at Devlin, then tilted his head at Conroy. I saw the anger well up his neck and settle somewhere behind his eyes. "No, no, don't even go there," I said. "Not in a million fuckin' years, bet my life on it." Devlin may have been a lot of things, but he was no rat; I was sure of this.

Pirelli and Conroy looked to each other once again and slowly walked toward the woman and Billy. Then Conroy stopped and turned to me, slowly, Pirelli hovering. "Then maybe it's your little pal Cholito ratting us out."

I was a second from cold-cocking him. Pirelli tried to say something, but I just held my hand up to him, not taking my eyes off Conroy. He was obviously trying to draw lines in the sand; I wasn't having it. "What, all of a sudden you ain't got no workers out here, John? Maybe it's the thousand motherfuckers you got out here working your dime, maybe it's someone from your past, John, maybe they were looking at you and while you were off taking a dump somewhere they saw me. So get this divide-and-conquer shit out of your head." I stepped very close to him; I wanted him to know that he should not try and create rifts between any of us, and if he wanted to take it a step further, I was with him. He simply looked away. He was good. He'd never once been baited into a fight; I was sure something was in the mail between the two of us. He then looked back at me and at Patty.

"If it's not that junkie, then it has to be Shah," John said. "They have to know we're in bed with him, even if he isn't the one who's rolling. They see the biggest dealer of boy right in our faces and the prick never gets collared . . . they must've thought he was papering us or think we been on his dick to get padded . . . so maybe they started an investigation behind it."

Either way this was cut up, we *were* in bed with the Shah, only thing was, he wasn't padding us, or at least I knew he wasn't padding *me.* That chilling feeling enveloped me again, the one that told me I really didn't know everything about John. Maybe he and the Shah had something hooked from way back in the day. Now I was full-blown paranoid—I needed to find out for myself.

"So, the Shah's reign of power is going to come to an end." John said this matter-of-factly, as if he'd already tact-planned it out, almost as if it had already been done. This raised me up. *Why would he pound his guy, one he's worked with for so many years, so easily so quickly?*

"That's a real scummy move, John," I said.

"What's the matter, this guy on your dick all of a sudden?"

"No, John, just wanna play it straight with our snitches, that's all, brother."

He moved to me slightly; he delivered the lines with calm clarity: "There is blowback firing right at us, and I know the prick for ten years. Safe to say, it very well could be him. Maybe it's not, but I ain't taking any chances. This motherfuck would do us in a hot fuckin' second. You, my man, are way too close to these pricks. You need to wake the fuck up to the fact that he is a scumbag drug dealer who's gonna get played. He ain't my friend, and he definitely ain't your friend, and don't ever forget it . . . and by the way, he's mine to do with what I like, not yours."

I had been incredibly naive to think that we were all gentlemen and that there were rules that had to be adhered to. The Shah was going to get got one way or another, with or without me, just part of the game.

I went home stressed. If I saw anything in my rearview—cars, trucks, bicycles, vendors, whatever—I'd think they were all watching me. I instantly was aware that I had a shelf life on this job, and it ended when they decided that my time clock would be punched for good. All these years I'd put in, and for what?

The drive home down those pretty streets didn't help these feelings of fear and paranoia and self-loathing for placing myself in this mess. Mia had been putting on a great face all these months, putting up with my bullshit self-centeredness. She accepted the fact that I would not meet any of her work friends for dinner, or go with them on their weekend sailing trips. She transitioned easily between her job and her home life while I dreamed of being back out in those ghetto streets. She and that house and our future had become inferior to me. My primary focus was to try and ride this investigation out without getting too bloodied, and then I would get out of the Badlands and into an OCCB unit to gain my gold shield. I still believed in the job and I still had a crazy jones for the street, but somewhere inside me I realized I'd have to settle down and create some kind of normal life with Mia.

The humming in my head was at a fever pitch when I rolled up to the front of our kick-ass house. I turned up the radio and let the car idle for a few extra moments because I knew once the engine turned off, that ringing in my ears was just going to get louder and louder. The only way I found I could stop the ringing was by drinking myself silly with a bottle of Jack Daniel's. Mia allowed me this vice; I think that she just wanted to see some kind of emotion from me, even if it was drunken nonsense. She had said many times that my silence had made her paranoid. I had to laugh at the thought. She had no idea what paranoia was, and I wasn't about to tell her.

She was preparing dinner in the yard, on the outdoor stove, when I arrived. She looked stunning, as usual. Of course, I didn't acknowledge this, I had other things on my mind. I went right to the bar and poured a giant glass of bourbon. The table was set beautifully with candelabras, a lace tablecloth, fine crystal; bouquets of flowers even lined the walkways. Candles in votive jars were hung from the beech tree, and more candles lined the deck that looked out into the endless blue of the Long Island Sound. I sat in the deck chair and drank.

She walked to me slowly, cautiously, and pecked me on the forehead; I felt her soft hand gently brush my chest. "Oh, honey you look so tired." She whispered this as she placed her face next to mine.

"Why are you home so early?" I asked, drinking the mind-numbing liquor without kissing her back.

She moved back to the oven. "Told you, baby, doctor's appointment."

It was at that moment that I saw something that did not compute—a cigarette butt. I bent down and picked it up. Then I walked to the garbage can, where there was an empty beer can. I picked it out, then showed them to her. "What's this?"

"Garbage?" She was cool. She was not guilty, but paranoia is as powerful a drug as TKO.

I walked to her slowly. "We don't smoke, and I haven't had a beer in this house in days, so . . ."

"So I gave it to the bathroom guy; why the big investigation?"

"Don't be sarcastic with me, Mia. Don't fuckin' do it. I deal with that bullshit all day long; I will not accept it from you."

She put down her utensils, tilted her head at me. I knew this was not going to be pretty, but in my mind I was right and I was going to find the bathroom guy and fucking shoot him.

"You will not accept it from me . . . excuse me! Who do you think you are, and what exactly is it that you're insinuating? Robert?"

She never called me Robert, and from her tone, I felt that I was overhearing another unhappy couple argue. I could not let it go. "What, you have a couple of beers with the bathroom guy, he comes back here, smokes a cigarette. You guys walk the fuckin' pier? What, Mia, fuckin' tell me."

She walked to me with a jump in her step. This was the first time I had seen this side of her. She was not of the streets, way too smart for me to play her.

"Ask me what it is you want to ask me, Robert." She was face-to-face with me; I knew I was already in it, though something was telling me to tail down and walk away. It was her eyes, full of anger but with a wanting behind them. I know that all she wanted was to be happy with me, for us both to enjoy this great life, but I could not break through this barrier I had to put up. I felt sorry for her, and I felt sorry for me, but I was a hardened animal by this point in my life. I had no time for any of it.

"You want to ask me if we fucked?" She smiled; she knew the buttons to push. "Yeah, we fucked on the pier"—she leaned really sexy, and whispered—"and he was fucking fabulous."

I grabbed her by her arm. "All of a sudden you're a fuckin' comedian?"

She ripped her arm out of my grip, fell backward, then jumped back in my face. She pointed her finger under my nose; she was seething. "Don't you ever grab me like that again, you hear me! If you think this is Brooklyn, you are sadly mistaken. You will leave that bullshit in the ghetto or wherever the *fuck* it is you got it, because there will be no next time, Robert!"

I pointed back in her face; I was not backing down. Though the truth is, I should never have been *up* to begin with.

"You don't know what the fuck is going on out there. How do you know who this prick is? He could be staking out the house right now. You're so wrapped up in all this high-society nonsense and living in some fantasy world in a fucking bubble that you don't have a clue to how easy you are, how easy anyone is! Do you know the fucked-up people who are out there, do you? Do you have any idea how fucked up a world this is?" I was livid. The image of that poor woman walking naked and blood-ied in the piles of garbage was something that was hard to forget. I saw Mia there, but I could not tell her. I was angry because I did know how fucked up the world was, and how, where we were living, was so not in the real world. I was wrong; that was as real as it gets.

Her face turned from anger to hurt in a flash, she looked

wounded; she backed away from me slowly and turned. There was a long, quiet moment, and before she walked inside, she said six simple words: "You're going to be a father."

Dazed, I stumbled backward into a lounge chair. That was the last thing I expected her to say. I felt as though I'd been kicked in the stomach by a horse—now there were three of us.

The time was right to do the Shah. We wanted him off the street before he could do any damage or before any one of these IAB pricks or whoever had the case could get to him.

John stood out of sight while I knocked gently on the dirty apartment door. The old bullet holes were now rusted in the fire-proof metal. I could hear a Spanish show on the TV, playing loudly behind the door. I knocker harder. The door opened and a woman who appeared to be in her eighties stood there. One of her eyes was glazed over with a gray film, probably from an un-treated cataract. Her skin was wrinkled and her teeth were rotted in her mouth, but she was dressed in a clean, neat, black day dress and wore rosary beads around her neck. She was smoking a thin brown cigarette, probably one she'd rolled herself. This woman was hard-core old-school Puerto Rico. The flag hanging in her living room said as much. She smiled when she saw it was me at the door and patted my back. She opened the door for me to come in. She didn't speak a word of English and my Spanish was as good as curse words and slangs, and that wasn't going to get me anywhere with this proud woman who had more than a handful to deal with, with her grandson Cholito. I smiled back at her and called for Cholito to come out. He moved off the couch slowly. His eyes were focused, so I knew he wasn't high. This would be good for me. He stepped into the hall and shut the door.

"Wassup, Tatico, a warrant come up on me or somethin'?"

I smiled; he was concerned that he might have caused me in-convenience. "No, brother, no." We walked to the dirty window that looked out into the atrium where children were playing, where children could so easily have been shot. "Cho, you gotta give me an honest answer, and nothing is going to happen to you as long as you tell me the truth, okay?"

He was seriously focused now; I really liked him when he was sober. I could tell he was a loyal grandson; I knew he gave her much of his earnings and then some. Cho's vice was not money, it was flecked powder. Before the junk found its way to his heart, he was probably a trusted friend. I reached out and placed my hand on his shoulder. "Did you ever tell any cops that we gave you drugs or money? Is anybody paying you to tell them about us? Just please, Cho, we go back, just tell me the truth."

He closed his eyes and shook his head no. He exhaled loudly and then he placed his hand on my shoulder; he truly looked as sad as I had become. "Oh, poppa, no, they got you on something? Poppa, no, you like my brother, man. Never, never would I turn on you, never." He didn't let go of my shoulder. This wasn't an attempt on his part to play me; he cared.

Conroy appeared behind Cho, who felt his presence and spun around. He was right up on him. "If you're fucking with us, I'm gonna come back and find you, because at that point, nothing matters. You feeling me?"

All Cho could do was nod. I touched his shoulder again, saw the distaste in Conroy's eyes. Cho turned to me, and the fear in his face was evident. I could only hope that he still trusted me. "We're going to do Shah." I whispered this. No one was in this filthy hallway, we'd swept it for bodies before talking to Cho, but I whispered it because I truly knew the depth of what we were about to embark on. We were going to take out the biggest drug dealer in Brooklyn, and a very wealthy one at that; his tentacles were far-reaching and very dangerous. "We'll need to know when and where it comes in."

He smiled weakly at me; I smiled back. John Conroy simply stared.

The sun was just rising over the low, beat-up mom-and-pop storefronts that dotted Third Avenue. There were junkies already lining up in front of the South Brooklyn Health Care offices, a fancy name for the local methadone clinic. Below, in the courtyard, a couple of crackheads were searching under benches and in the overflowing garbage cans for empty crack vials. They would get a penny for every vial they turned back in, much in the same way I used to collect cans for pennies when I was a child.

She walked slowly across Nevins Street, occasionally stopping to check on the baby that was apparently sleeping comfortably under the periwinkle blue blanket, on her way toward Baltic Street. Though it was before six in the morning, she walked as if it were three in the afternoon, not a care in the world, just out for a stroll with little Johnny on her way to the playground. When she reached Baltic, I saw a car door open and close quickly in the middle of the block. "There's gun number one," I whispered. The dude who stepped from the car was big, with the physique of a bodybuilder. *More jailhouse muscles,* I thought. I'd never seen him before. He walked in front of the woman. They never made eye contact or had any other discernible communication that I could see. He loped into the atrium at the far end of the projects; she followed. They both headed straight to the building. Another man who was as big walked from the north end of the projects and followed the woman; he was approximately forty feet from her back, almost the exact distance the lead gun was. "There's number two," I said. They entered the building. Conroy and myself exited the hallway and climbed one flight up the fire stairs. We were now two flights above our target apartment. The intelligence we'd received from Cho was that the lead gun would take the elevator with the woman while the second gun would sweep the stairway for bodies, moving one flight above the apartment to check to see if there was anyone above. Then he'd walk down and enter the apartment with the other two mules. This was done to the letter, with much precision. The Shah's crews were paid well because they were highly skilled. He was a smart businessman, that was a given. "You receive much of what you pay for," he would say. His drugs were primo and his workers were professional. The heroin game is short-lived and dangerous, though Shah had played the game way beyond his own life expectancy because of his excellent business acumen. That is, until today. *Shah has a shelf life too.* I smiled at the thought. This actually might work. These projects were no longer going to be run under the dictatorship of Shah King and company or, for that matter, John Conroy. It was going to be open season on everyone.

We heard the second gunman's footsteps reach the landing below us, one flight above the apartment. We then heard him descend two floors and the fire door close. We moved quickly down the stairs and John moved into the hall, charging for the door before it closed. He just made it in, kicking the door wide open. Shah did not know we were there until we were in the apartment. He was still sitting on a tattered couch drinking coffee from a Styrofoam cup, with another man, Spanish, who I'd also never seen before; the skinny chick with the baby carriage, and a black woman, probably a blood relation to Shah, who appeared to be in her thirties and was wearing a housecoat, which told me they were using her place to deliver. When he saw Conroy's gun and our convergence method, he knew he was being played. He jumped up off the couch and yelled, "Chill, motherfuckers chill!" to the three other men in the apartment. We were seriously outmanned and outgunned, so I was locked and loaded. First one to make any move was getting a hot one, and then I probably was not going to stop shooting. The stakes were much too high. If I was going, so were they, all of them.

The men raised their hands in the air, listening to John's commands. The Shah just stood in front of the table, his arms outstretched, palms facing the ceiling. They didn't move, he didn't move, not because he was listening but because he was confused. Was Con actually playing him?

"Con, what the fuck, son, what the fuck you doin'? Tell a nigga' this ain't what it appears to be!" His voice pitch was high, though he was trying to keep it together, not looking at the lowly aide-de-camp—me—once. This was a Brooklyn thing between John and his bitch, or vice versa.

"Tony, shut the fuck up and put your hands up!" Conroy called him Tony, something he'd never done before. I saw the realization of the situation in the Shah's eyes when he heard it. He slammed his hands across his outer thighs three times, quickly, as if he were on the brink of a temper tantrum.

"Oh, motherfucker, motherfucker, you motherfucker, Con, you cunt motherfucker. I thought we was partners, you white cunt motherfucker!" He was livid, screaming, with his eyes closed. He knew we had him, he knew we were going to do what we did best, and that was to put him away for a very long time behind our great acumen, testilying in court. The Shah was *got!*

Suddenly he stopped screaming, looked at Conroy, and said to him calmly, "Fuck am I screaming about? You right, son, you bagged us correctly, so we pay the tax . . ." He pointed to the carriage, then he waved his hand around the apartment. "Do the do, Con, take it all."

I wasn't naive or stupid. I knew there was a lot of pure gack in the carriage, I knew there was going to be a lot of armament in the apartment, and I most definitely knew there was going to be much cash in the apartment as well. I don't care who you are, the thought of turning a blind eye in a situation like that is going to cross your mind. This was no IAB setup, as we'd gleaned from Cholito, so no one could have known we were hitting the spot. We didn't even tell Cho if and when we would, and we only did a tour change four hours prior to the operation. So this was a highly compartmentalized, seamless plan that even our bosses were not aware of. I quickly remembered my suspicious feelings about the two; maybe they had been down this road before, and maybe Conroy had erred. In any case, I was not going to be the patsy like so many other cops who got dragged into a bribe and never got out. Before allowing Conroy to even think about the answer to the offer, I stepped up to Shah, who still hadn't acknowledged my presence. I pistol-whipped him over his right eye and it squirted blood immediately. He was stronger than I'd expected, or maybe he was too stunned by what he saw as Conroy's betrayal, but he only stepped back in a daze. Soon though, that familiar look of pain crawled across his face; it felt really good to give this prick that pain. It was not nearly what he deserved behind what he'd done to me and Conroy and Cho, but it was a start.

Conroy screamed, "No, no, no, Rob. Goddamnnit, no!" He

spun his gun at each of the other men and the two women. I just watched the blood dribble through the Shah's fingers and down his thick forearm. I liked the sight of his blood, and I liked the fact that I was the one who'd opened him up. I was not focused on Conroy or the other animals in the apartment, only this scumbag in front of me. I wanted him to step to me, but he did no such thing. He just stood with his hands pressing the gash above his eye. Still he did not look at me.

I moved to the rear of the apartment, swept through the rooms as Conroy called for backup. The rooms were empty. I then moved to the baby carriage, pulled the Cabbage Patch doll out from under the periwinkle blue blanket, and tore up the thin cushion; there taped to the bottom of half-inch plywood was the end of Shah King's reign—one kilo of 96 percent pure heroin, about $130,000, which would have been whacked up into thousands of dimes of lesser purity, and that's where all the money would have been made. Not today, I thought. I looked up and smiled at the Shah. "You are so fucked . . . *Tony.*"

This must've been quite the pill for Conroy to swallow. He was the biggest felony-arrest cop on the job, and that was due in part to the man we'd just arrested. It was clear that not only was the Shah's reign in the streets over, John Conroy's reign could have just ended as well—and that had to suck.

Conroy took the collar. The Shah, whose real name was Anthony Huggins, did not say another word to us. He also refused medical aid, and I was more than happy to oblige. We arrested all of them—the two women, and the three other men in the apartment, split them up and tried mightily to have each of them roll on the others, but they'd been down these nasty roads before, so we got dick out of them. I left after we completed the paperwork, to attend to some pressing personal business.

took a cab to 55 Water Street, which was half a block from the South Street Seaport. Mia was not expecting me; I wanted her to know that in spite of my actions, deep inside I loved her and was thrilled that she was pregnant.

The receptionist rang her while I sat down in the ultramodern lobby. There were wraparound windows looking to the far reaches of New Jersey on one side, and to the other side, the place where I had just played a dangerous game of cops and robbers—the Badlands. The second I saw the Statue of Liberty, I got that feeling that I wanted to get back there. Then I thought about why I was here and I had to suppress my anxiety and urge to sweep the streets again. *Tomorrow is another day,* I thought.

She stepped into the lobby, completely off guard. Her hair was up in a bun, revealing her diamond earrings. Her silk Hermès blouse was unbuttoned just above her breastbone. I tried to get past the anger welling up in me when I saw this—I was sure that the other men on this floor must've had quite the field day fantasizing about what was underneath. I let it go. She smiled as she crossed to me and kissed me full on the lips. She noticed the bag.

"What's in the bag?" She smiled, knowing that this was an apology, so there must've been something good inside.

"We have a dinner reservation for five-fifteen at Flutie's. You cool with that?" I asked her this quietly. I did not think that the receptionist needed to know that I was on my knees.

"Meet you there in half an hour." She kissed me again; I noticed her leg rise off the floor gently. I took this as a good sign. She did still love me, and I did still love her; she had to have known this. I smiled and turned to leave. The receptionist buzzed the glass door to let me out and I moved to the elevator. I turned to look back inside the lobby and Mia was still there watching me, a sad look on her face. I felt a knot ball up in my stomach; I tilted my head at her and she sadly mouthed the words "I love you."

I was sitting at the south wall of the restaurant. There was a big window that overlooked the East River, but more important, it faced the Badlands. Of course, not one person in the restaurant knew this. How could they? Three quarters of the patrons were tourists without a clue, and the rest of them were the very three-thousand-dollar suit-wearing clowns I was sure were trying to look at Mia's tits any chance they got. I felt some resentment toward these guys. They were as much a part of the problem as the Shah Kings and the rest of the slingers and gunners out there. Supply and demand—these cats were happy to be away from Brooklyn, but they'd certainly keep the dealers in business by having their cocaine and heroin delivered so they could speedball their way into oblivion in the privacy of their gated communities north, east, and west of the city, thus enabling the dealers to branch out into the environs of wherever the fuck it was they wanted to sling. Back in the seventies it was called white flight; now it was simply known as young, upwardly mobile professionals moving out, leaving the boroughs to be swept clean by guys like me. I began to look at anyone who was not in the mud with me, fighting the animals, as frauds. They were as guilty as the dealers and shooters themselves. It was a twisted and paranoid way of thinking, but it helped me straddle both of those complicated worlds, and as I finished my third Jack Daniel's I felt good, a certain self-righteousness came over me, knowing that I was doing something noble. I sat there in the restaurant with all the chattering and clanging of silverware and felt the butt of my gun. That to me was worth more than any material happiness. That was as real as it got, and Shah King could vouch for that.

Mia made her way to the table. She sat next to me and held my hand. "Ooooh, Momma needs a big, fat cocktail, but the doctor says different . . . maybe just a glass of wine." She looked at my drink, then at me. "You okay, baby?"

It seemed that she was so cautious of my moods lately; I felt terrible that we had gotten to this low point in our marriage. I smiled back and kissed her. The waitress came over and Mia ordered a chilled bottle of Puligny-Montrachet. I, of course, knew nothing of wines other than the fact that the ones she ordered were expensive and went down really easy.

I placed the baby blue Tiffany box on the table. Mia loved buying, but she especially loved receiving. Her eyes filled as she removed the tasteful, thin paper from within the box. Her long, manicured hand moved slowly up to her mouth; she then reached over and hugged me. She removed the sterling-silver rattle that had the engraving "Mia and Rob's baby." She blotted the tears that now fell freely from her eyes. I loved her deeply at that moment. I wanted to make things right, but the words didn't come to me as easily as they once had. I tried.

"I know things haven't been . . . like they were, lately, and I'm so sorry, Mi, so sorry. More than anything else I want you to know that I'm excited about the baby, and I love you."

She cupped my hand in hers; she paused before she spoke. "I miss you, Rob. I miss talking to you. Can we be honest with each other? No judgment, just us talking like we used to?"

I wiped the tears from her eyes. I held her tightly and whispered, "Of course we can."

"I feel that maybe you have moved beyond me, that you outgrew me. I even feel that maybe there's someone else." She dropped her head and stifled a whimper after she uttered those words. I knew that that would hurt her to the core, the betrayal of the trust that we shared. There would be no coming back from that. I was terrified of losing her, but, more important, of hurting her that deeply, because I had already crossed that fucked-up bridge. I felt the guilt rise up within me and I held her hand reassuringly.

"Honey, no, it's not you, it's not you . . ."

"Rob, please. Don't say it's you. Please don't disrespect me with a tired old line like that. I want you to tell me what's wrong. Is it me? Is it something I can fix?"

"No, it's not you . . . I don't know why, Mi." I was finally getting to the truth, to what was really at the core of who I'd become. I felt my throat closing at the realization that I was lost and getting more lost by the second. "Sometimes it's like I'm just dead inside. I don't know. I've become . . ."

"It's the job, Rob, I see it, I see the change in you . . ."

I was outted by the brilliance of this woman and frightened because it was true. I had to reassure her, tell her that she was wrong, dead wrong.

"Mia, you'll see; now that there are three of us, I put in for a transfer to get my shield. It's easier work and there won't be that much overtime. I'll be able to spend more time with you watching you get chubby with that beautiful baby. Honey, it's all going to change now. It's right there in front of us. You'll see, I promise."

We hugged, she whispered her love to me in my ear, I closed my eyes, and when I opened them, there it was, staring right back at me, my other lover, the one who, even with Mia in my arms, I really wanted to be with—the Badlands.

12

Borges

The call came over the radio while we were tossing a blue, customized Corvette on Hamilton Avenue. The driver had no license or registration, but the last thing we wanted to do was run the plates for fear that it might come up 10-16, or stolen. Then we'd have to take a GLA, or grand larceny auto collar, which was a bag of shit we did not want. I cuffed the Dominican man to a fence and he watched as John tossed the front and I did the rear; that's when the transmission was broadcast over the radio: "Numerous calls, 10-10 man down, possible DOA, rooftop 120 Center Mall." I looked at John, and without waiting for his response, I slammed the trunk closed, uncuffed the nervous man hooked on the fence, and said, "Catch you next time." He jumped into the Corvette and sped off. I was sure there was something in the vehicle, but I also felt that our every move was being video recorded. As John pulled out, I peered into suspicious-looking cars and vans and on top of buildings. I even found myself searching the inside of the car for bugs or these new gadgets called lipstick cameras—a miniature audio/video camera that is three inches long, half an inch thick, and can be secreted anywhere in the vehicle, recording your every move.

There were already a number of RMPs in front of the building. PDU was also there, and more cars rolled up. This told us the job was founded, or real, and someone was, in fact, lying dead on the roof. As we moved toward the farthest building west in the atrium, I searched for Cho. He would know who the victim on the roof was and, more important, who'd clipped him. He was nowhere in sight, though a dead body generally does that to business. The drug trade doesn't stop, it just moves indoors or to secondary spots, away from the police activity.

There was a crowd on the roof, mostly cops: uniforms, anticrime, and PDU guys from the 7-6. I figured this had to be a good one because already the instamatics were flashing, and I heard guys describing the wounds and laughing. There was a bunch of neighborhood street kids behind a yellow line set up by the first unit on the scene. I saw Borges, Cho's newest street steerer, looking over the shoulders of one of the locals. He made eye contact with me, then dropped his head quickly. I found that odd, as he had been trying his damnedest to ingratiate himself on my dick for the past year. I wanted to see if I knew who the victim was, so I pushed past the onlookers and that's when I saw them. The black Converse high-tops. They were unmistakably his: scuffed, worn, grayish on the sides. Holes were developing in the rubber bottoms. I had told him I wanted to get him a new pair; he'd just laughed and said, "Nahh, poppa, these kicks like me; old school, worn, and Chuck Taylor comfortable." I had bought him those Chuck Taylor Cons. I stopped short. I knew it was him, even though his face had been torn apart by a large-caliber bullet, one shot dead center.

I backed up slowly, feeling the sticky roof tar under my feet. I had to inhale deeply. The last thing I wanted to do was puke, but I felt it rising from within. It wasn't the nasty visual, a purple-reddish half-dollar-sized hole where his nose once was, his eyes swollen shut, the bone fragments of his face turned outward, giving him the appearance of gouged-out watermelon. It was who he was. My heart was broken, by a twelve-bag-a-day junkie named Theobaldi Rodriguez, aka Cholito.

I looked to Conroy, who didn't seem bothered by the scene at all. I wasn't surprised, hell, if it were anyone else, I wouldn't have thought twice about it, but John, he seemed a little too cavalier. He was even joking with some of the uniforms on the roof.

Some more in-the-dark fans buying more of King Kong's bullshit,
I thought. I knew my days were numbered with super cop. Hell,
I knew my days were numbered period.

Something was nagging at me. I began clocking the crowd
again, making eye contact with Borges. Again he dropped his
head and slowly started to wiggle backward, away from the
scene. This time Conroy had noticed. He had to have been thinking exactly what I was—if anyone knew about the death of my
buddy, this scumbag would. We stepped toward him . . . and he
ran. He was discreet enough about it to not raise up any of the
other cops, making it to the door and wrenching it open. I was on
turbo drive, so he'd just made it to the first landing when I
grabbed the back of his hair, twisting hard as he fell into the steps,
hitting three or four of them before he stopped rolling. I was on
top of him before he could move. John was right behind me and
slowly walked down as I jack-lifted Borges into the wall. I
pointed in his face and yelled, "Don't you ever run from us, you
little spic, you hear me . . . Ever!" He grabbed the side of his
head that had hit the steps, but I would not allow him that comfort. I grabbed his hand and slapped him hard in the face; again I
pointed at him, saying, "Motherfucker, you are a cunt hair from
joining your partner up there. A fucking cunt hair, you hear me!"
I didn't wait for the answer, BANG, I slapped him again.

He was dazed, though I had his attention. Out of breath, he
said, "Okay, Tatico, okay, you got my 'tention."

Conroy knelt down and asked him calmly, "What's with the
running bullshit?"

"I'm . . . I'm a scared a you two, Con, that all, just scared,
son. Streets be talkin,' sayin' I'm a get fucked up next, you can
understand my nerves, yo."

Actually, I couldn't. We had never dealt with him other than
to find out where Cho was dealing. It just was not computing.
"What in the fuck are you talking about?" I asked.

He would not look me in the eye; I could not tell if this was
street skiffle he was trying to sell or if it was the truth, "Why we
bullshittin' each other, C? Word's out you two on a tear. After
you's did Shah's spot, we's all out a work . . . next thing you

know, my man up there with a hot one in the face . . . you know how the shit roll, down ma'fuckin' stream."

I was trying to put it together. I stared down at this helpless fuckup. Conroy did the same. He then asked, "Who did Cho, Angel?"

Only now did Borges raise his head slowly and look directly into our eyes. He looked at me and then at John without saying anything. Conroy broke the silence. "All right, take a fuckin' walk."

He slowly stood up and headed down the stairs. He stopped on the landing and looked back up. He wasn't as helpless, or as frightened. He even smiled as he walked back up toward us, nodding his head as if he was giving us the punch line to a long joke. He stood below us on the steps. "All right, yo, seein' how I was wrong about the whole nine, you know, I was bullshittin' y'all. I am still, you know, working . . ." He pulled a wad of cash out of his pocket, opening it up like a green bouquet loaded entirely with twenties. He extended his hand to us, smiling. It was a blatant and poor bribe attempt.

That's when all the lights were suddenly turned on. John and I knew it the second we saw the bills; Angel Borges or whatever his name was, had made the fatal mistake of overplaying his hand. No dealer in the street sells twenty-dollar bags; everything is broken down in dimes, dimes of boy, dimes of girl, even the jumbo crack vials were in denominations of dimes. Dealers do not make change in the street, that is the law. We knew he had to have been at the federal level—no street cop worth his salt, and even the imbeciles from IAB, would ever make that mistake. The flash of red I saw must've hit John at the same time because we simultaneously slapped the cash out of his hand. I grabbed him by the neck and John swung wildly, glancing the side of his face. He started to cover up. I threw him to the ground and kicked him in the back. I had a clean shot at his head and was about to stomp when Conroy lifted him off the ground, slamming him into the wall. He squeezed his neck; I thought he was going to strangle the life from him. I didn't care.

"You have got to be kidding, you rat motherfucker! You

can't even bribe us correctly, you dumb, smelly spic! Who is it you're working for?" Borges's air was cut off, he could not talk, his face was turning blue. John wasn't looking for an answer; it didn't matter who he was working for. "You lookin' to tool up on us, what, riding the pad, or selling, you think you got us selling? Because if that's what you're out here to collar us for, the cell at Federal Plaza better be big enough for all of us, you little spic, 'cause you were out here dealing for almost a year. Or that don't count, you can deal, but we can't, the feds got the *jugo* we ain't got, huh? FBI crime is more important than NYPD crime!"

Snot was shooting out of Borges's nose, his eyes were bulging; meanwhile, there was a small army of cops and bosses thirty feet above, maybe some who were part of the whole scam. I grabbed Borges by the hair, ripping him away from Conroy, and he began to cough and choke. I turned him to face me. "You go back and tell those hack wanna-be cops at 26 Federal Plaza that we're out here doing our jobs. We ain't selling smack or steering, we're locking up the animals you steer for and sell to. What'd you do, grab some junk from the property clerk's office and give it to Cho to get on his dick? Poor junkie didn't even see it coming, did he? You motherfuckers make me sick. I'd fuckin' put one right in your head if we weren't here, spic." I calmed, though, so many thoughts were running through my head. "The only difference between you and that poor bastard on the roof is, he had heart and he knew who the fuck he was. Can you say the same?" We left him there, struggling for his breath.

The hypocrisy of it all was so thick I could have choked on it: The FBI were dealing to try and get two cops who they, mistakenly, thought were dealing. Conroy was right all along. They saw us swinging off of Shah's dick; in their eyes we were as dirty as he was. My life was full of gaping black holes, I had entered into something there was no way out of; it was all starting to unravel. I hated everything and everyone.

I was moving ahead of Conroy, toward the car; I needed to get out of the area, needed to think, clear my head.

"Cho was ratting on us and he didn't even know it." Conroy was summarizing the situation like it was the end of a movie with a twist ending, and he seemed to enjoy breaking it down. I turned and glared at him. "Bro, at least try and hide your contempt. Guy was just murdered . . . I mean, what the fuck, John."

"Rob, he was another junkie snitch. Don't get all twisted over this, it's all part of the game."

"Fuck the game, John, I liked the guy, I fuckin' liked him. He didn't deserve to die."

"Shit happens, pal." He said this coldly as he walked past me; at that point I was scared, not of him, but of what he was capable of and the fact that he probably knew more about this than he was leading me to believe. It was clear that I couldn't trust him any longer. He continued to talk as we approached the car. "What we should be worried about is not the feds. We should be worried about our job, IAB. We have to assume that they initiated this whole abortion and the feds saw easy targets and jumped on the bandwagon. We have to assume that anything we ever did or said to Cho was reported to them by Borges and then back to the feds. We could really be fucked here."

"You know what, John? I don't give a fuck, I really don't. Let them come and get us."

I got in the car, and the truth was, I didn't care. The game was over; it was clean-up time for whoever it was who had the case. We were going to get called to the mat and there was nothing we could do about it. We played hard and were going to get hit hard. Conroy seemed different, not as aloof as he'd been earlier. John Conroy, when you got right down to it, was as human as the rest of us, no more, no less, and John Conroy, alleged supercop, Mega Man, King Kong, was scared.

The sergeant's locker room was behind the big desk in the precinct. Mahoney would change, sleep, and have the occasional cocktail there before, during, or after each tour. There was a twin bed situated in the corner of the twelve-by-twelve room. There were a few lockers along one of the walls, a small desk, and a TV jerry-rigged for cable. It also was equipped with an ancient VCR that showed all of the illegal porn and "faces of death" tapes procured from search warrants. He poured another three fingers of good mash into my Styrofoam cup.

"I don't know what these pricks could want from me, Tommy, I really don't."

"Well, the desk just received a telephone message that IAB and the special prosecutor's office are working the homicide with PDU."

This hit me like a bullet. "They think *I* did Cholito?"

"You and Conroy are who they're looking at." I was speechless. They were no longer trying to hide the fact that we were suspects; that meant that they had to have pretty compelling evidence. Mahoney asked me evenly, "Do they have you, Rob?"

"No . . . Not that way."

"Well, how *might* they have you?"

"Nothing that counts, I don't think. Tommy, I never stole, used, or sold junk, never took a dime. Cholito probably got hit behind his dipping habits or for rolling over on the Shah. Why in the fuck would we kill him?"

"Well, if I was an outsider looking in from Poplar Street* or the SPO's office, I'd say he was clipped because you two found out he was working with IAB. Dead guys generally make terrible witnesses."

"I'm not the one who thought that—" I caught myself from further implicating Conroy, but as far as I was concerned, it was as clear as a bell, and it made perfect sense; but could Conroy have actually pulled the trigger? I suddenly realized how twisted the whole scenario was becoming. Cholito was my friend; I'd tried to protect him, and by doing so that left me vulnerable to my partner and the job because I got so personally involved. I lost an incredible street asset, but more important, I lost a friend. And I was now accused of murdering him. I felt myself falling deeper into a hole I could not climb out of.

---

*Poplar Street in Brooklyn Heights is where internal affairs was located.

"Well, Rob, this turns out to be another IAB crusade; no one is safe, no one. We could all end up in the fuckin' can."

It was going to add insult to injury if other cops got jammed up behind this investigation. I knew that every cop in the entire zone had to have known about the now-open case on me. I was a leper in the street and on the job. The last thing I wanted was to have other cops hurt behind my jones, but there was nothing I could do to stop it.

B eing out on the streets was no longer fun for me. I now knew what it felt like to be the chased, what it meant to be someone's jones, and it sucked. Still, I didn't see myself as a victim. No, I was a player in a high-stakes game, and I was the underdog. It was catch-up time and I needed answers to the many questions that still remained unanswered; topping the list was to find out who'd killed Cholito.

The tension in the car between Conroy and myself had gotten to the point where we spoke to each other only in response to job-related issues. Cholito was not brought up at all, nor the investigation, for that matter. I needed to separate myself from John, needed to sever our ties and go out on my own and look at the whole picture with a fresh set of eyes. This was the first time in my career that I did not want to be at work. The problem was that I did not want to be at home either; many a night during that dark period I found myself driving aimlessly in the farthest ends of the boroughs. I'd even slept in my car when the paranoia got really bad.

Some mind-numbing days and nights had passed. As I was cruising the streets, I saw a thin man of medium height with nappy dreads and some gold make me. The second he made our ride, he took off. He ran across Hamilton Avenue, dodging the cars that were speeding toward the Brooklyn Battery Tunnel. I was right behind him, so I had to do the same, and the closer I got to getting hit by one of these cars, the worse it was going to be for him when I caught him. Both of his hands were out, pumping with each stride, so I wasn't as inclined to think he had a pistol on him, though strangely enough, this was the first time I had chased a man when my gun was not out. I honestly didn't care that he could have pulled out and taken me down without me returning fire. I heard Conroy hit the siren, trying to get across the six lanes of avenue, but the traffic was heavy on both sides and the cars were moving too fast to stop on the median. Conroy's presence, or lack thereof, didn't matter because at this point, he was a liability to me. I also knew that if we were being followed, there was no way in America that they would be able to maneuver through the traffic and down the one-way streets without being seen. That was good for us and bad for this poor schmuck. He turned south on West Ninth Street, which traversed straight from the Badlands and into a high-end neighborhood called Park Slope. An arm of the Gowanus Canal was on my left when I caught him. He actually tried to jump into the canal, which I took as a positive, because he was scared to death. Maybe he was wanted on a body or two, maybe he knew something about Cholito, maybe we could strike a deal and barter.

I had him facedown in the embankment, which was knee-high deep in muck and garbage. I tossed him quickly for a pistol; there was none. I was out of breath and covered in the same shit he was; I was hot, dirty, and paranoid; I wanted this part of my life to be over with, I wanted to find the answers I was searching for; I hated these streets, hated Conroy, and hated myself.

He did not resist and was quiet, too quiet. I dragged him up to the street and started to walk him back toward Hamilton Avenue. Conroy had made it across the avenue and was now flying down Smith Street to find me. I waited for him on Ninth Street, where it was desolate; I wanted complete privacy to question the man. After Conroy pulled up, I opened the rear door, threw him in the backseat without cuffs. He wasn't armed, so I was not in fear of my life. I jumped in the front and pointed to an abandoned dry dock that ran parallel to the canal. It was far enough down the embankment to be hidden from the street. As we rolled, we didn't say anything to each other. I can only imagine what this guy was thinking, though he did not try to run or talk his way out of this. He had to have known who we were; maybe he'd seen us in the

Badlands. I turned to him when Conroy switched off the engine. "You know who we are, yes?" The man was shaking, and he wasn't faking it—his teeth were chattering and his lips were caked in dried saliva. He nodded quickly in the affirmative. "So what'd you take off for?" I asked this calmly, but I felt a surge of anger building, I was hoping this would end quickly and that he'd have something more than lies and nonsense to tell me. I was a raw nerve and didn't have time to fuck around.

"I had a little bag a coke on me—"

Before he'd finished the lie, I swung hard with an open fist, catching him squarely on the cheek. This was going to be an ugly display of every bad emotion that I had tamped down for the last six months—Cho's murder, my duplicitous partner, the streets, all of it was ready to erupt out of me. I grabbed his ear and pulled him to me, so close our eyelids were touching. "Now before this goes any further, let's stop the bullshit, okay? You know exactly what we're about and you know you aren't getting collared behind a bag of coke, so let's start over or on Jesus Christ himself, I'm gonna throw you into that canal, you hear?"

I pushed him with such force into the backseat that he slammed off the rear window. Conroy looked at me, unsure. He had to know this wasn't good cop, bad cop role playing; this was all bad cop, bad cop.

"Just tell us why you made us chase you. Don't be afraid, we know everyone is running scared out here, we just want to know why." Conroy asked this calmly.

The man nodded again, wiped his mouth, and dropped his hands into his lap, interlocking his fingers. He did not look at me, just stared directly at Conroy. I guess he thought he'd made a connection with the lesser of the two evils. He was wrong. "You right, man, I gots a bullshit bench warrant and—"

This is where I lost total control; reasoning, logic, any street communicating skills that I had developed over the years vanished. I had become as vacuous and dark as the streets I had patrolled for so long. All of the hatred erupted out of me like a hammer striking the primer of a .45. I was a perfectly placed .45 hollow point and this man was in the wrong place at the wrong time. Gun in hand, I leaped over the backseat. I felt my foot kick Conroy in the head in my need to get over the seat and at the man. I did not care, this was sudden-death play; there was no turning back. I struck him once on his forehead. The man tried his best to cover up, but I was too quick, I hit him with everything, my elbows, fists, feet; I had my knee jammed into his neck so I would cut off his breathing, incapacitating him further. "What did I tell you? You wanna play us like some third-grade boons?" The words came out like screeches you'd hear late at night in an insane asylum. My lips were caked with white foam and spit flew out of my mouth as I continued to pummel him. I wanted more, I wanted Conroy to see where I was and, more important, what *I* was capable of. Though everything that occurred here was not premeditated; it was all real, raw emotion; the action just gushed out of me, and there was no stopping it. I lifted my gun up close to my face, I opened the chamber, I dropped all the bullets except one to the floor, I screamed, "This is what it's like, this is what it feels like, you little animal." I placed the round back in the chamber and spun it before snapping it shut. My knee had the right side of his terrified face jammed into the dirty seat. He was able to see my incensed rage with his left eye; I noticed that he tried to close it; that is when I jammed the barrel of the gun into his eye, forcing it to remain open. "Tell me, you motherfucker, tell me why you ran."

"Officer, please; please." He was crying; he had to have known this was as real and as out of control as it could get. He had to have known that I would have killed him and dumped his body; I was not thinking at all.

Click.

The man screamed, I felt his body go limp, I heard Conroy scream something; I turned on him wildly. "You, you motherfucker, you, shut the fuck up 'cause I got something for you too." I turned my attention back to the man; I cocked the hammer. "You still wanna play, huh, you cunt . . ."

"Everyone knows you two are hot . . ."

It was hard to understand him, as he was crying and shaking. "What do you mean hot?" I screamed.

"In the street, they be sayin' you's killed that German on the roof."

"Who, who said it?"

"I don't know, Officer, they just be sayin' it, I just heard . . ."

"Which one of us?"

"What?"

I screwed my gun deeper into his ear. "Which one of us killed Cho?"

"I don't know . . ."

Click.

The man closed his eyes as he wailed; Conroy was screaming at me, though all I could decipher were loud static noises from both of them.

"Was it me or was it him? Who are they saying did him?"

Conroy kicked open his car door. "Get out of the fucking car, Rob, or I'll shoot you right there, right motherfucking now." His words and his tone brought me back to the cold reality of what I had done. There was now a crying man underneath me and I was holding a gun to his head. I had to catch my breath. I jammed the pistol into my waist and jumped back into the front seat; I did not look back at the man. "Get out." I said this quietly. I heard the door open and close, footsteps scrambling quickly away from the car. I flipped open the door and got out, leaned against the front fender, inhaling deeply. Conroy approached from behind, his footsteps heavy. "You stupid motherfucking psycho."

I felt his big hand grab my shoulder as he spun me around, off of the car. I was spent, nothing left to fight with. He reached down, quickly relieving me of the gun. He then swung an arching roundhouse, glancing off the left side of my head. I didn't care if there was more to come, and there was. He swung again, this one caught me just under the chin and I fell back into the car, hunched down, covering up. I felt both of his hands grab at my head as he screamed, "You could have killed him." He launched me off the car and I hit the pavement hard.

"The gun was empty, the gun was empty," I screamed back at him. I heard him step back. Conroy pulled the gun out: *click,*

click, boom. His face said it all. Maybe there was the scintilla of hope that there wasn't a bullet in the chamber, that it was all a well-executed charade to get at the truth, but there was, and he'd realized how genuine the last ten minutes had been, and how over the edge I had truly gone. I suddenly realized the same thing.

We watched each other for what seemed like an eternity. He then just shook his head. "No wonder Devlin dumped you . . . you're out of control. It's over, man, get yourself a new partner." He tossed the gun at my feet as he walked to the car. Then he turned back to me. "Another thing. You think I killed that little German dope head, then have the balls to say it to me like a man. Don't try and beat it out of some poor nigger."

He sped off, leaving me on the dirty dry dock. The tide was low and the haze and the heat had made the stench stronger. I started to heave and then it all came up. Maybe the ghetto was trying one last time to cleanse me, though I knew it was not going to be that easy to absolve me of the dirt I had ingested. I wiped the sweat from my face, though all I accomplished was smearing more of the sticky vomit, mud, and garbage on it. I was now one with the garbage. *Garbage in and garbage out.*

I was dried up emotionally, walking around in a catatonic state. Mia tried to talk to me, but when she would initiate any conversation, I'd turn away from her. I'd become accustomed to sleeping on the couch when I was at home, which was no more than two days a week. As bad as my life had become in the street, it was worse at home. Mia drifted away, becoming less and less inclined to want to have any conversations with me. We were living in a dark and cold world together, coexisting in a loveless and bottomless pit. I knew deep inside that I was wrong, wrong about everything and so wrong about not getting the help from her that I needed, but the truth was, I was ashamed by what I had become, and my hell would only get worse.

• • •

She needed help with the groceries. The doctor had warned her that her cervix was weak and that she would need to eliminate any excessive stress from her life. When she told me this, I don't really remember, because I was living in my self-absorbed little cocoon and I was the only person who was hurting. She wasn't facing the homicide charges that were sure to come. She wasn't looking at twenty years of hard-core time for murder; I was. In reality, what was happening to me was happening to her and that beautiful little baby forming inside her.

I stepped out of the supermarket and did a 360 around the perimeter of the parking lot. I knew they were there and I was worried that the scumbags were going to arrest me in front of Mia. I was still living the farce that I could ride this out and things would return to normal between the two of us, but I was so far off the cliff with everyone and everything in my life that the simple task of breathing was day to day for me. She recognized my jittery paranoia. "What's the matter?" she asked coldly as she walked by.

I held on to the packages tightly and gritted my teeth. *I feel like I been bingeing on crack for five days and am stressing over a motherfucking come down, so leave me the fuck alone.* I felt like screaming this into her well-appointed ear, but all I could do was scream it inside my own head, keep it for the rest of the psychotic internal monologues that I'd been having of late. "Nothing, nothing is wrong, let's just get home." Again I turned to check the lot; I did not see any PD cars or unmarked federal cars. Everything in the lot had a price tag well above what the year to date said on my year-end net paycheck. There were Jags and Benz station wagons, there were BMWs and a sweet, fire-engine red Alfa-Romeo idling behind Mia's Volvo, blocking us in. A man of about thirty was sitting in the driver's seat talking to a woman standing at his window; she was dressed like she was going for tea at La Goulue, on Madison Avenue. I looked at both the man, who wore tennis clothes, and the woman as I opened the trunk to the Volvo and threw the groceries in; then I slammed the trunk. I felt their eyes on me as I got in and started the engine.

I searched the lot once again for suspect cars, up in the air for suspect helicopters. I was ready to go in cuffs. I scanned the rest of the lot with the electric right-side-view mirror. I realized that Mia had been watching me carefully throughout this. I quickly looked away from her and saw that the Alfa had not yet pulled out to allow me to drive away. I beeped.

"What, you're not going to check the undercarriage for bombs?"

"Oh, is it time for your comedy set to begin, Mi? Can we wait till we get home so I can pour myself a quart of Jack?" I beeped again.

"You know, there's medication for the onset of OCD, Robert."

I wiped the sweat from my brow. I did not take my eyes off the man in the red Alfa. I beeped yet again. "Yeah, well things are a little rough at work . . ."

She opened a magazine and turned the page roughly. "Yeah, yeah, yeah, I'm very aware that things are bad at work, what else is *friggin'* new." She was angry, which made me angrier. I beeped again.

"Fuckin' typical"—I whispered this—"bitch."

I saw her head snap toward me. "What did you say?"

"You fucking heard me."

Mia had changed from a soft-spoken and analytical person to one of fiery and spontaneous action, thanks to me. She grabbed hold of my face and I pulled away, opening a nice gash on my chin from her nail. The sight of my blood must've given her great pleasure, I thought, but there was a long line of people wanting some of my flesh and some of my blood. "Do you see what's happening here, Rob, or are you that fucking blind . . . you're blowing this, or do you even give a shit?"

I beeped again. "You knew exactly what it was you were getting in to, so if you're looking for pity, stop off at Mortimer's after work and tell it to someone who gives a fuck. That place is loaded with you Wall Street victims."

"No! Bullshit! I had no clue this was what my life was going to turn out like; sleeping alone, no friends, I can't even get laid by you. I try to talk to you, because maybe I see that there is a glimmer of light left in your eyes, but all that really is, is the sad reflection of what used to be there. You walk around like a goddamn zombie and I'm supposed to just sit back and make sense of it all, and now you're going to vilify me for telling you how it really is. I'm done, Rob, so fucking done with it all. And I am not going to raise a child in this environment, I'm not. Goddamn you, I am not."

"What is it that you're saying, Mi, huh, say what the fuck it is you want to, stop talking in your Wall Street lawyered-up gibberish and be motherfucking assertive in your own quest for the truth, you fucking crybaby. Try it, Mi, the truth will set you free. It works for me."

"You want the truth"—she pushed the rearview mirror toward me—"take a look, Rob, take a good look, because that person there is the person who is going to end it all for you. You're on a crash course with yourself and I'm getting out of the way before I become just another dried-up fatality. I'm too smart and too good for that."

While she ranted, I saw nothing but the man who was boxing me in, wearing his pretty little snow-white tennis suit and being jerked off by the Jappy North Shore socialite in training. I beeped for the last time, holding my hand on the horn. I heard the buzzing in my head explode into a cacophony of white noise. The blood rushed through my neck like a runaway locomotive, the throttle pushed to maximum. The last thing I heard was, "I don't know who you are any longer, Rob."

I slammed my hand on the steering wheel over and over, and squeezed my hands over my ears. I wanted to keep the train from hitting the wall, but there was no turning back. "I'll tell you who I am. I am the asshole who gave you everything you wanted. I allowed you to lead me around like a little lapdog and I am fucking sick of it and sick of you. I am the asshole who allowed you to rope me into this pretty little house in the pretty motherfucking scumbag suburbs. I never wanted this life, never, but I motherfucking did it for you. I'll tell you what motherfucking else I did not want . . ." The words came tumbling out. I wasn't sure that I meant them, but they were said and she heard them as clear as a bell. I was so off the reservation that there wasn't time to just stop, apologize, and try to get my shit together. All I saw was the dick blocking me, in the red Alfa.

Mia looked away from me. I saw her touch her stomach, but not consciously. She was cold, succinct, and incredibly sad when she said, "You son of a bitch." Her head dropped, I heard her whimper, and she said it again quietly, to herself. "Son of a bitch."

I felt the guilt ride up from deep inside my guts. I shook it off and slammed the steering wheel again, over and over. I screamed and wailed because of where I had ended up. All the promise had turned to diseased shit. I kicked open the door, and through the red veil that was before my eyes, I actually think that the man gave me the finger. I walked to him on a mission, ignoring the woman. I pushed her out of the way. The driver was stunned. These things just don't happen in Great Neck, Long Island.

"You scummy motherfuck, you want to die, don't you . . ." I ripped open the door quickly; he did not have a chance. I grabbed his ear and chin, pulling him upward; I knew that if he did not remove himself from the seat of the car, his neck was going to break. A little trick I'd learned in the academy and used to pull perps out of cars. As I twisted with all my might, he lifted himself off the seat and fell out, hitting the ground hard. Mia was screaming, but again this was just white noise to me. There may have been people watching, but I was out of my mind. I screamed in his face, spittle hitting him. He was covering up. My gun was exposed, in my waistband. He was scared, but I didn't care. He'd so blatantly defied my simple request to move his car and was now the black-dot focal point of all my rage. "You don't wanna move your car, I'll motherfucking move it for you." I ran to the car, placed it in neutral, and pushed it forward; it picked up momentum and probably would have jumped the curb, hurting someone, had it not been for a speed bump that slowed it to a stop. I turned back and ran for the man. He raised his hands in a defensive gesture as I faked with a right uppercut, then I hit him flush with an overhand left. He hit the ground. "Now, you cunt,

I'm gonna pull all the bitch out of you. I am gonna fuck you dry."
I pulled my leg back wide and was about to kick his head; had it
not been for the screams of Mia I quite possibly could have killed
this man. The tunnel vision was gone, my peripheral vision told
me there were many people watching. Mia ran to the Volvo and
dropped her head in her hands. I caught my breath and moved
quickly to the car. Luckily, the car in front of the Volvo had
pulled out, so I was able to drive forward without any of the by-
standers taking down the plate number.

A utility van was parked in front of a power pole a half block
from my home. I saw it the second I made the turn around the
bend. I was tempted to ram it, go out in a fiery ball of semi-
glory—*Disgraced cop rams internal affairs OP van. Cop killed,
but he got three rats on his way to hell, so it's a wash.*

I pulled the bags out of the trunk and pretended I didn't see
the van. The cold sweat dripped down my back, giving me a de-
pressing chill. I was nauseated knowing that I was now being
watched. In the kitchen Mia was sitting in a chair, stunned. This
afternoon she had met someone she had never seen before and
had encountered a horrible display of humanity that she'd never
want to bear witness to again. My focus on her and the pain she
was dealing with was minimal at that moment. I was so focused
on that phone on the wall, the wires that were connected to it,
and, most important, who was jacked into those wires. I was
standing in the middle of the kitchen staring at it. I must've appeared to be in some sort of drug-induced state.

"I want you to be careful about what you say on the phone,
Mia."

She tilted her head from the polished tile to the vicinity of
where she had heard my voice, but she didn't look at me.
"What?"

"Some nonsense is going on at work . . . and . . . I think the
phone . . . well, it may be tapped."

I moved to the bags, quickly removing the groceries. Her response seemed to take forever, but it came. "My phone is fucking
tapped, Rob!?"

I tried to cover as best I could. As I continued to remove the contents from the bags. I didn't turn to her, sure that she'd be able to read the myriad emotions on my face—disgrace, embarrassment, and fright. "Don't make a big deal out of it, Mi, just watch what you say."

"I want you to tell me what in the hell is going on, right this second." Her tone was clipped and harsh. The last thing I needed was to be scolded by someone who I'd tried for years to keep in the dark about the dark.

I walked out of the kitchen and said, "It's nothing, it's just procedure." I entered the big family room, cold and empty of even the smallest remnants of a family. I looked at the front door, thought about going out there to get some air, but they were there, so I charged up the stairs toward my bedroom, where I hadn't slept in months. I lay on the bed hoping she wasn't coming up, though I heard her feet, heavy on the steps. I pulled the pillow over my head; I was trying to block out the buzzing, it was not going to stop, I'd had it all day; the door swung open, and I felt her hand swipe at my foot.

"It's procedure to tap a cop's phone?"

I still had the pillow over my head, but no matter how hard I tried neither she nor the buzzing was going away. She ripped the pillow from my face and threw it across the room. She pointed in my face, dangerously close. She was not my beautiful wife any longer, she had become one of them. "What do you think I am, an idiot? Do you actually think you're that enigmatic, that you're that much a fucking mystery? Well, you're not. You are as simple and as telling as the next scared little boy playing policeman, except I know you, Rob, and I know you've done something and gotten into trouble and GODDAMN IT, I WANT TO KNOW WHAT IT IS YOU HAVE GOTTEN US INTO!"

The word "us" was what did it, and I was glad she had said it because it opened up the gates to the hell I'd been living in. I kicked at her, though thankfully, I missed her. I shot off the bed and charged for the first hard object I could find, the hand-carved cherry-wood vanity that her mother had given us as a wedding present. With every last ounce of strength, fortified behind the hatred and rage that now made up who I was, I hit the eight-thousand-dollar Italian vanity, and then I hit it again, and again. I screamed violently, "You're just like the rest of them, aren't you? You have fucking betrayed me just like the job has betrayed me. My own fucking WIFE! What have I gotten US into, US? All these years I have been trying to keep you out of it so you could not see or know what it is like, so you would not have to see the same horror I have seen, so your eyes would not be as gray and colorless as mine have been becoming, so I could still know that there was something worth doing this for, YOU! And you turned on me like everyone else. You want to know what I did?" I moved to the dresser, as good a piece of furniture and as solid. I slammed my fists into the top, knocking off her perfumes and her trinkets and her hair clasps and our wedding picture in the antique silver frame. "Men who would chew your uterus out and fuck me in the ass for fun I have had to get into bed with. I have had to befriend them, play the fucking game with them, and then lock these motherfucking animals up, all in a cocksucking day's work. Okay, maybe I didn't do it the way it was supposed to be done, maybe I had to play the game hard, but what do you think would happen if every cop in the city did it the way it says to do it on motherfucking paper? You could not walk the streets, they would own me, you, the kids; it would be hell on earth, the same hell that I am now motherfucking living in, you betraying CUNT!" I ripped open the closet door; I pulled out every piece of clothing that I owned and started to tear at them, the hundred-fifty-dollar T-shirts that I never wore, the Gucci loafers that I never wore, the Armani suits that she'd bought for me and which I never wore. I tore them at the seams; her head was down as I destroyed the material matter that she had collected for me throughout the years, her way of showing me that she cared and loved me desperately, I destroyed it all. "This, this means nothing to me, give me that little motherfuck-ing spic back, that is what means something, he should be alive. It wasn't my fault, it wasn't my motherfucking fault. They think I did him and took drugs and stole motherfucking money, and I never took a fucking dime; and don't think that we didn't have plenty of chances to take; I could have had millions by now.

These cunting blood-clot whores are trying to put me in jail." I tore the buttons from my shirt, I ripped it off my back, I slammed my fists into my chest, I grabbed at my cheeks; there was no realization of pain, I was already in too much pain. I saw myself in the mirror, and the image was horrific; there was a split second of recognition and that is when I charged it and slammed my fist into it. It was leaded glass, so thankfully it only cracked and my hand was not opened to the bone. I spun on her and charged; her head was in her hands, part covering herself, part hiding from the animal that had transformed into more of an animal right before her sad, scared almond eyes. I pulled her to her feet, I shook her with everything that I had left in me; I wanted to shake the love out of her, I wanted her to see me for who I had become; I knew that it was all over, now *she* had to know. Mia was crying; I grabbed at her face roughly, saying, "You look at me, you motherfucking look at me or I swear I'll do us both right now." And in that moment, sadly, I was capable of doing just that, ending it all. She was crying, I did not care, she did not want to look at this man; I did not care, this had to be said. "LOOK AT ME!" I shook her violently, she went limp, she stopped crying, her eyes were glassy and red, though now she was drop-dead focused on the blazing intensity that was *my* eyes. The buzzing and ringing was loud, I screamed over it, "You want to know why I don't want to have a baby? Because we live in a rat-infested sewer, a filthy toilet bowl full of maggots is what this city is, it's what the world is, and nobody gives a fuck, not a fucking soul, no one! And I see it more and more every day, the children are walking piles of flesh ready to be sucked up and dumped with the rest of the garbage this city wants to burn, and the only ones who stand between the babies and the furnace are saps like me! ME! The politicians don't give a fuck, the bosses don't give a fuck, I GIVE A FUCK! ME! And when I go, when all the other fall-guy cops go, it is all fucking over, and you can move to Kings motherfucking Point or to Bangor motherfucking Maine or wherever the fuck it is that you think you're going to be safe and that's when you are going to realize that I was right, and there is not a good goddamned thing you can do about it!" I searched deep into her eyes, I was looking for any door that was closed, I wanted every inch of her opened, I wanted all of her, much the way I had years before, except that was a different time and I was a different man. "There is no sense to any of this anymore, none. There is no sense to anything any longer, it is over, *we* are over. Mia, I am who I have become; and you want to know why? Because if you want to fight them, you have to BECOME THEM!"

We stood eye to eye, so close I felt her heart pounding against my chest, her breathing rapid. The ringing in my ears wasn't as powerful, her voice was low and raspy, tears pooled in her eyes and slowly drifted over her cheekbones, resting somewhere on her neck. "Then what's the difference, Rob, what's the difference?"

She was right, there was no difference. I had come to know that, it all came down to those three words. And now she knew it, knew that I was no different from the animals and monsters I had been chasing, period.

I released my grip on her arms. There were welts on them. I shook off the realization that I had caused those welts, but those were the welts that would heal, with time, they were the only bruises that would heal.

She backed away from me. I turned, ashamed of what I had become, ashamed that I'd allowed this beautiful girl to get caught in the same dark web I was caught in, but for me, there was only one way out. I heard the door close gently behind me, then heard her car start. I didn't move until long after I heard its soft engine disappear down the road, which was once the road I had lived on and been so deeply loved on.

13

"G.O. 15 Not in Effect"

The bathroom was cleaner than most of the other police-owned facilities. I wondered why, then it dawned on me that the walls must have been scrubbed clean once a week behind all the nasty graffiti left by the hundreds of cops who had the misfortune of excreting in this building. IAB was a miserable place to find yourself in, especially if the notification you'd received told you to report with your PBA attorney and that G.O. 15 was not in effect. That little footnote meant that if you admitted to any crime during the interview, you could be charged and arrested for it. Cops usually received notification that G.O. 15 was *in* effect, meaning he'd receive immunity from any crimes he admitted to during the interview; my notification read that G.O. 15 was *not* in effect.

Conroy and I were in the bathroom at IAB looking out the window onto Poplar Street, in Brooklyn Heights. We turned the faucets on and checked all the stalls. We didn't think the room would be wired, as that would be illegal, but we could not be too careful. My back was to Conroy as I lazily studied the tiled walls for any discernible graffiti markings. I was glad I'd taken the ten milligrams of Valium Patty had given me; I was able to think without feeling the mega hits of anxiety rush through my body, which was a torturous feeling.

"Our memo books read the same, so as long as we keep our

stories the same, they got nothing." He said this as he dabbed water on his face; he did not look at me and I did not look at him.

"What stories, John?" I said this with the slightest hint of sarcasm, but it wasn't a dig at John, it was just the way it came out. He still didn't look at me, but the comment must've ricocheted into an open wound because he barked back quickly.

"Any of our collars, what in the fuck do you think?"

"Don't know what to think, you're the pro at this, John, remember? You're the one who's been down here so often you have your own coffee cup." That *was* meant to sting, and sting it did. Conroy snapped the faucet shut and moved closer to me; I still didn't look at him. I wanted to show him what it felt like to have an indifferent and condescending motherfuck of a partner.

"What, all of a sudden this bag a shit is my fault, Rob?"

"Not saying that, John."

"Well then, what in the fuck are you saying, buddy boy? Don't play me, or this abortion, like that, son. I didn't make you do anything you weren't willing to do; as a matter of fact, it was your dime what got you into the detail in the first place, and your dime that busted you and that Devlin kid up; you are here because you placed yourself here. It's hard to play victim when you're the one holding the bat, *sabe*?"

He turned from me and moved to the window, lit up a cigarette, and stared back out into the street. I could not let the moment go, I wanted him to know a couple of things and one of them was that I didn't trust or believe anything he said. "Hey, John, between a couple of old buddy boys, did you do Cho?" I smiled at him as he slowly crossed to me. He rubbed his big hands along my back and chest, obviously searching for a wire; then he smiled.

"We weren't here right now, I'd put one where the one in Cho should've went." He lifted his thumb and forefinger up, pointed it between my eyes; he then took one last look at himself in the mirror and turned to walk out. Before he reached the door, he whispered back, "On that note, you can go fuck yourself . . . Tatico."

• • •

T he room was half the size of the interrogation room in the
7-6; if it was six by six, it was a lot. It seemed like a jail cell
equipped with a small table and four chairs. These rooms were
meant to be small. Up close and personal is how the rats liked to
play it; they didn't have the balls to get up in the guts of the
streets, so they waited till they could corner the cop in a room
just like this one, and then try to play hard-nosed policeman. It
was old-school mentality and any salty cop could see right
through the charade that these cowards performed daily. I especially was in no mood for game playing. I wanted to get back into
the street and somehow redeem myself. My PBA attorney had
been inside the room waiting for me. Richard "Ken Doll" Irvman was retired from my job, and from what I understood, he
was quite the piece of work. He was a detective who'd gotten
bounced back to the bag, or sent back to uniform patrol, behind
an unfounded allegation that he was a hired gun for Leroy
"Nicky" Barnes, out of Harlem. Nicky Barnes was a major
player in the heroin trade back in the seventies; he never rolled
on Irvman once he himself was collared, even though he rolled
on more gangsters than Sammy Gravano did years later. But the
job, IAB to be exact, didn't give a shit and banished the rising-
star detective to a place called the 5-2, in the northernmost section of the Bronx. This was a geographical death sentence for
Irvman, who lived with his wife and two kids on Staten Island.
To arrive on the job at seven A.M. would take between an hour
and a half to two and a half hours, all depending on traffic. Irvman toughed it out, riding out the next twelve years in uniform,
way up in the tit end of the Bronx. He made it work for him. En-
rolling at Fordham University, studying law, and graduating top
of his class. When he retired, he began working as a lawyer for
the PBA, and God bless him and the guys just like him, they
hated IAB almost as much as the poor schmucks on patrol did. I
surmised that Irvman would defend any cop in these tight,
scummy IAB cubicles, for free.

Irvman was a handsome man in his mid-forties; he looked

like a Ken doll, which would account for his nickname. He was slick in physical appearance, though his fifteen-hundred-dollar-suits and Ivy League good looks paled in comparison to his intelligence about the job, the rights of the cops, and his incredible knowledge of the law. He was wearing a black Brooks Brothers cashmere blazer with double venting in the back. He wore beige khaki trousers that seemed hand sewn, a crisp white Armani button-down shirt with a forward-point collar, and a gold Turnbull and Asser silk tie. *No wonder these pricks were gunning for him. He's a male model with a law degree,* I thought. He winked when I entered, then patted me on the back. "Rob Cea, long time, my friend, long time; how's the family?"

We had never met, but he wanted the two IAB knuckleheads who followed me into the room to think we were two old buddies, just kicking it hard, old school. They were two friends, and we were two friends, and Irvman knew he was smarter and slicker than these two asbestos-suit-wearing rats. Irvman dressed the part because he liked to flaunt his success in front of these scumbags who'd tried to put him down in much the same way they were going to try and put me down. He didn't look at the two cops, he just patted my shoulder and continued. "Jesus, Bobby, you're looking good. Annie keeps asking me to invite you over, but we just opened another practice out on the island, so I been crazy busy. Maybe you come out to the club, we play the back nine after we resolve all this nonsense here, yes?"

I smiled; he was good, very good. I actually believed every word he said. I was tempted to slip him my number after the interview. "Yeah, Rich, definitely. Tell Annie Mia has been asking for her as well. Tell her to give a call, we'll set something up."

He sat in the chair and pulled my chair close to his so that we could discreetly communicate with each other during the interrogation. The two cops sat side by side at the small table and one of them snapped on a tape recorder. Irvman, to add one final piece of dramatic flare, snapped his fingers lightly and said, "Oh, Bobby, almost forgot . . ." He pulled a leather cigar holder out of his jacket pocket and discreetly handed me a Cohiba. He whispered, though loud enough for the two imbeciles to hear,

"Cuban, pre Castro." He gave me a million-dollar wink and I was now completely eased of whatever tension the ten milligrams of Valium could not ease.

Lieutenant Ferber was about the same age as Irvman, though he looked fifteen years older and wore cheap rubber-soled shoes, a Macy's off-the-rack brown suit, a beige shirt, and a chocolate tie. He was trying hard to stay attuned to the fashions of the day, as I noticed a *GQ* magazine on his desk when I passed, but Lieutenant Ferber's curtains just somehow did not match his carpet. His partner was Detective Cesar Mendoza, a guy who would not pass muster in an opium den. Medium size, he wore blue polyester pants and tie with a long-sleeved light green shirt that rode up his arm as if it were cut too short; it was also stained in the pits. A tattoo peeking out from under his shirt told me he might have done undercover, or UC work in the office, or had once been a UC in narcotics. That didn't surprise me, as the narcotics units ballooned so much after the inception of crack that they had to pull in any minority who had two years or more on the job without really checking their qualifications. The UCs in the narcotics units were a crack pipe away from being perps themselves; that would certainly explain this greasy Puerto Rican's choice of assignment, IAB; so Richard Irvman and myself, we were in grand company.

Ferber pulled a pair of thin bifocals from his pocket, then leaned into the microphone trying to act very much the guy in charge. "This is Lieutenant Jeffrey Ferber of the internal affairs bureau. I am with Detective Cesar Mendoza, shield number 616. We are conducting an inquiry into the death of Theobaldi Rodriguez, also known as Cholito. Present at the time of the inquiry is Officer Robert Cea, shield 17750 and his PBA-appointed attorney, Richard C. Irvman." He looked up at me over the bifocals, which perched at the bottom of his long, angular nose. "Officer Cea, where were you on the evening of September 15 at approximately 2300 hours, of this year?"

"Can I check my memo book?"

"G'head." I flipped open my blue memo book, my bible. Any job that a cop went on had to be placed in that book, even his days off. Everything a cop did while on patrol was by strict order supposed to be in that book—it could either save you or sink you.

"I was RDO."

"Not an emergency day or a chart day, it was an RDO?"

Irvman tapped me once under the table with his foot, then looked at his manicured nails and said, "He already answered, next question."

"Do you remember where you were?"

"Yes, I was home with my wife."

"How could you be so sure?" the greasy pint-size detective asked. Now, he was not my superior, he was just a detective, which is basically a glorified patrolman who doesn't have to wear a uniform, so he should not have been asking me any questions. I felt Irvman about to speak, but I beat him to the punch. "You are?"

"Detective Mendoza."

"So why in the fuck are *you* asking *me* questions?" Irvman smiled, then kicked me gently under the table. The lieutenant briefly looked to the detective, then back to me.

"Officer Cea, try and refrain from cursing." Ferber nodded to the tape recorder. I glared at Mendoza, saw his face flush. He could not take any type of confrontation. *If I wanted, I could have you easily, you fuckin' coward.* This I thought as I fantasized about meeting him on a Badlands roof. *I'd have you in a dress and lipstick selling cigarettes and blow jobs, you wormy rat.* I turned my attention back to Ferber. "How well did you know Theobaldi Rodriguez?"

"Not well, he was just a street guy I'd see in passing around the Red Hook Houses."

"Was he a drug user?"

"Yeah, he seemed like he may have used drugs."

"Did you ever witness him taking drugs?"

Irvman's foot tapped ever so gently against my foot. I knew what that meant. "No, never witnessed him using narcotics."

"Did he ever give you any information?"

"Occasionally, in passing, he'd throw me a bone if there was someone around who was wanted."

"You ever throw him any bones in return?"

Irvman immediately raised up, "Phrase the questions professionally. No, no wait, let *me* rephrase that . . . as professionally as *you* can." He now glared at Ferber.

"Did you ever give him gratuities in exchange for this information?" he asked coldly.

"No."

"No money?"

Irvman kicked me twice; I could feel from the taps that he was getting angrier by the second, though he remained just as condescending and cool. "He already answered. Next question."

Ferber tilted his head at Irvman. He was flying very high in very thin air, way out of his league. Irvman ate up guys like Ferber before his first shit in the morning. "Any bargaining if you ever caught him with anything?"

"I never caught him with anything."

"Ever give him any drugs?"

The questions were starting to hit home. Of course I had done that and so much more. Hell, I'd cooked up for him with drugs, I'd stolen for him. I was trying desperately to remain as cool as Irvman was. "That's a crime, I would never do that."

It was now time for his performance. Ferber leaned in and searched my eyes; I was sure not to look away, tilting my head at him and hoping he'd recognize boredom and nothing else. "You never gave him any drugs?" This was asked with mock disbelief. I heard Irvman laugh sarcastically.

"I never gave the man drugs."

"Did you ever witness PO John Conroy giving him any drugs?"

My answer wasn't as quick; this was the first time Conroy's name had been brought into my inquiry. I wondered why. I also wondered what his answer to that question would be once it was posed to him. "No, never witnessed John Conroy giving him *drugs.*"

"Do you have any information regarding the death of Theobaldi Rodriguez?"

"No."

"Any idea as to why he might have been murdered?"

Irvman grabbed hold of my leg before I could speak. "Don't answer that." He leaned in and shook his head slowly at Ferber. "That's a question for one of the street mopes who knew the victim, or it's a question that needs to be asked of homicide or the PDU guy who caught the case. It is, however, not a question for my client. Next question." He leaned back in the chair. The truth was that I did have ideas as to who the shooter might have been, that the bullet had come from one of two people, and the man in the room directly next to the room I was in was one of those people. This I could not tell them; my suspicions were probably going to the grave with me.

Ferber smiled. It seemed as if he knew something I did not know. All the Valium and Richard Irvmans in the world were not going to make the if-they-wanted-me-they-had-me feeling go away. Ferber snapped the recorder off. "No worries, we're through here." "Through" sounded like "true." He turned to Mendoza. "Make copies of his memo book from June twenty-eight to September twenty." He didn't look at me. "After he gets a copy of your book, you can go."

"Bobby, let's go to Montague Street for lunch, my treat," Irvman said as he stood, brushing his pants off. He was about to step out of the room when he noticed me staring at Ferber. I wanted to make eye contact with him, wanted him to know the truth about me, about what I'd tried to do. He still would not look at me, his way of letting me know that he had some sort of control. I could not let the moment pass. I stepped to him.

"I didn't commit no fucking homicide, Lieutenant. I am a good cop, regardless of what you people may think." My tone was deadly serious. Coupled with the fact that I was physically very close to the man when I said it, he had no choice but to look at me and respond.

Ferber looked at me, then back at Irvman. "You mind if I have a few moments with Officer Cea alone?"

Irvman scowled at Ferber, then placed his hand on my shoulder and started to lead me out. "Yeah, I mind." If looks could kill, Ferber would have been a corpse. "C'mon, Bobby, there's a bottle of VSOP with our names on it and a very cute bartender who we're going to make very happy waiting for us at the Montague saloon."

I stopped. "No, Rich, I want to."

This time he leaned into me so Ferber could not hear. "Bobby, this prick is not your friend. These guys would turn their mothers out to sell tricks if they thought they could collar a cop, you understand?"

I looked at Irvman. He had to know from my responses and attitude during the interview that I wasn't going to give the lieutenant dollar one. "Rich, I know what I'm doing, I won't hurt myself, trust me, I just want to let scumbag know the witch-hunt he's on is gonna get him dick."

He squeezed my shoulder and whispered, "Don't talk into the recorder, don't let scumbag bait you into anything, and if that suck-dick detective comes back in, walk the fuck out, 'cause then they're just playing you. Call my office immediately if you get any notifications from these pricks about charges and specs. I'll talk to you either way next week . . . You did good today." He moved toward the door. "All right, Bobby, I'll meet you at the bar. I'll order the oysters Rockefeller. Hurry though, because they're delicious . . . and I'm hungry."

He winked and was gone. For some reason, I was able to breathe easier being one-on-one with Ferber. I knew who he was and what he was all about, but if I was going down, I wanted one of these talking heads to understand what I was all about. I also thought I would be able to Geiger-count how much trouble I was really in from the way the conversation went. Ferber leaned back against the desk. "What's your definition of a good cop, Officer Cea?"

I folded my arms, though I tried very hard to appear friendly. I wanted to lull him into giving me something, anything; after all, he was no different from the thousands of other street punks I wormed info out of daily. "A guy who's out there every day locking up animals who'd kill their babies for the almighty dollar or a vial of crack. I am stopping crime, not committing it."

"You ever break the law, Cea?"

I wanted to say no, that the laws I broke were not for any

personal gain, that they were twisted and manipulated for the good of all of us, for the good of the five-year-olds who never had a summer vacation because they weren't permitted to play in the streets of the Badlands. The laws I broke were without question only directed at men who would not think twice about killing any one of us, regardless of sex, age, color, or creed, and the sad thing about all of it is, without men like me who would dare to question these laws, which are built solely to protect only the bad guy, the streets would be owned by the animals I tried so hard to arrest. Democracy in a place like New York City doesn't work, the reason being, it's too diverse. Ask Rudy Giuliani, who reigned as an absolute monarch, and dragged the city kicking and screaming into lawful prosperity. His "monarchy" allowed every cop in the city to get right the fuck up in the face of the animals who ran the city under the administration of the fabulously inept David Dinkins.

Ferber continued. "Ever let a misdemeanor slide in order to get a felony? Because you do know that's a crime. If you do that, then what's to stop you from letting an A two felony go in order to get an A one felony? Maybe a rape for a murder?" Ferber wasn't telling me anything I didn't already know. What Ferber failed to mention was that this bargaining occurs every day between the defense attorneys, the prosecutors, and the judges. Sammy Gravano admitted to killing nineteen men, but because he was the only rat they could get to testify against a bigger scumbag, John Gotti, well then he was treated with kid gloves and allowed to serve only a five-year sentence that ran concurrently with his testimony. Which means that when he was done telling his tales, he was a free man, and that was after admitting in open court to his own atrocities, including killing his wife's brother. Why was it okay for the federal government to do this on such a grand scale? Because it's the only way to beat an unbeatable foe.

I did not have the patience or the time to school Ferber on the intricacies of the street. He wouldn't understand it anyway. I let him continue, I wanted him to tell me what it was they had, without him really telling me, and it was working famously. The more he talked, the more he liked the sound of his own voice. He was no different from every perp I'd ever locked up. Give them a loud-enough microphone with a long enough cord and they were certain to hang themselves. I now understood why Conroy was always so eerily quiet; he was clocking *everyone.*

"You ever lie to get a collar or a conviction, that's a crime." What he had told me so far was that I had turned a blind eye to some offenses in the streets, and I had test-i-lied, and so far he had nothing. "What about drugs? Would you consider a cop who gave drugs to a junkie in exchange for information a bad cop?" This was the area that could quite possibly put me away for a very long time. I had given many snitches in the street bags of dope for info. Cholito was the man who'd received most of the street gratuities, but there were hundreds of others just like him, and lots of them were still alive. If they were collared, it would not take a great leap of the imagination to allow myself to think that they were turned by these pricks; they would be offered immunity for their crimes in order to testify against me, for my crimes. More nauseating hypocrisy.

"'Cause that's the same as selling drugs. That, in my book, would make you no different from every Shah King the street can shit out." As we eyed each other, I felt a brick of bile develop in my throat. He had told me what I had feared the most. All their information was coming from John Conroy's ho, Shah King, and I was mightily fucked. He smiled and I noticed that his teeth were tobacco stained and chipped; he leaned in for the coup de grace. "It doesn't seem like you got an answer for me there . . . *Tatico.*" He had the Shah, he may have had Conroy, and he certainly had me, hell, he even had my fucking street name. I did not answer him; I can only hope that my eyes did not give away my absolute fear. He turned from me dismissively and moved to the door. Before he opened it, with his back to me, he quietly said, "If any of these allegations against you can be substantiated, I am personally going to take your shield away, and all the Richard fucking Irvmans on planet earth are not going to stop me and save you . . . You have a nice day." He walked out of the room. Those stinging words lingered. I had the feeling of sinking defeat. They had me, and goddamn, they wanted me. It was just a matter of time before it all ended.

I rolled up to the rear gate of an abandoned Christmas-decoration factory on Columbia Street. The scarred building was northeast of the Red Hook projects and was situated on one of Brooklyn's many lonely, forgotten docks. I looked up to the roof of the building and noticed the giant plaster Santa Claus that looked out into the East River and north of the city. Years of abuse and neglect had made him quite the image. Bullets had sheered off the right side of his face, leaving Santa with a permanent and hideous scowl, smog from the East River's ships and the Brooklyn-Queens Expressway's car traffic had turned his once-bright red coat and hat into the color of granite.

The pier was full of marked and unmarked cars; suits, uniforms, cops, bosses; a harbor-unit boat was anchored between two ancient cement piers, guiding a team of divers searching for clues. It was an impressive giant, working crime scene. I wasn't looking for anyone in particular. I'd signed out at the precinct a half hour before, but something had led me there. I moved through the crush of cops and saw her, lying on her belly, her face turned toward the entrance of the pier, welcoming all who have come to do their jobs. The killer wanted to leave a lasting impression. He was an artist, still life, postmortem his specialty.

She was completely naked and lying on top of a mound of garbage, the bottom part of her torso facing north while the top part of her torso was arched up and her shoulders and head were facing south. She seemed twisted in midair. I saw a black, bulbous spot where her eye once was. Her other eye remained intact though it stared up to the sky, milky and vacant. Her arms were tied behind her back with what appeared to be thin panties, and a brick was jammed into her mouth. I moved closer. I heard cops talking to me, though I continued to move forward, not acknowledging any of them. That's when I noticed the pipe that was protruding from within her; it ran in a big arch three feet from her body and was jammed into the ground, giving her the appearance of floating in space. Why doesn't someone remove the fucking pipe, give her one last bit of dignity? I thought. She was smallish, maybe 105 pounds, olive skinned, Hispanic. I felt something I hadn't felt in years, a deep sorrow for this woman. What she must have gone through before the Monster allowed her to die. I also felt deep hatred and so much anxiety that I wanted to scream. I wanted to go back out on patrol and stay in the Badlands until I could meet Mister Monster. I wanted to gently remove that pipe from this poor beautiful shell of a woman and keep it until I found the animal who had perpetrated this crime. Then I would use the pipe on him, as meticulously as he'd gone to work on this helpless and blameless victim. I felt a kinship with the Monster; the kinship was knowing that we were going to end up in the same place, only I was the one who was going to put us both there. I felt a hand on my shoulder and Patty Pirelli was behind it. He looked somber. This was particularly tough for Patty. He could kill anyone twice and not give it a second thought, but when it came to brutal victimization of a woman or a child, Patty was as soft as the rest of us.

"Rob, what are you doing here?"

"I went in to sign out, heard it over the radio. It's fucked up, man."

Again he held my shoulder. Patty was comforting, and a leader in his own way. Different from Conroy and different from me or Devlin, you knew he'd been in gnarly situations before, on and off the job, and whatever advice he gave you was from experience and the heart. He truly was a good man and a great cop. If Patty made it to the twenty, he could definitely fill Richard Irvman's Ferrigamos with much ease. "Hang tough, bro, long as they don't have a wire or tape, it's all good."

I did not remove my gaze from the woman in the pile of garbage. I shook my head slowly, "Not that Patty, this. This is fucked, brother. This is so fucked, look at what this scumbag did, motherfucking look." I barely uttered these words; it was more of an affirmation to myself.

Patty watched, as helpless as I was. "He likes it here, Rob, and that's a good thing, because we are here." I nodded. I wanted to survey the area, to feel the dirt where my man walked, to breathe the same air as he did. I wanted to be consumed by the

Monster, because in my world, dog eats dog, or in our case, monster eats monster.

I spotted Mahoney standing back, allowing the crime-scene unit to sift, take pictures, and collect what evidence they could. In a garbage dump on a two-hundred-year-old pier I wondered how one deciphers what is evidence and what is just plain garbage. Again I was proud to be in the presence of these men who were digging in hundred-year-old shit all for the same cause, to avenge this woman's death. Mahoney walked toward me and Patty, a black canvas bag strapped to his back. He too patted my shoulder when he reached me. "You all right, kid?" I nodded. The vibe was somber all the way around. He reached into the bag and pulled out a police sketch of the wanted perpetrator. "This is from the Hamilton Avenue rape. It's going out today. According to her, it's dead on."

I took the sketch from Mahoney; it wasn't as clean as a photo—they never are—but there was something familiar about the face. I could not put my finger on when or where, but I knew I had seen this man somewhere. The trick was remembering where and then working backward from there. Knowing that I had crossed paths with him excited me, and knowing that we would cross swords almost gave me a hard-on, just like the ones IAB and the feds now had for me. I crossed to the woman. All I could do was shake my head. Patty joined me again. "Rob, man, you look terrible. You can't do anything here. Go home, get away from all of this for a day or two. None of this . . ." He half-nodded to the woman and then he raised his chin toward the projects, which were now casting a dark shadow over Red Hook, in the distance. "Not any of it is worth it. Life is too short, *paisan* . . . this job just isn't worth it."

I didn't look at him; I looked from the sketch to the woman. "It *was* worth it, Patty, it really was."

"All right, brother, I'll see you on the six to two."

He walked away. I still could not take my eyes off the woman, even though her face was almost beaten off. I could see that she must have been pretty. I also saw in this lifeless body the one person I could always count on and rely on to give me great comfort—I saw my wife, Mia. I saw her lying there, helpless, defiled and dead. I wanted to help her, to pull that pipe from within her, I wanted to hold her and tell her it was all going to be all right, I wanted to feel her skin on mine, I wanted to apologize for everything that I had put her through, I wanted to open up to her, allow her into my world, to be one again. The clouds that were hanging over the Red Hook projects were now crawling northeast; they were almost overhead when a clap of thunder jolted me. It was time for me to get my life back, if it wasn't too late.

The rain eased up once I drove over the Kosciusko Bridge, on the BQE. The traffic was still bumper to bumper, but that was okay because I needed time to gather my thoughts. I wanted to be crystal clear in what it was I had to say. I wanted her to know that the flaw I had found in myself would be corrected and that I would give up everything to gain her respect and trust once again. I pulled off the Whitestone Expressway onto Twentieth Avenue and slowly made my way through the middle-class neighborhood. The homes were upscale for any borough in the city of New York; the people were a little different as well. They knew what they had, twenty minutes into the city by car, though divided and segregated from other neighborhoods by the Long Island Sound, parts of the Hudson River, LaGuardia Airport, and four superhighways. This part of Queens was one of the gems of New York. Whitestone was safe a hundred years ago and it was going to be safe in another hundred years.

The only spots that were available were a block and a half away, on 147th Street. I walked down the tight one-way street of neatly kept one-family homes. The people of Whitestone took great pride in their homes. There were rose gardens and fragrant shrubs, there were potted plants placed dramatically on the brick steps leading up to colorfully painted front doors. This was the place that should have been in my progression up the geographical ladder. I had skipped this perfectly landscaped little neighborhood; I'd gone from low-end Brooklyn to high-end Kings Point. I'd missed a rung, though I was glad that Mia had not. I knew she was grounded behind all of this comfort and that was why she was going to make the place I called home, Kings Point, work for both of us.

I rang the doorbell and the lights came on in the inner porch. Mia's mother, a short woman nearing seventy who always wore black, peeked from behind a lace curtain. You could see that at one time she'd been as beautiful as Mia, with smiling eyes. Not tonight though. I could see she was sad. I had always liked this woman even though she spoke very little English and I spoke even less Italian. She opened the door and smiled weakly. I knew she wanted this to work, that if it could be repaired, she was a good ally to have.

"I'm sorry I'm here so late; is she still up?" I asked this quietly; she touched my arm and pulled me into the house. After she closed and locked the door behind me, she took my coat. She was a good woman, and I knew Mia was as good. I only hoped Mia felt the same about me.

"*Mia è stanca. Piano, piano, si?*

I smiled at the sad woman. She was loyal to her daughter; she was asking me in simple words that I would understand to go easy, that her daughter was tired. There was something else in her eyes, though I did not know what. I gently kissed her cheek and moved inside.

The house was dark though the kitchen light was on. The house always had an amazing aroma, and tonight it was anisette and coffee. Mia's mother's kitchen was the center of their family's universe. Everything that was of any consequence was discussed in that room. Mia was sitting at a large oak table in the middle of the room; two empty espresso cups were on the table, one for her and one for *Mommina.* She was wearing a robe, and she looked tired, her face drawn and pale. I wanted to cry the second I saw her. I had never seen her look so worn down, and it was all because of me. I crossed to her slowly. "Mia . . ." I whispered this half to her, half to myself. I slid a chair next to her and sat very close. "I'm so sorry, honey, I'm so sorry." I reached out to her, I laid my hand on her shoulder, but she just vacantly stared into that coffee cup on the table. I imagined this was what she'd received from me, day after day, evening after evening. There was a moment of silence. She was guarded, but I truly believed that she had to have known how deeply I loved her, that I did still care in spite of everything I had said.

"Mia, I want you to get your things, and I want you to come home."

Slowly she brought her eyes to mine. I could see traces of her steely fortitude. "Why . . . Why am I going back to where you never wanted to be in the first place? Why would I do that?"

I lowered my head. This was not going to be easy. I had dropped too many bombs on her.

"Mia, those things were said out of context and in a fit of rage. You have to know that I didn't mean that. You have to know you're my soul mate. We are one, Mia, we always have been. Please don't hold those terrible things I said against me. There is too much between us."

"No, Rob, too much has *passed* between us; so much has passed that it can never be the same. Do you realize that in all the time we have been together I have never really met any of your partners from the job, and you have never met any colleagues of mine from work? You talk about me living in a bubble . . ." She shook her head slowly and pointed her finger somewhere in my direction. "You are the one living in a bubble."

"Mia, the men I work with are different, they don't understand that there is a line that separates work from reality. These guys carry it with them twenty-four/seven, and the last person I wanted to be privy to all that crap was you. They do not know how to leave it at the precinct . . ."

"So what's the answer, Rob? Just staying at the precinct longer and longer so you never actually have to leave it? At least they do that . . . They go home . . . You and I are roommates on different schedules who do not speak the same language."

"We do, Mia."

"We don't, Rob. As a matter of fact, you don't even speak. I'd have preferred to have heard all of the horror stories. At least I would know how to help, maybe comfort you, maybe we would have been able to work through some of those issues you felt the need to keep me in the dark about. That's what I thought marriage was supposed to be, a partnership where two people work out issues for better or for worse. But me, I have nothing, just a man I hear enter the front door at four A.M. The only chance I get to feel his lips on mine is when I have to sneak a kiss while he is asleep on the couch, which is also the only time I get to see him. Yeah, that's a great life and a perfect marriage. Rob, I tried, but I'm tired and I'm through."

What she was saying was true, every word of it, but I could not give up on us that easily. I was as strong willed as she was and I would figure out a way to make this work. I would not allow her to raise a baby, my baby, in a broken, loveless home. She was a good woman and was well on her way to being a wonderful mother, but I wanted to be as brilliant a father. I had seen the scars that broken homes indelibly leave on babies; they lose what they need the most in life, trust and faith.

I dropped my head on her shoulder. "Mia, I don't . . . I *can't* lose you, I can't. I love you too much and I love this baby too much. If anything, we have to give this one last chance to survive, for this baby. Mia, please, don't think of me, think of the baby."

I didn't want to use that card, but I felt my grip loosening; Mia had a heart, and I know she wanted this baby as much as I did. She dropped her head and quietly sobbed. "You never wanted the baby, Rob, never, and that hurt me the most. I'm giving you your out Rob . . . Take it, just go."

"I know where I went wrong, Mia, and I know how to get back to that place. I know how to change all of this."

"Robert, I see how much hate there is in you. That you can't change."

She delivered the line with ice-cold incisiveness, and she was right, and it stung because of its dead-on, pointed clarity. I felt the lump in my throat swell; I needed to hold on, though what the fuck for? This was what it was all about, dropping my guard, allowing myself the comfort that she so freely offered me, and then I cried. I held her close to me and I cried, and for no other reason than that I needed to let it out. All of the pain and hurt and anger I had walled up inside; the crying felt good, and I thought, *Why didn't I do this so long ago?* When I looked into her eyes again, she was no longer crying. Her eyes were a mix of confusion and hurt. "I don't want to be that way any longer, Mia, I don't."

"Maybe this job brought out the person you really are deep inside, but you have become the person you have hated the most. Rob, there is no difference between you and them; you yourself said it the other day, and now there is nothing . . ." She held my face in her hands and made a point of focusing on my eyes. *"Nothing* left between us. Nothing, Rob. It's all over."

"Mia, we'll start over. I'll quit the job; Mia, we're going to have a baby, please." I felt a hot desperation crawling in my chest.

Another moment passed between us; her eyes were suddenly sad again, and then she said, very quietly, "There is no baby anymore."

It took a moment for it to find its mark, but it did. I didn't want to believe what I had heard. I tilted my head at her, unsure.

I felt myself stand. She was sobbing again. That's when the severity of it all hit me, it felt like a .45 slug had crept up under my vest and gutted me cleanly. I was now a festering, open wound. I slowly stepped back away from that woman sitting in the chair who had just given me a death sentence, that woman who'd handed me a gun with one bullet and set me adrift in an endless sea of loss. I knew that nothing in my life, or what was left of it, would ever be the same again. In that split second, she completely redefined my whole existence.

I moved quickly through the living room. I saw her mother sitting in the dark, crying quietly as I walked past her. I stepped out into the pounding rain, crying as I walked aimlessly in the middle of the street. I had nowhere to go, and no one to go to. I was lost. I had instantaneously become just another victim . . . of myself.

14

Redemption

I sat in my car and stared out into the rain. I felt it tug at me from under my wet shirt, biting me slightly, nipping at my lower back, trying to get out. I was completely spent of all emotion. There was nothing left. I reached around and felt the wet wood on my palm. I loved the way it felt in my hand. Those Pachmayr grips were for pussies. This is how the Colts were designed, hard and cold in your hand, letting you know they were there and ready to do damage. I opened the bullet chamber and checked the load, though that was an empty gesture. I was always strapped heavy. I swung the chamber shut and raised it up to my mouth; I closed my eyes, felt the cold steel touch my lips, tasted the metal. It was much like the taste of blood, which I'd grown to like. I pulled the hammer back, felt my heart pounding. I should have pulled the trigger instantaneously, but I didn't. I grabbed the port of the gun to steady it from shaking, but now both hands started to gyrate, and that's when I started to think. I thought of my brother, Jeff. He would be the one the job would call, he was the one person I'd put on my ten card* to call in case of emergency. I loved him and I didn't want him to have to identify his cowardly brother with his head blown up on a lonely block

---

*NYPD ten card is an index card with pertinent contact information on every officer. All official equipment, including serial numbers, are listed on the ten card.

somewhere in Queens. He didn't deserve that; I certainly did, but Jeff didn't. Then I thought of Cholito and his death. I figured if I pulled the trigger at that moment, this would be a ground ball for all the parties involved to close out the case on me. I would certainly be the one who had murdered him. I squeezed my eyes closed and pulled the gun out of my mouth, dropping it onto the floor of the car. There was a better way to do this. If I was going to go, I was going to take the filth with me. I started up the engine.

B illy met me at the last table of Farrell's. It was in a section south of the moneyed area known as Park Slope, the bar a neighborhood staple for over 120 years and the second-oldest bar in the city; it has always catered to city workers, mostly firemen and cops; it was a place to go to unwind, where there would be no posturing because there were never any women in the place. As a matter of fact, women were not allowed in the bar until the mid-seventies when the actress Shirley MacLaine had demanded to be served. She was, and that changed the clientele in the bar forever, though not much. Farrell's was the one place where you could go to sit, sip, and talk quietly.

I had already had three shots of Jack, but tonight I did not feel any of its calming effects. It was just liquid that had no bite and no particular taste to it. Billy was sipping his pint as he leaned in across from me at the table so that we were almost eye to eye. It felt good to be with him again. I knew that if I was going to get something back, it was going to have to start here. I wanted him to know everything that I had felt and what kind of impact he had had on me. I knew I was going to go out of the picture eventually, one way or another, and I wanted him to understand that he was truly my hero. He was the real thing, and he needed to keep on doing what it was that he was doing.

"Things happen for a reason, Rob, she had a reason to do what she did, and there is nothing that you can do to change that, but you can learn from it, man."

Just his voice was soothing to me. I wondered where I would

be if I'd taken his road back in the 6–7, if we'd both gone to the study sessions together and worked our way up the ladder through the civil-service tests. We'd still have been salty behind our time in the Badlands, but we'd be bosses and that much more valuable to the job, to the people of the city of New York. Billy was going to do great things on the job and certainly in life, this I was sure of.

"I miss talking to you, man."

"Me too, Rob. Remember what I used to say: We don't know where each other is, we can't protect each other."

I nodded. "I'm glad you're here."

"We'll get through this, and everything will be the way it used to be and you'll be stronger from it."

"Remember the rape victim from Hamilton Avenue?" I asked this quietly. He nodded. I wanted to take my time with this. "I was watching you that day . . . the way you handled her. We were all afraid to step up to her because of what she'd been through, but you . . . you were there, you put the blanket around her, you spoke to her, you made her feel like it wasn't her fault and that she was still a person. You cared, Billy . . ." I looked into his eyes. "I wish I had that."

"You do, Rob, you do, man. You care for these people, I know you do. None of these guys out here know you like I do, none of them." He tapped his heart. "I know what's going on in here, brother. You're here for the same reason I am. We just do things differently, but we're looking for the same results, give a little comfort back. Don't beat yourself up over this, Rob. You've done a lot of good out there. Guys on the job thirty years have not come close to doing what you did. You should take comfort in knowing that." I still didn't look at him. I was embarrassed because I didn't want his praise, although getting it from him helped close some of the open wounds. He placed his hand on my neck, then tapped my shoulder, saying quietly, "You know, Rob—and this goes for everyone I have worked with since I been on the job—when I know you're working, I know that if the shit hits the fan, you are not far behind, that everything is going to be all right. We all do, and you know what? As cops, we can't ask for anything more than that, to feel like there is someone out there who is going to help. So you help, bro, you help all of us get through the tours."

More than anything else all I'd ever wanted was to be relied upon by the men I was lucky enough to serve with. I felt that even though I'd lost the way, maybe I had helped somehow, maybe I had put another cop killer away before he was able to take one of us out, or maybe I did stop another senseless murder, maybe it really all wasn't for nothing. I did, however, know that my time left on the job was limited. I'd seen it all and pretty much done it all; whether I was going to jail or getting bounced from the job or going out by someone else's hand didn't matter, this was the instance in my life when it was time to turn a page. If I was going out of the picture, I wanted to at least go out trying to do what I originally came on to do, fight crime.

I stood up, and Billy did the same as he reached out to my shoulder. "Rob, stay at my place tonight, don't drive all the way back to the island."

"Nah, Billy, Patty's doing a six to two. I'm meeting him at the precinct, then we're going back to his place. I'm gonna stay there for a while . . . there's nothing left for me on the island, she's, you know . . . gone for good." No beautiful pregnant wife, no home, no plans for the future, it was just me, and I had to deal with that fact, period.

Billy stepped close to me and we hugged; for some reason I felt that that was the last time we'd ever be that close, I felt like I was saying good-bye; I held him tightly, then broke away and never looked back.

I drove over the Third Street Bridge, going the wrong way, but it was the quickest route to the precinct from the Slope. There were no cars at this time of the evening in that part of town, unless they were bad guys, and that too would have suited me just fine. The waterway underneath was just another section of the Gowanus Canal, which once carried boats with goods to different parts of the city. This was once the Erie Canal of Brooklyn.

Now it was a sludge-filled vein in the Badlands. The streets were empty and dark; the streetlights in the area were ancient, though remarkably, still functioning, washing the landscape in a soft, dull bath of white light. I noticed the pictures of the Monster plastered all over the walls of the abandoned factories, on the street poles, on doors, on rotted, dead trees. He was there, just staring back at me in that odd, ugly white light. It was his eyes, so fucking familiar, it was killing me to know that I had met him before, but my mind was blank. The slower I drove the more his face came into focus, like film slowing down, until I stopped. Click, click, click. I had my foot on the brake just as I rolled over the bridge. It was me and him; I must've stared at the image for five minutes and that is when I was jolted back into my seat. I felt like someone had reached inside me and flipped the on power switch. I jumped out of the car and charged across the wet street to the poster, screaming, *"MOTHERFUCKER!"* I tore the picture from the cracked redbrick wall, did a 360, and ran to a phone at the base of the bridge. I dropped in change and dialed quickly. "Put Pirelli on the phone . . . Patty, it's me, I made the motherfucker, I made him, Patty, meet me at the Tuff Gong, no lights, no sirens Patty . . . Hurry!" He knew what I meant. Come quick and stealthy, do not raise anyone up to the fact that we are on our way. That is just the way I wanted it. *No lights and no sirens.*

I pushed through the door, the place busy as usual, my favorite bartender slinging Hennessys and Cokes and bottles of Guinness to his third-world customers. I barely glanced at him because he was not my target, and there he was, my old friend Rudy. Everyone knew a white cop had entered. Most of them had seen me there before, so they figured it wasn't a roust or a shakedown for guns. They were half right—*Rudy* was going to get shaken. In one swift move, I pulled the skinny pipehead off the stool, dragged him into the bathroom, and threw him into the same sink that Conroy had.

He screamed and held up his fists like a boxer; I must have humiliated him in front of some crack whore because his back was way up and he was ready to fight. "What the fuck, C? You didn't have that ma'fuckin' strap you wouldn't be nothin' but a punk-ass white cunt."

He was just reiterating what every street mope in the world says and wants to believe, that we cops are soft without our guns, I promptly lifted my shirt and did a 360 for him; my gun was still on the floor of my car. "No straps, Rudy, it's just you and me."

He went jailhouse on me, which is what I figured he'd do. Once an animal knows he's going to have to fight and he is not intimidating in the least, he usually tails down. No big surprise, but this wasn't about me rolling on a dirty bathroom floor with this slug. This was a search-and-destroy mission.

Rudy lowered his hands and smiled. "Oh, you think a nigga' gonna lay down for that old one? Shiiiit, C, I'm too ol' school for that bullshit now. You gonna bait me into something and then you got the power to end me up north. I mos def ain't havin' it though."

"You shut your mouth and listen the fuck up, 'cause I ain't got the time to fuck around with you." I ripped the picture from my back pocket and unfolded it. "Where is he?"

I studied him and watched his face come to the realization just as mine had minutes before; he grinned and was now playing the game of take and take. "Fuck is that, C?"

"Rudy . . . Tonight is not the night to play jailhouse nigger. He's the motherfucker you sold the gun to, the scumbag I let walk the fuck out of here, the same motherfucker who you beat for jumbos. Now, who is he and where is he?"

"Ohhhh shit, yeah, that do look like that Herb motherfucker. Yeah, that cryin' little bitch was in here not long ago. Ma'fucker graduated to the good stuff, son! He needed to pull a come down, bitch must've been basin' for days, dirty like a ma'fucker too. Lookin' to score some a the TKO, but you niggas torpedoed that the fuck out the water, so nigga be jonesin' hard."

"Where'd you send him; is he still here?"

"What's in it for me?"

"What?"

"Hook a nigga up, son, give me a little somethin' keep my

shit goin' for a couple a days, you know, like you used to do for that little German ma'fucker. Keep the thug weekend goin', yo."

I had nothing on me and I didn't think I was ever going to have anything on me ever again, on top of which, I didn't want to play the game that way any longer. I was through with the dirtiness of it all. I closed my eyes tightly. "No, Rudy, it ain't like that anymore."

The door swung open and Patty entered with his gun in his hand. He was sweaty and out of breath, though he looked prepared and ready to do damage. "Rob, what the fuck is going on?"

"He knows him, Patty, he knows the motherfucker." I looked right in Rudy's eyes when I said this; even though he was from the street, I was hoping he would recognize the need in my eyes. "Do me this one square, Rudy, help us out."

He laughed and looked at himself in the mirror, the wrong posture to take now that Patty was in the room with us. "A square? C'mon, son, Shah did you niggas a square and look where it end him up, dime and a deuce up north without passing ma'fucking go, please, nigga, please! Gimme a good bag a something and the nigga's in your lap."

"Rob, I just tossed someone. I ain't sewered it yet. Give it to the little boon and let's do our work."

I felt the surge of hatred pour out. I wanted to play it the right way and I wanted the Monster, but I did not want Rudy to call the play. I charged him and grabbed him by the throat to squeeze the life out of him. He started to swing at me, and he did connect with three or four good shots, though I felt nothing. I screamed, "Tell me where he is." He kept swinging and connecting. I felt a gash open over my hairline and blood trickling down the back of my neck. This sent Pirelli into a feeding frenzy. A cop's blood spilled in another cop's presence was never a good thing. Pirelli separated me easily from Rudy, then hit him once in the throat, sending him immediately to his knees in a fit of pain. Patty was a force of nature once the bell was rung. I knew Patty was going to kill him, and that would end the Monster's connection to the Badlands and my connection to the Monster. I realized that the rules of the game were not going to change, not because of me, and definitely not because of any street perp. This was a game of take and take some more until all the chips were on the table, last person standing wins the pot.

I ran out to his car, double-parked in front of the bar. The driver's door was still open, and while there was a crowd in front, no one dared go near the cop's vehicle. They knew Patty, some of them intimately. I ripped opened the glove compartment and, sure enough, rocks in a plastic sandwich bag were ready to be dispensed. I ran back into the bar before it was too late. I kicked open the door and found Pirelli still working on him, though he didn't even look winded. I struggled to pull Pirelli off of him, and dropped the bag into Rudy's lap. He looked up to me with swollen eyes. "You my nigga, C, you all that, son." It was as if he had never been touched and nothing had occurred for the last five minutes. He smiled broadly though his teeth were cracked and blood oozed from many parts of his head and face. "Nigga comin' back tomorrow. He knows I'm opening up with new product. I sold him enough for the comedown."

"What makes you sure he'll be back?"

"I'm not, but I know the powder I laid on him is gonna get him back 'cause it almost as good as the TKO, and like I said, this nigga gots a new jones, son. You see, he be around Flag Pole lookin' for my cure. He a convert, C."

I gambled that evening. Pirelli followed me toward Flag Pole and then into every building we had ever entered. We circled back around through the neighborhoods and found ourselves in Gowanus. Again we searched buildings, parks, the subways. The streets were empty, the subway platforms were empty. I walked up the steps from the BMT line on Third Avenue, Patty walked up the other side. We both noticed the car at the same time, an unmarked LTD with tinted windows. IAB or the feds most definitely. We both moved to it simultaneously. By the time I had charged out into the middle of the deserted street, it had pulled away. Patty crossed to me.

"Rob, they're shutting us the fuck down. We have to chill till this thing blows over, we have to go easy; right now we're out here on patrol and neither of us is on duty, let's not let this get out of hand."

The rats had twisted my balls; there was a woman killer on the loose and they were fixated on me. I turned from Pirelli, not looking back. "Whatever, Patty, whatever you say."

The days passed and there was no sign of Rudy or of the big, ugly man from the poster. Patty was okay with it because we were starting to see more and more cars leapfrogging us in the streets. One would follow us, turn off, then another would pick up our tail, turn off, and then another. There were three cars on us most of the time. We were their straight eights. Patty had the right idea: *Let the shit blow over. Sit tight in the box and it will all go away,* he said, and he was half right. I should've sat it out, but I didn't, I couldn't. The days were long and the nights were longer. I was a nomad just moving through time. I had become fixated on the Monster because that was all I had left. I wanted what remained in my life to mean something, to get that last bit of *jugo* from the job, and most of all, I wanted the pain that was mightily inflicted to end.

The End

The rain was coming down in sheets; it was hitting the car like marbles, nonstop *ping-ping-ping-ping-ping.* I was peering through the downpour in the unmarked shitbox Delta 88. Between intermittent swipes of the windshield wipers, the streets of Red Hook were empty; they seemed almost clean, though I knew different.

I felt the rats behind me, two, maybe three car lengths, possibly an OP van or a nondescript Toyota though it was hidden well. Maybe the banged-up "Puerto Rican" car service *can.* These motherfucks were there, I could feel it, watching my every move. I felt scummy knowing they were there. Probably in their thirties, couple of minorities trying to fit into the hood, two PRs, maybe two dark-skinned ja-baps. I rolled down the window far enough to catch some of the rainwater from the gunpowder clouds. The sudden bursts of thunder, the eerie quietness of these battle-weary streets all enhanced my feeling that this was the perfect day for the end. I rolled up the tired window and ran the water through my long, unkempt hair. It felt good though that moment was as fleeting as all others had become. Mia popped in and out of my mind. I could actually smell her scent. It was usually on her neck, at the point where her shoulder flowed out like a piece of art, that her scent was the strongest. My God, how I missed that scent.

The smallest memories are the ones that hurt the most. *Stop fucking thinking, Rob, stop fucking thinking PLEASE!* I kept repeating this over and over. I squeezed my eyes closed, tight, trying to release the hurt, but it wasn't happening.

I looked in the rearview mirror, trying to clock where exactly the rat patrol was. They were good, but not as good as me. I mean, if I really wanted to, I'd pull the Delta out, give them a tour of the Badlands, and lose them within minutes. No matter what, these were still my streets and I owned them. But it wasn't about that anymore.

I caught a glimpse of myself in the mirror, the first in a long time. Hair matted, three-day growth on my pasty skin, eyes sullen and circled. I had a strong urge to spit at that animal that stared back at me, but why dignify that thing with a response? Any reply to that thing in the mirror would just deepen the self-hatred, and at this point all I motherfuckin' wanted was to live through the numbness without feeling today, because this was the end.

A blast of thunder rattled the car. Patty's eyes opened into thin red slits.

"You still there, Rob?"

"Yeah, go back to sleep, brother."

Within seconds he was out cold again. I stared at him; he was as much a part of me as the streets were.

I noticed one of the street mopes moving in and out of a doorway. I knew him and he knew me. He nodded to let me know in our coded street language that there was someone else out there watching. He tapped his eye twice, telling me there were two of them and he pointed with his chin at approximately eight o'clock to the rear of my unmarked, which told me exactly where they were. Then he raised his fist in the air and disappeared into the driving rain. It felt good knowing that there was someone out there who was still kicking back to me.

I rolled the window down again, the smell of the ozone dissipated into the natural smell of garbage. Low tide in the basin; this didn't help. The mire from the canal and the urine from the streets were too familiar. This was the deepest part of hell, Dante's ninth circle. Home, where I belonged. Dealers and their jumpy customers started to appear magically, as if they'd never left the Hook. All lined up in their usual spots, waiting to serve or be served.

"Flacko," a painfully skinny, part-time burglar, full-time junkie with a twenty-bag-a-day boy jones, made his way over to the car. He didn't give a fuck that the other street mopes saw him talking to me; I was dead meat on the street, a fried afterbirth. Everyone knew that I was shut down, so I guess Flacko felt very safe. What they didn't know was that today I was on a mission! *Good, let Flacko think he's safe, everyone else will think the same thing. Maybe that will bring the meat right to me.*

"C-dog, what up?" Raspy and ratty, that's what he sounded like, his vocal chords long since destroyed from the streams of chocolate heroin he booted into his throat. It sounded almost like a sexy whisper. I smiled through my anxiety.

"Yo, you gots any Newports or double Os, bro?"

"Flacko, how long you know me?

"Yo, you been around this block, C."

"So you ever see me light up?"

"No, poppa, but that don't mean nothin', yo. You could be one a them bum smokers, you know, bummin' a Marlboro here, Camel light there, you know how that shit go, C." He smiled, teeth dark brown, like the color of dried blood after days in the heat. They were cracked, as were his lips. He was a poster boy for the Badlands. He'd be the perfect public-service announcement: "Mothers, don't even think about moving here. I could be your kid." He leaned his slight frame nervously from side to side; he looked at Patty, who was snoring louder than before. Flacko pointed at him with his thin caked-up lips. I almost laughed.

"You wanna wake him and ask him?"

Flacko pulled away from the window, laughed nervously, his attempt at a whisper making me reach in to hear. "I ain't wakin' that crazy 'talian ma'fucker, C. I ain't got time for a short beat down, yo!"

This annoying little junkie with the chalkboard voice all but put a smile on my face. "Didn't think so."

He smiled back, but there was something behind the smile, some sort of air of entitlement the little spic had, it was almost a superiority he had over me. He started to junkie-strut away, laughing as if he knew something I didn't.

"See ya on the cell block, C. C'ya, wouldn't wanna be ya!"

That laugh tore through me like a .22-cent nickel behind my ear. Should I pull the little junkie's head through the window, roll it up, and drive to Coney Island for some fries? *Fuck it.*

"Not if I see you first, Fucko."

He moved down the street quickly; he had to know the ice he was on was about to crack. "The name's Flacko. You all right, C, you all right."

His voice trailed away. I just let it ride because today was going to be a good one, I felt it in my soul, and Jim Morrison's lyrics were penetrating me deep inside, floating in and out of my consciousness like a halcyon haze.

"This is the end, my only friend, the end."

I always liked that song and today maybe it would be my anthem.

Patty rolled over, opened one very bloodshot eye.

"Fuck you talkin' to that little German for?"

I half-glanced at him then, back out in the street. I wasn't in the mood for a "why me" lecture though I knew it was in the mail. He must've seen the jones that was betraying my eyes; I know he'd seen that look a thousand times and I know he never liked it once because there was always something attached to it. A chase, gunfight, then the never-ending allegations. Patty really didn't give a fuck, but he knew the climate was not right for one of my infamous "test-i-lies." He sat up slowly and squinted out into the street.

"Fuck are we doin' in the Badlands?"

I tried to tune him out, keep focused on the movement that was before me. He rubbed his big, manicured hands through his hair, then pulled from a bottle of Evian. He poured some on his hands, then washed the bourbon-tainted sweat from his face. He poured the water down his neck, letting it cascade along his chest; he started to come back to life. I, of course, waited for the inevitable fucked-up other shoe to drop.

"You know who's out here, right, bro? This is a straight eight, Rob, no fuckin' around."

I didn't answer; he must've gotten a taste of the odd electric vibe I was emitting because he moved in a little closer, not taking his eyes off me once.

"Are you fucking kidding me? I don't feel like getting jammed up today, Rob. Let this shit blow over first. It always does. These motherfuckers are up our asses dry. You understand me?"

I took my time with the answer or maybe I really didn't hear him or just didn't give a fuck. I was definitely watching my favorite channel though, Columbia Street.

He straightened up in the seat and with surgical calmness allowed for me to hear his unwavering, deadly serious tone, he asked the question that was as loaded as both our Glocks.

"Say you fuckin' *sabe*, Rob, say you motherfuckin' understand!"

I too knew this man sitting next to me as well as he knew me. He would not ask a third time. I nodded with as much indifference as I could. Though I really could give a piece of welfare cheese on "Federal Friday."

"I understand, Patty, but remember, there's no such thing as a straight eight, not in Brooklyn there's not. Your words, not mine, *paisan*."

He didn't like the comment, I could see the anger bubbling; he slightly cocked his head toward me, trying to decide if he should swing or elbow. I could see him unconsciously hold on to his hand, trying to suppress his first instinct, which was probably both, swing and elbow.

"What are you now, all of a sudden some fuckin' homo village poet, a word wizard? You got some stupid shit playin' off in your head I don't know about? What are we into playin' word games, tryin' out for '*Wheel of . . .* fuckin' Jeopardy?'"
He stared at me long and hard; hangover or not, he was going

to knock the fuck out of me before he allowed me to fuck myself, but more important, he did not want me to play into IAB's rat trap. They had monster woodies for me and anyone associated with me. They were just waiting for me to fuck up. He drove on, hard.

"Listen to me, buddy boy, they think they got you on a body, you understand? We're on the fuckin' cusp here, you get it! Do not fuck around or I swear to Jesus on the cross I'll bust your hole out right here, right now."

I turned to him with absolute distaste because the words and all the miserable drama were caught in my throat, so much so that I wanted to vomit.

"I fuckin' hear ya, Patty."

"You're goddamn right you do, and I would definitely chill with the attitude, as you can see I'm in no mood. *Capeesh?*"

I turned to him, my voice ringing with sarcasm.

"Always the wise guy, right to the bitter end, huh?"

He was confused, bordering on a Chernobyl-type melt-down. He decided against the explosion; better to lose the battle than get raped in the war.

His famous last words: "Fuck you."

I thought about that for a second, his last words, much like the last words General Custer must've uttered when he rode into the valley of death: "Where in the fuck did all those Indians come from?" Or the mayor of Hiroshima's last words: "What the fuck was that loud noise?" Patty's weren't so eloquent, but they spoke volumes. "Fuck you." Two words could not be truer, *I was fucked!*

He slid back down into the dirty velour seat trying to relieve a cramp above his ass; he turned away from me.

"Today is a straight eight, partner, straight fuckin' eight."

Patty had made his point severely and quite clearly, he and only he would be the one who would air me the fuck out had I any ideas of actually playing policeman again. But I did not care, I *wanted* to die, and I *wanted* to take the Monster with me, and Patty just wasn't convincing enough for me to listen to his logic.

• • •

quickly moved back to the hunt. *They're all out today. Excellent.* I immediately spotted two Dominican boys. Right off the banana plantation, or ganja field, or cocaine lab, or whatever the fuck they're selling these days in the good old DR. They tightened up the second they saw me. This told me that yeah, they're dirty, but they were scared to death. These little mopes were carriers. Couple of ounces at the most, probably pink Peruvian girl. They quickly turned from my car, walking northbound into the packed square of projects. They figured to get lost among the other dealers and buyers, but I knew exactly where they were. They truly must've been imported from some ghetto in the DR within the last week, because they were not up for the game. Not mine anyway. They'd be some other mildly sharp cop's overtime relatively soon. They were definitely not in my playbook, lucky for them. Today was their day. *Today's gonna be a good day!*

I scanned every person who moved through the projects; not one man, woman, or child went unnoticed. Then suddenly another ray of light poked through the quick-moving clouds, it seemed to shine on my Chevy. I squinted across the field of projects. *Could it be?* My hands started to tremble with anxiety. The man; big, black, very muscular. Face so familiar, so fucking familiar. *Was that the bell I just heard, start of the game? Could it be?* I prayed. *C'mon, motherfucker, be the one.*

My eyes pierced through him like a diamond-cut bullet. I wasn't made yet, so it was tough to gauge the level of play. This was as tight as it was going to get; the current running through my body told me this and it never betrayed me. It was like a hit of pure Bolivian marching powder. I searched quickly through the one-on-one photos, scanning each picture, mind racing like a NASA DSL. *Murder? Which one and where? Gun was used, yes . . . no. C'mon, hustler, who the fuck are you? Where you from, player? Murder . . . yes . . . pictures? Posters . . . ? Torture? RAPE! MONSTER!*

The lights were suddenly all turned on. My eyes opened

wide, my desperation turning wild with hunger. My heart was beating out of my chest, eyes dilating. I had my mission; it lay right in front of me. This was it . . . the end!

I flipped open the car door and jumped out like a coked-up jackal, didn't bother shutting it or looking back when my radio tumbled to the ground. I didn't care because this wasn't about backup, this was between me, the Monster, and God.

The jolt of my movement woke poor Patty. He must've been confused, thinking, *Where the fuck is Rob?* Had to be his first thought; then he must've caught me moving like a bullet train cutting a wide path through the filthy atrium. I heard him scream, "Fuck, you motherfucking cunt." He slammed his big fist into the dashboard. I was so sure he'd rather shit out a hub-cap than do what he had to do now, and that was run, run to save his crazy partner's life.

Junkies and perps froze when they saw me coming, though they were not on my list today. I only had eyes for the big, bad-ass black man. I was flying, moving at the speed of light. My feet felt light under me, skating almost. It felt like my first chase, my virgin voyage. I was reborn. I knew this was it. As I ran toward him, everything seemed to fall back into order, the way it was years before. I was laser guided and locked on a man who was as bad as they came. It was just the two of us, with no need for test-i-lying because this was as legit as it could get. I was a cop again, and as fleeting as that moment was, it truly was the last time I was going to feel that way. This I knew, and I wanted to feel all of it, every rush of air, every odor, every scream that erupted from the air around me, and to this very day, I can still feel all of it, everything that occurred in those last few conscious moments. The irony was not lost on me that I felt so alive, yet deep inside I knew I was heading right for my death, or at least that's where I hoped I was heading. I truly felt that if I did accomplish what I had set out to do the moment I laid eyes on the Monster, well, then everything that I had gone through would have been worth something. I would trade my life to squash his, and goddamn, I was cool with that. It was all going to be A-OK, because I'm okay, you're okay.

The Monster was moving, looking for a score, couple of jumbos to rekindle his deadly inner inferno. He laughed as all the dealers and street mopes stepped aside. Did they feel his awesome presence, did they feel his power? I wondered, did he get wood behind his incredible aura, did they all know Monster was back on the prowl, looking to do his nasty work, the work he loved almost as much as the man now closing in on him at the speed of light had once loved his work?

The Monster saw the fear in their faces; they were scared, but not of him and his tremendous stature. Something was happening, something else. The Monster turned and saw me. Moving stealthily, smart bomb zeroing in and he was the target. I was going to get in deep, I was going to chew through barbed wire to get me some payback, *and here I motherfucking come!*

I saw him back away and stumble over an ankle-high chain divider. He scrambled to his feet and rocketed into the building door with such force it was torn cleanly from its rusted hinge. He moved with ease in the maze, as if he had been here before. Maybe watching for another victim to prey on. Well, now he was the prey. He hit the stairway taking three or four steps at a time, moving with incredible speed. He glanced over his shoulder. I wondered if he'd recognized the crazed cop who was chasing him.

I heard him moving above; the thuds on the steps sounded like muffled cannon shots. He must have been scared. *How's it feel, you motherfucking rapist, you twist, you scumbag? Can you feel me coming to get you, to finish our business; today is our day, tree jumper!*

I hit the stairway. *He's going to the roof, good.* I jumped on the elevator and pressed the button to the top floor. Tactically not a smart move, but my gut instinct told me he wasn't thinking coherently. He would keep moving up till he hit daylight, then cross to another building's stairway from there and work his way down. I just had to catch him before he realized he'd have to jump thirty feet across and seven stories high to do so; these projects are made of fireproof stone, there are no fire escapes, and knowing how desperate he was, that would be his move, hell, it would be my move if I were him.

The elevator creaked shut, then started up with a bang. My every sense was heightened. That bang from the elevator's pulley sounded like an explosion, the urine in the corner smelled like it came from a pack of ghetto dogs. I even thought I could smell the alcohol from the old Magic Markered graffiti that covered the metal walls. The excitement was roaring through my body, my hands were sweaty and shaking.

"This is it, motherfucker, this is it. I got you and you got me." I whispered this to myself; it sounded gentle, as if I were talking to Mia before we made love. "Focus, Rob, here and now."

She didn't belong here, I did not want to taint what was left of those beautiful memories we had once shared. I shook off her image again, as hard as it was. I had to focus and finish what had been started too long ago.

I dropped down into a combat position inside the metal box. I figured he might second-guess me and would be waiting outside the door; at least that was what I hoped.

The elevator slammed to a halt, the door slid slowly open, into darkness. My heart was pounding so hard I felt my pistol bounce with each beat. I was slowly able to decipher my surroundings—a torn, bloody mattress was jammed into the stairway; sinewy condoms, crack vials, more graffiti, used Tampons, bloody hypodermics, a dead cat, all littered the landing. Underneath me the broken glass sounded like a symphony. He must've shattered the fluorescent light. *Old trick, scumbag, but I'm glad to know you're here.* I stopped for a moment, trying to adjust to the darkness. *Is he close, right next to me, is this getting the sick fuck off?* I listened for breath, an alien heartbeat, anything. Then I heard the *whoosh* of air, but it was too late to react. A sudden and intense pain exploded from my wrist, I hit the ghetto carpet hard and heard my Glock clattering down the stairs. Then another *whoosh* and I felt the same explosion of pain above my nose. Blood started to fill my eyes though I was just able to see the big silhouette emerging from the darkness, standing above me like an animal unsure of its kill. He calmly raised the two-by-four and brought it down with such ferocity, even I was impressed. I moved just enough not to take its full impact. Still, it felt like I'd been hit with a rocket-propelled grenade.

Scumbag tossed the wood and charged for the roof. Instinctively, I grabbed for his leg but swiped at nothing. A blast of light cut through the darkness and I saw him leap out onto the roof like the uncaged animal he was. I got to my feet, slid back down hard, in either his blood or the blood that now ran in rivulets down my forehead. I stumbled up the stairs. My head felt like it was in a hydraulic vice. I knew I had a concussion or worse—a great start to the magic that I anticipated. Though the blood was dripping down my neck and my wrist was starting to swell, oddly enough I still felt strong. I felt as though I was home watching a movie that I had seen before, one whose ending I knew. All I could do was laugh, and that fucked-up, twisted, sinister laugh told me I was at the right place and in the right time in my life for it to be the end. I was out-of-control insane. On a suicidal quest.

I shouldered the door with everything I had; I figured I'd push him back if he was out there waiting. When I burst out onto the tar, he was nowhere in sight. The summer sun was dropping behind the Statue of Liberty. I spun in every direction on the roof, *C'mon, player, where you at? It's time to tail up,* I thought. I heard those sirens in the distance. I could only imagine that Patty was somewhere out there, charging from building to building, out of time and just about out of moves. What good would a million strapped cops do without clear knowledge of my whereabouts?

I moved cautiously along the edge of the roof. I'd seen that trick before. Hang down, let go, keep your arms outstretched, and pray you catch the window ledge on the next floor. If not, it's one ballsy yet messy way to go.

He wasn't there. All that was there was the sound of the street traffic way below, oblivious to the destiny that was about to unfold seven stories above. The sirens were getting close. If I could hear them, so could scumbag. I had to move quickly. Then . . . *click.* I felt the unmistakable cold piece of metal stab the back of my head gently. If you've never experienced a loaded gun placed at the base of your medulla, the feeling is very similar to driving down an icy mountain in the dark at ninety, with no brakes. You know you're eventually going to stop, but with really extreme and fucked-up results. All I could do was close my eyes and finally say hello to the Monster, look in his eyes and see my prey. I turned slowly; I did not want to raise scumbag up, not yet anyhow.

My man was exactly as I remembered him. Big face, pockmarked, with thin lips to match his thin evil eyes. He had horrific body odor. Rapists generally aren't out to impress the Bettys— pain and damage, that's what they're all about. His hand was open to the bone, probably from smashing out the light in the hallway; the gun was covered in blood. He was shaking starting to hyperventilate. Maybe it was the come down from all the ghetto girl, maybe it was his insanity. In any case, I noticed and I fucking liked the vibe the Monster was emitting. This was going to be good.

"I don't wanna do you . . . Could'a did yous in the st-st- stairs . . . Ain't gonna do the man, but I is wa-walkin' the fuck outta here."

His words slurred together childishly, the speech impediment making him all the more scary to me, making this the perfect endgame. He was shivering, his hand was trembling. I waited, then I smiled at him. He looked confused as I shook my head no.

"C'mon, brother, don't pee in my kicks now. We got history, you and me, you know this, yes?" I waited for him to respond, but I'm sure he didn't know what the fuck to make of me. Had I been of sound mind when we had this little rooftop cluster fuck, I'd probably be dead because there is no way in America I'd stare at that two-inch biscuit for that long a time without jumping off that roof. No, the end is always about re-demption.

"Now don't bitch out on me. You and me are gonna get up in each other's guts. Tell me I'm wrong. Show me how you can man up, like you did to all those women."

He did not know what to make of me. The white cop who was clearly out of his mind and definitely outgunned at the moment. He tilted his head toward me.

"You on the wr-wr-wrong end a da' p-p-pipe . . . You ain't s'posed to be smokin', yo' . . . But this nigga' will smoke ya punk ass l-like the chump you is."

I stepped a little closer. I needed to knock him off balance even further, confuse him into dropping his guard ever so slightly, and then we'd go.

"Nigga, did you just say chump, or jump, 'cause I don't un-derstand a fuckin' thing you're saying. What is it, you suck a lot of cocks, that why you talk like a little bitch with braces? You do suck some dick, this I know, so you must be sucking some Al-abama blood snake or something 'cause you really do talk like a fuckin' retard."

He flinched slightly; I could see he was trying to decipher what jailhouse game I was working on him. I kept going.

"That's it, you suck dick, you're a retard and a smelly, ugly motherfucker too. I got four words for you, take a fuckin' bath. You take it in the ass I bet, am I right?"

His bloody gun hand started to jerk. I was getting the reac-tion I wanted, disorientation. This had to be a first for him, on the right end of a chewed-up trey-eight and being humiliated by some white cunt cop.

"Yeah, you're definitely a booty bandit, all you tree-jumping rapists are. Listen, there ain't nothing wrong with sucking a dick or two, but that whole ass-play thing, that's a little fucked up. Me, personally, I don't like taking a hard shit, let alone hav-ing some jailhouse baboon stick a dick in my ass and lay some boy butter on me. I mean, that's gotta hurt, no? But then again, we're back to that whole retard thing, so I under-stand . . ."

The sirens were getting closer. I had to force him to make the move. I leaned in for supreme effect.

"You fuckin' nigga."

I could see his finger grabbing at the trigger. He wanted to blow a quarter-size hole right through my forehead, probably dig out a piece of gray matter, keep it as another one of his trophies. Something else to jerk off to later. I could see he wanted off the roof without having to do a cop. He was up to five women by this point; did he think that killing a cop would make his sentencing any worse? *In prison a cop killer is miles up the food chain from where the rapist sits, you fucking moron. Make your move,* I thought. He wanted out before those sirens turned into angry cops, game faces on, locked and loaded for bear. He started to hedge. Did he think this was a wash? *Not today, pal; this isn't close to how the end is going to be played . . . Fuck it!*

I looked into his eyes and prayed that my peripheral vision was on. As if lightning shot from my arm, I grabbed hold of the bullet chamber. I'd disarmed enough perps in my time to know that as long as my hand was on that chamber, the scumbag would not be able to fire the revolver. Now I saw the anger in the Monster. Close combat would be the only way to do this; I pulled him to me. He was concentrating on pulling the trigger, he had no choice but to increase the body count. This was good. I was able to twist the gun into his stomach; if by chance the gun was going to explode, fuck face was taking the first hit. We fell to the roof ledge; I started to scrape his bloody hand along the cement roof cap. I scraped harder, he screamed. I actually saw the wound separate into bright white bone under the grayish tissue. I was transfixed by it for a moment. He was screaming loudly now; I wanted to inflict some pain on this animal before the real redemption was to begin. I was in a zone. Everything around me disappeared, especially the noise; those annoying sirens, so many of them blaring out surreally in different rhythms. The teakettle whistling two stories below, the motorcycle rumbling down the street. It was as if the house lights had dimmed and the show was just beginning.

Boom! He was able to get a shot off, I saw it just miss his lower torso; the discharge from the chamber turned a patch of skin on his stomach the color of burnt opium. Again he wailed. My nostrils flared at that familiar, acrid gunpowder smell, the smell I had also learned to love.

I began to slam the Monster's hand into the four-foot cement ledge. He could not hold on to the revolver any longer. It slipped out of his hand, and down to the ground, way below. He quickly wrapped his arm around my neck and easily threw me to the tar. He straddled me, then wrapped his hands around my neck. I noticed his one hand; it was a bloody mess of flesh and bone, and with every scream he let out, the wound would pump faster. I was covered in his blood and mine. *This is how it's supposed to be.*

He held me pinned with one hand and grabbed me at the shoulder with his other. I knew his next move was to throw me from the roof. He was so strong, this wouldn't take much effort on his part. However, that wasn't part of the plan. I started to dig in the small of my back. *Where are they . . . There they are . . . Which hand is closer . . . Pumping wrist . . . CLICK-click-click. CLICK-click-click.* We were now one, cuffed together, fused at the wrist. If I was going over, he was coming with me. I could see his confusion turn to realization, which turned to utter rage. He now screamed like a wolf caught in a bear trap. It rocked me to the core of my miserable dirty soul. I now had a sense of what fear this animal's poor victims must've felt when they met him. He lifted his head up and slammed it into my left cheekbone. I actually felt my eye droop as my orbital was crushed. Nausea started to overtake me, the pain was that intense. I could barely speak. "G'head, you motherfucker, do what you want to do. Kill me, do it now." Sensing defeat, he howled. He began to swing hard with his free hand into my head. I could not fight back, though the truth was, why fight back? I was spent physically and emotionally. The pain was unimportant; I was numb and already dead.

The Monster stood up in what would be his final display of absolute fury, and it was majestic. He slammed me across the tar roof, trying to work his way to the door. I kicked out with whatever strength I had left. He stumbled forward. I was starting to lose consciousness, though I wanted to see this to the end. He stood up again and stomped me in the ribs. It felt as though my lung had popped inside me and suddenly I could not breathe. I heard myself wheezing, and tasted bile and that distinctive copper taste that only occurs when you've swallowed too much of your own blood. As he tried to rip the cuff off my wrist, I heard my own bone start to crack. It was at this point that he paid deep attention to the work he was very good at—torture. He kneed me just below my rib cage, grabbed the back of my head, and pulled me up to him. Face-to-face, inches separating us. I can only hope that I showed scumbag that he did not command fear in all who encountered his wrath, I can only hope that I smiled as I said this: "Finish it, you fuckin' coward!" I coughed out a sack of frothy blood into his face. He replied with insane anger, opening his mouth wide, revealing the large, cracked tobacco-stained teeth. He bit down hard. I roared in pain as I felt him moving through what was once my nose, then into the bone. He pulled away. His mouth was full of blood, my blood. He hit me again and again, anywhere he saw flesh, indiscriminant explosions of pain, and the light slowly faded. I remember the sensation of being in a pool, only I could not see anything. I was cold, very cold. And I heard two loud bangs that were echoed and from a distance, they sounded like they were shot from within a tank of water. That's when I saw her, Mia. She was floating above me, years ago, innocent of all hurt and pain, beautiful, so alive. I saw the baby, my baby, the baby I never knew, though the one I was sure I murdered. I saw me, crisp blue uniform, shield glowing in the sunlight. I can only say that at that moment I finally felt the redemption and peace that I was seeking. Everything suddenly went billowy white and I was finally . . . free.

Through the blackness I heard an echoed siren somewhere overhead. It was the siren from the marked RMP that was transporting me to Kings County Hospital. I tried, but I could not open my eyes, I felt fluid in my mouth, then I felt a hand tilt my head and fluid drip down my neck and down my back. I gagged, then heard men talking. A woman's voice was in and out; I assumed these were the doctors and nurses who were tirelessly trying to save the unrecognizable man on the hospital gurney, and then there was nothing but the stark cold reality of . . . nothing.

6

"Endgame, Baby, Endgame"

I felt pressure on my foot. My eyes fluttered open and eventually a room came into focus. Everything had a dull sheen to it, even . . . Mahoney? Yes, Mahoney was bent over, looking down at me. I realized I was in a bed; when I went to move, I felt the bandages on my arms and wrists and I felt a cloth around my head and neck.

He was smiling and I think I smiled too, but I was too fucked up and medicated to know. I tried to speak, but nothing came out.

"You got him, Rob! Positive from the chick on Hamilton. He's gone, baby, you did it. And here's another one—narcotics collared some mope on a separate B felony. He started to drop bombs for the narcotics guys, gave up a shooter for a body. You know where?" He laughed and shook his head. "Red Hook, some roof in Red Hook, a German named Cho. He gave us the shooter, we got him and the gun. He was an outside hire by the Shah to clip him for the rollover, just like you said."

A hand reached in to touch my shoulder. I felt a lump in my throat when I saw it was Billy. I started to cry, though it was silent. I felt the tears stinging the skin around my nose and lips. He dropped his head, as I am sure he felt the same emotion. He looked up at me with his eyes full. "They dropped the charges, Rob. The whole thing's a fucking wash. Endgame, baby, endgame. You did it, buddy, you solved some bodies and you showed 'em, you showed them all."

When I woke again, the room was empty. Doctors came in and out, probing me to see what was going to be fixed and what wasn't. None of it mattered to me. The scars that the plastic surgeons might or might not be able to hide, the bones that were fractured and broken, all of it would remind me of who I was, what I had become, and what road I had lived on and almost died on. To get to where I was and to get through what I had survived had set the stage for me to become the person I wanted to be.

I knew that if I survived the Monster, everything in my life was going to change. Mia helped facilitate that. The job for me was finished, I knew I could never delude myself into thinking that I was still a good cop; I had seen and done too much to ever really cleanse myself of all the sins I'd committed and been privy to. My life as I once knew it was over; it was now up to me to make it better.

Maybe it's better and maybe I'm a better person now. I don't know.

I served for three more years, doing things the right way, living my life in such a way that I could look in the mirror again. Yes, the wounds healed, and most tell me I look like nothing ever happened. But I know it did—you better fucking believe it—and, yes, the scars run deep. But, you know what? Hope runs deeper.

Epilogue

Anthony "Shah King" Huggins was found innocent of the crime of the homicide of Theobaldi "Cholito" Rodriguez. Looking at a term of no less than twenty years had he gone to trial, he pleaded to a lesser charge of possession with intent to sell and was incarcerated for a term of three years. Upon his release, Huggins realized he'd lost the projects to upstarts half his age. He developed an irreversible heroin addiction and overdosed in 1995 on his own drug, called "3 and out."

Demetrius "The Monster" Burroughs was positively identified by two of his victims through a photo array. He expired two weeks after his capture, of complications due to bullet wounds he'd sustained during his arrest.

John Conroy took three civil-service tests, passing all of them. After two years as a captain in a Manhattan north precinct, he was promoted to the rank of deputy inspector. He is currently working in a quiet detail in a quiet section of northeastern Queens.

Patty Pirelli made it to the rank of detective second grade out of the organized crime control bureau; he retired in 2002 and is living in Miami Beach, Florida, where he operates and is partial owner of his family's restaurant.

Billy Devlin is a captain working in a joint task force with an unidentifiable federal law-enforcement agency; he has no plans to retire.

Mia, from what I understand, had remarried. I know nothing of her current life—where she is, does she have children, has she found her inner peace? I hold nothing against her. She was right, as she usually was, about my having become a monster, among many things. I never got over the loss of our baby, the final bond between us. Throughout she was crying out for help and I wasn't there to give it to her. I believe that if we hadn't lost the baby Mia and I would have found a way to love each other again; but, in the end, things might have gotten worse. With this loss, we were now truly through.

As for me, I eventually left the job. I realized that life did not begin and end in an unmarked police car. Life for everyone was going to go on, whether I strapped a gun on or not. Everything wasn't so damn immediate and I wasn't going to die if I didn't allow myself to. I began to write about my life experiences, successfully transitioning into television and movies. I learned to like myself again, but more important, I learned to trust and love again. I met and married a beautiful woman, Lisa, who I had two beautiful children with. I learned that the rush of chasing a murderer with a gun pales in comparison to the rush of watching my nine-year-old son hit a home run, or to the joy I get listening to my six-year-old daughter sing a pretty song in French. I truly believe that everything we go through in life, good and bad, makes us the person we are to become. The key is to learn from those experiences and use the incredible power of hindsight. If that is the case, then I thank God for every moment I spent in the Badlands. Because the love I see in my children's eyes tells me just who I've become . . . simply, Dad.

ACKNOWLEDGMENTS

Above all else I must acknowledge my wife Lisa. Her compassion, strength, and capacity for love are endless. Throughout this process she has been an absolute rock and a sounding board for creativity. She has been on this ride from the beginning and I love her deeply for it. I am truly the luckiest man alive. My life story was kept alive by many people, but no one more so than Lou DiGiaimo and Lou DiGiaimo Jr., both champions of mine in Hollywood and New York. I owe a great deal of thanks for their tenacity, determination, and friendship, and for their unwavering beliefs in my abilities as a writer. My book agent, Ian Kleinert of Literary Group International, has also believed in this project from the start and I'm grateful for his passion, innovative approach to business, and his mind-blowing work ethic. He's become more than my agent, he's become a fast friend and has navigated this unfamiliar terrain for me better than I could have ever imagined. Special thanks to my editor, Mauro DiPreta, for having absolute and complete faith in this book and more important, in me. He more than anyone else molded this into what I think is something special. He's given me incredible confidence with thought-provoking insight, creative input, and a no-nonsense approach to his work. He inspired me daily as I worked damn hard to maintain his trust and valued leadership. Joelle Yudin, the associate editor of this book, has been an enormous help in alleviating and troubleshooting problems before they occurred. Big ups, Joelle, for staying on point with books and other research material I needed to stay focused while writing this book. Thanks so much to Larry Becsey, my film and TV agent, for building a solid alliance and trusted friendship. My brother, Jeff, and sister, Dawn, have given unconditional support and love throughout some really dark moments in life. So many unbearable nights were made bearable because of the special bond we three share to this day. No written or spoken word can express the depth of my love and gratitude. I want to acknowledge Nana and Gramps for the love they gave so freely and for the love they continue to give. Mark Cianciotta was there for me on *the* darkest day, and I'll never forget you for it. Danny Gray, my oldest and dearest friend, was one of the first to read the unedited manuscript, as his opinion mattered greatly, and I thank you for your patience and suggestions. Kevin Diehl also gave support and advice after reading an early first version and I thank you and miss you. Big ups to Pete Smith for showing me how it was *all done* way back in the day. Others who were steadfast and true throughout the years are Vincent and Michael Cea, Dana Dolce, John "Cumumba-Jumba" DeSilvia, Kenny Becht, Ricky Stewart, Pat Cuomo, Larry Dolce, Michael DeMartino, Chris Lavasseur, Don Oriolo, Jerry Schatzberg, Russ *"Where's-My-Thousand-Dollar"* Lyster, Janet Punzi, Luca Palanca, and Joseph Farkas. I want to thank my mom, Joyce, for instilling in me a thirst for life and the courage to never give up on hope. A day hasn't passed where I haven't thought of your warm embrace and your calm, encouraging soft voice. I love you and miss you.